Monstres
Vol. 4: Night of the Ladykiller

Joann SfAR • Lewis TRONDHEIM

Guest artists:
Night of the Ladykiller: Jean-Emmanuel VERMOT-DESROCHES
Ruckus at the Brewers: YOANN

NANTIER • BEALL • MINOUSTCHINE
Publishing inc.
new york

Also available in Dungeon:
Dungeon, Zenith, vols. 1, 2: $14.95 each, 3: $12.95
Dungeon Early Years, vols. 1, 2: $12.95
Dungeon, Twilight, vols. 1, $12.95, 2: $14.95, 3: $12.99
Dungeon, Parade, vols. 1, 2: $9.95 each
Dungeon, Monstres, vols. 1, 2: $12.95 each, 3: $12.99
Also by Trondheim:
Little Nothings, vols. 1, 2, 3: $14.95 each
Mr. I, $13.95
with Thierry Robin:
Li'l Santa, $14.95
Happy Halloween, Li'l Santa, $14.95

Add $4 P&H first item $1 each additional.

See previews and more at
www.nbmpub.com

Write for our complete catalog
of over 200 graphic novels:
NBM
40 Exchange Pl., Suite 1308
New York, NY 10005

Little Guide
to Dungeon

The Early Years present the creation of Dungeon

Zenith relates the height of Dungeon

Twilight tells of the demise of Dungeon

Dungeon Monstres retells great adventures of secondary characters

Dungeon Parade is between volume 1 and 2 of Zenith with funny stories of Marvin & Herbert

Dungeon Bonus is little surprises...

Find out more at donjonland.com (you'll have to decrypt the french)

T 108492

ISBN: 978-1-56163-608-2
Donjon Monsters, volume 5, La Nuit du Tombeur,
Sfar – Trondheim – Vermot-Desroches
© Guy Delcourt Productions - 2003
Donjon Monsters, volume 6, Du Ramdam chez les Brasseurs,
Sfar – Trondheim – Yoann
© Guy Delcourt Productions - 2003
© 2011 NBM for the English translation
Translation by Joe Johnson
Lettering by Ortho
Printed in China
Library of Congress Control Number: 2011902447
1st printing

Night of the Ladykiller

SFAR & TRONDHEIM ; Color: Walter
Art: J.-E. VERMOT-DESROCHES

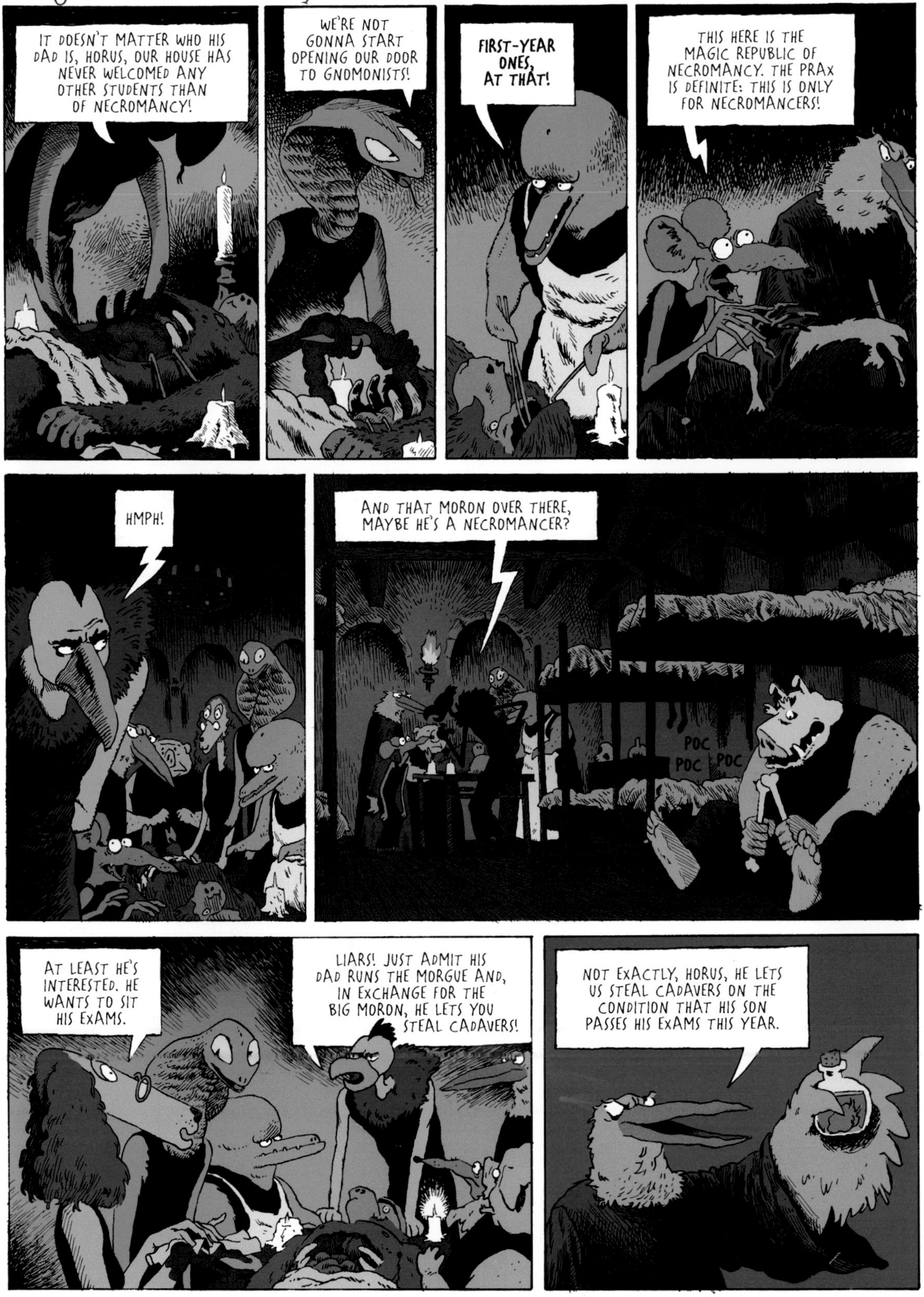
IT DOESN'T MATTER WHO HIS DAD IS, HORUS, OUR HOUSE HAS NEVER WELCOMED ANY OTHER STUDENTS THAN OF NECROMANCY!
WE'RE NOT GONNA START OPENING OUR DOOR TO GNOMONISTS!
FIRST-YEAR ONES, AT THAT!
THIS HERE IS THE MAGIC REPUBLIC OF NECROMANCY. THE PRAX IS DEFINITE: THIS IS ONLY FOR NECROMANCERS!
HMPH!
AND THAT MORON OVER THERE, MAYBE HE'S A NECROMANCER?
POC
POC
POC
AT LEAST HE'S INTERESTED. HE WANTS TO SIT HIS EXAMS.
LIARS! JUST ADMIT HIS DAD RUNS THE MORGUE AND, IN EXCHANGE FOR THE BIG MORON, HE LETS YOU STEAL CADAVERS!
NOT EXACTLY, HORUS, HE LETS US STEAL CADAVERS ON THE CONDITION THAT HIS SON PASSES HIS EXAMS THIS YEAR.

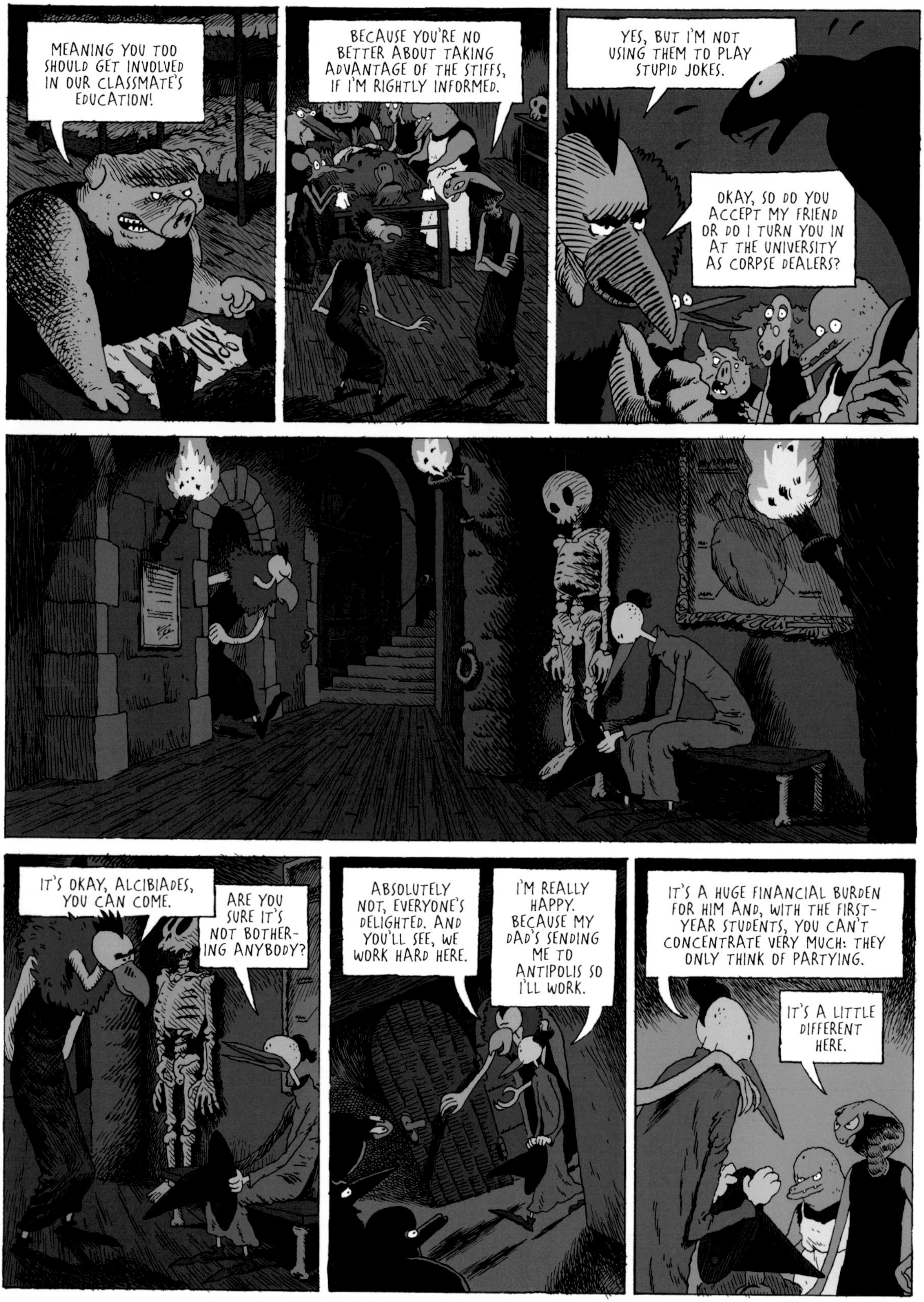
MEANING YOU TOO SHOULD GET INVOLVED IN OUR CLASSMATE'S EDUCATION!
BECAUSE YOU'RE NO BETTER ABOUT TAKING ADVANTAGE OF THE STIFFS, IF I'M RIGHTLY INFORMED.
YES, BUT I'M NOT USING THEM TO PLAY STUPID JOKES.
OKAY, SO DO YOU ACCEPT MY FRIEND OR DO I TURN YOU IN AT THE UNIVERSITY AS CORPSE DEALERS?
IT'S OKAY, ALCIBIADES, YOU CAN COME.
ARE YOU SURE IT'S NOT BOTHERING ANYBODY?
ABSOLUTELY NOT, EVERYONE'S DELIGHTED. AND YOU'LL SEE, WE WORK HARD HERE.
I'M REALLY HAPPY. BECAUSE MY DAD'S SENDING ME TO ANTIPOLIS SO I'LL WORK.
IT'S A HUGE FINANCIAL BURDEN FOR HIM AND, WITH THE FIRST-YEAR STUDENTS, YOU CAN'T CONCENTRATE VERY MUCH: THEY ONLY THINK OF PARTYING.
IT'S A LITTLE DIFFERENT HERE.

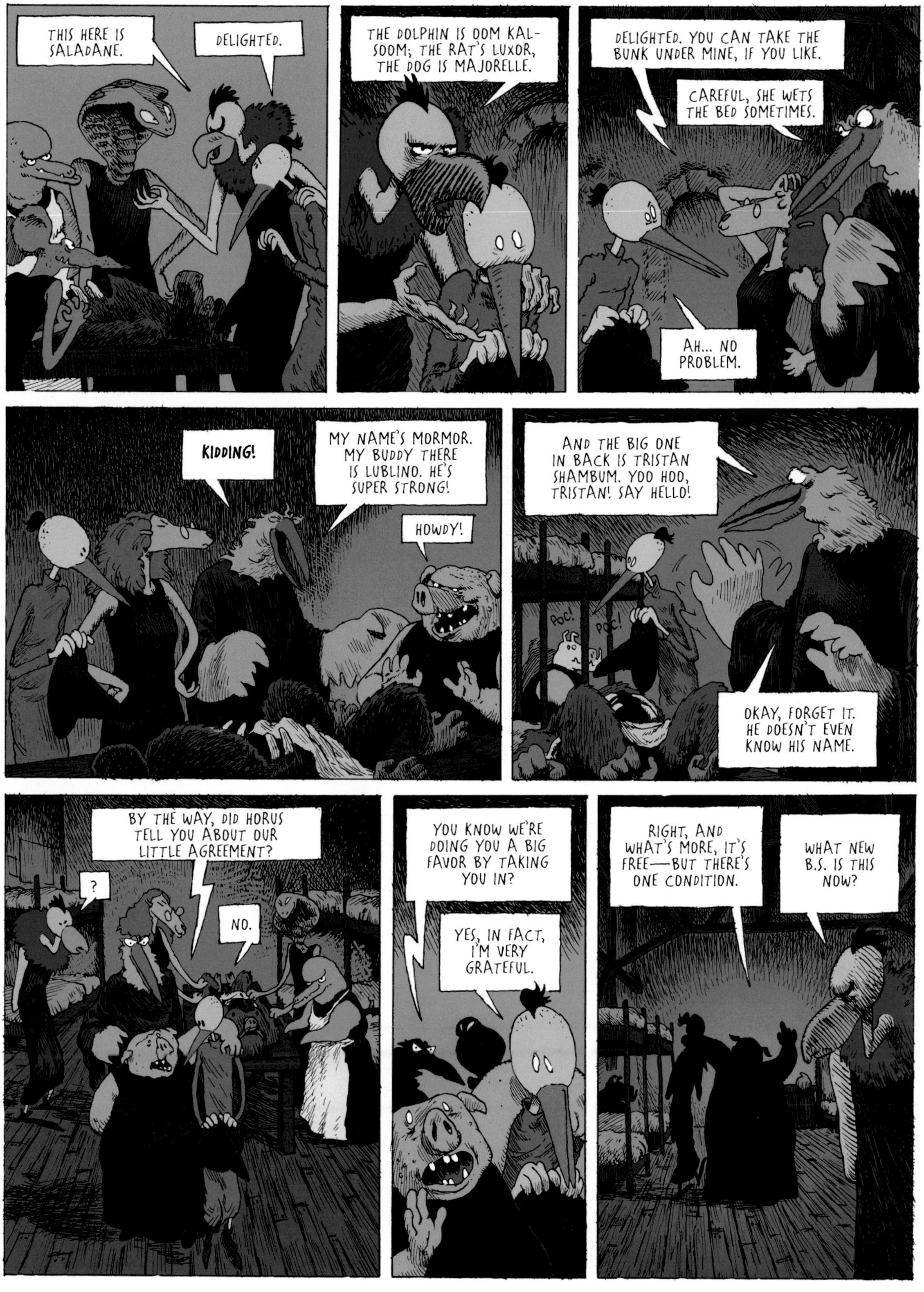
THIS HERE IS SALADANE.
DELIGHTED.
THE DOLPHIN IS OOM KALSOOM; THE RAT'S LUXOR, THE DOG IS MAJORELLE.
DELIGHTED. YOU CAN TAKE THE BUNK UNDER MINE, IF YOU LIKE.
CAREFUL, SHE WETS THE BED SOMETIMES.
AH... NO PROBLEM.
KIDDING!
MY NAME'S MORMOR. MY BUDDY THERE IS LUBLINO. HE'S SUPER STRONG!
HOWDY!
AND THE BIG ONE IN BACK IS TRISTAN SHAMBUM. YOO HOO, TRISTAN! SAY HELLO!
POC!
POC!
OKAY, FORGET IT. HE DOESN'T EVEN KNOW HIS NAME.
BY THE WAY, DID HORUS TELL YOU ABOUT OUR LITTLE AGREEMENT?
?
NO.
YOU KNOW WE'RE DOING YOU A BIG FAVOR BY TAKING YOU IN?
YES, IN FACT, I'M VERY GRATEFUL.
RIGHT, AND WHAT'S MORE, IT'S FREE—BUT THERE'S ONE CONDITION.
WHAT NEW B.S. IS THIS NOW?

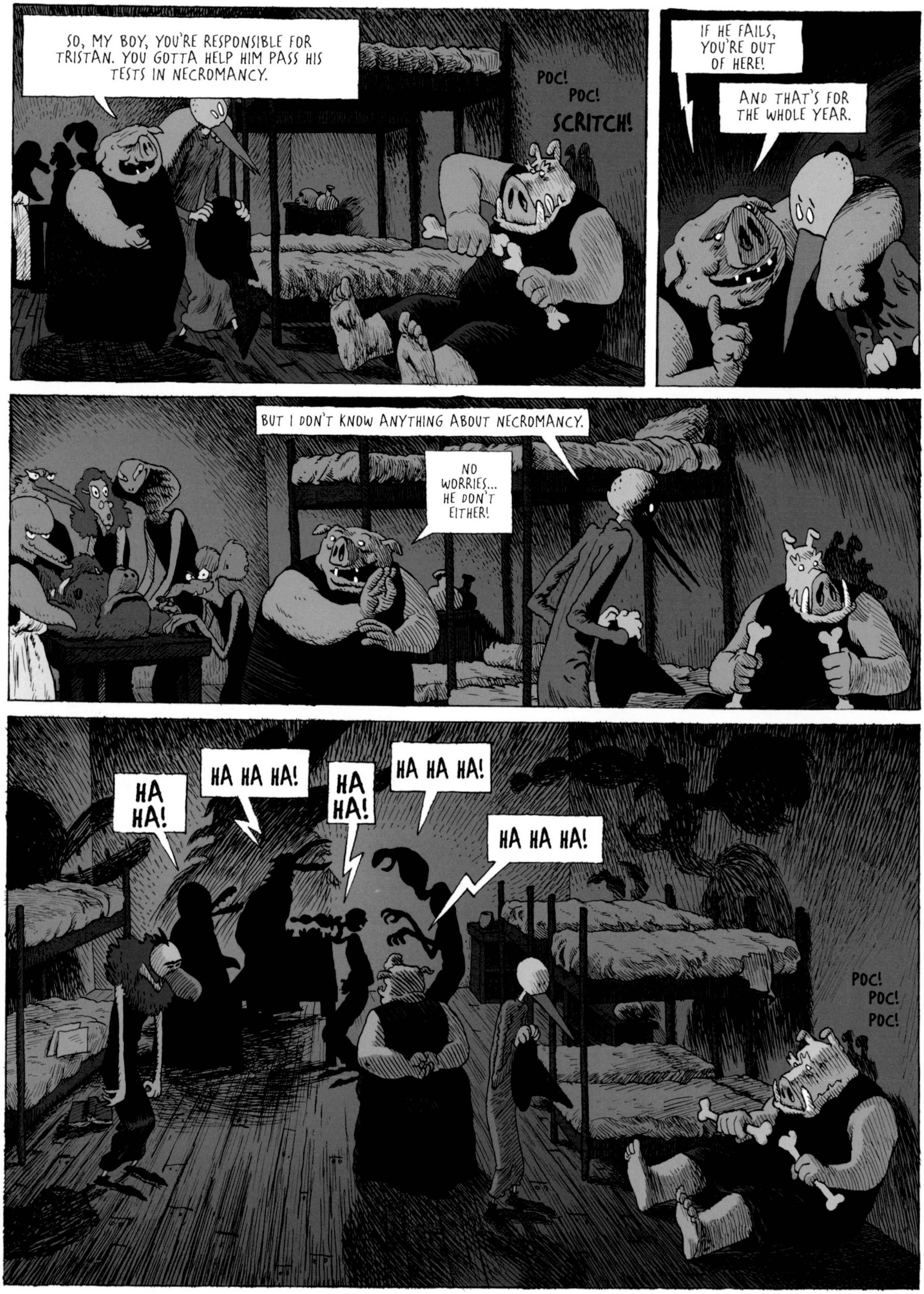
SO, MY BOY, YOU'RE RESPONSIBLE FOR TRISTAN. YOU GOTTA HELP HIM PASS HIS TESTS IN NECROMANCY.
POC! POC! SCRITCH!
IF HE FAILS, YOU'RE OUT OF HERE!
AND THAT'S FOR THE WHOLE YEAR.
BUT I DON'T KNOW ANYTHING ABOUT NECROMANCY.
NO WORRIES... HE DON'T EITHER!
HA HA!
HA HA HA!
HA HA!
HA HA HA!
HA HA HA!
POC! POC! POC!

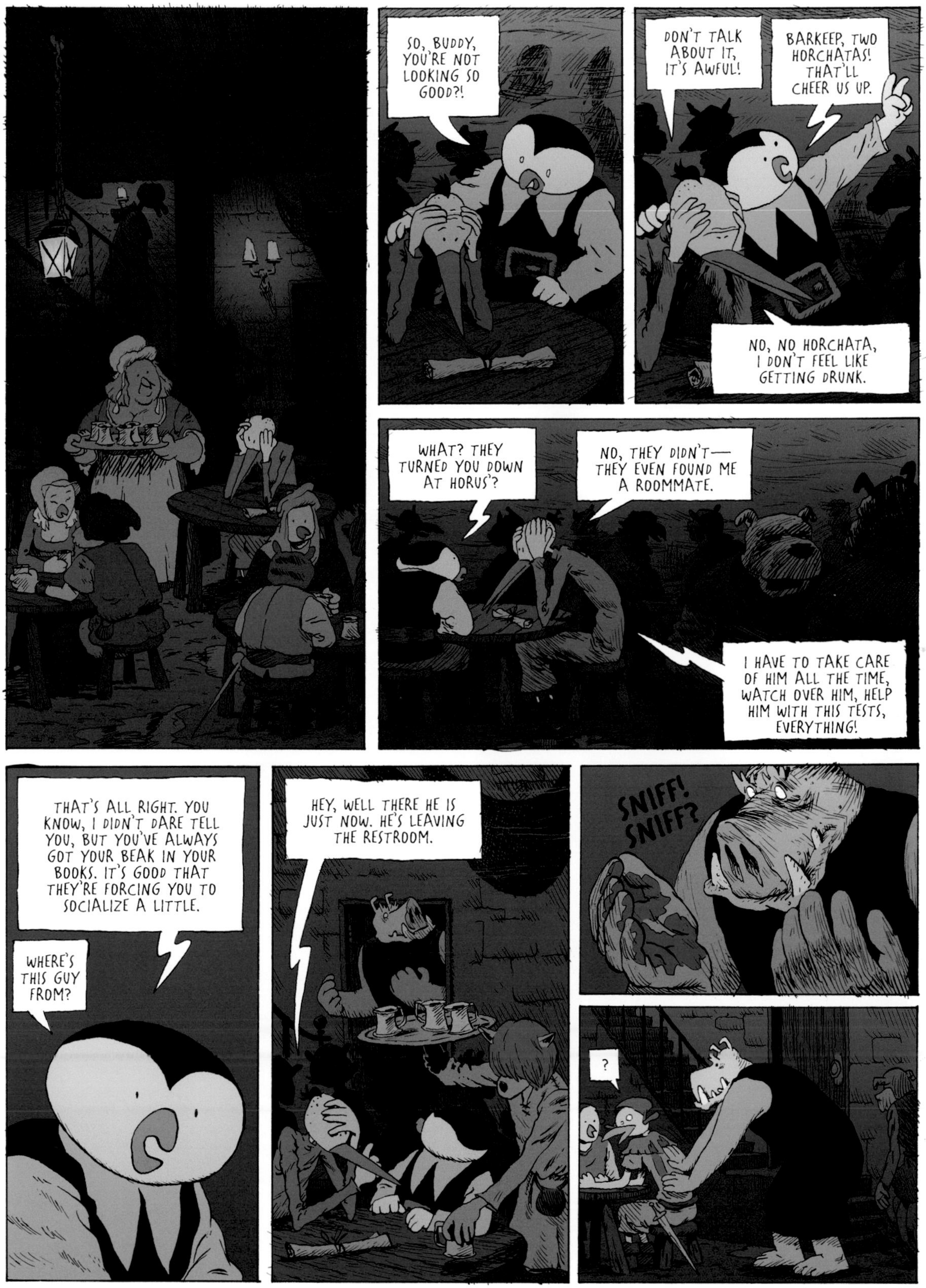
SO, BUDDY, YOU'RE NOT LOOKING SO GOOD?!
DON'T TALK ABOUT IT, IT'S AWFUL!
BARKEEP, TWO HORCHATAS! THAT'LL CHEER US UP.
NO, NO HORCHATA, I DON'T FEEL LIKE GETTING DRUNK.
WHAT? THEY TURNED YOU DOWN AT HORUS'?
NO, THEY DIDN'T— THEY EVEN FOUND ME A ROOMMATE.
I HAVE TO TAKE CARE OF HIM ALL THE TIME, WATCH OVER HIM, HELP HIM WITH THIS TESTS, EVERYTHING!
THAT'S ALL RIGHT. YOU KNOW, I DIDN'T DARE TELL YOU, BUT YOU'VE ALWAYS GOT YOUR BEAK IN YOUR BOOKS. IT'S GOOD THAT THEY'RE FORCING YOU TO SOCIALIZE A LITTLE.
WHERE'S THIS GUY FROM?
HEY, WELL THERE HE IS JUST NOW. HE'S LEAVING THE RESTROOM.
SNIFF! SNIFF?
?

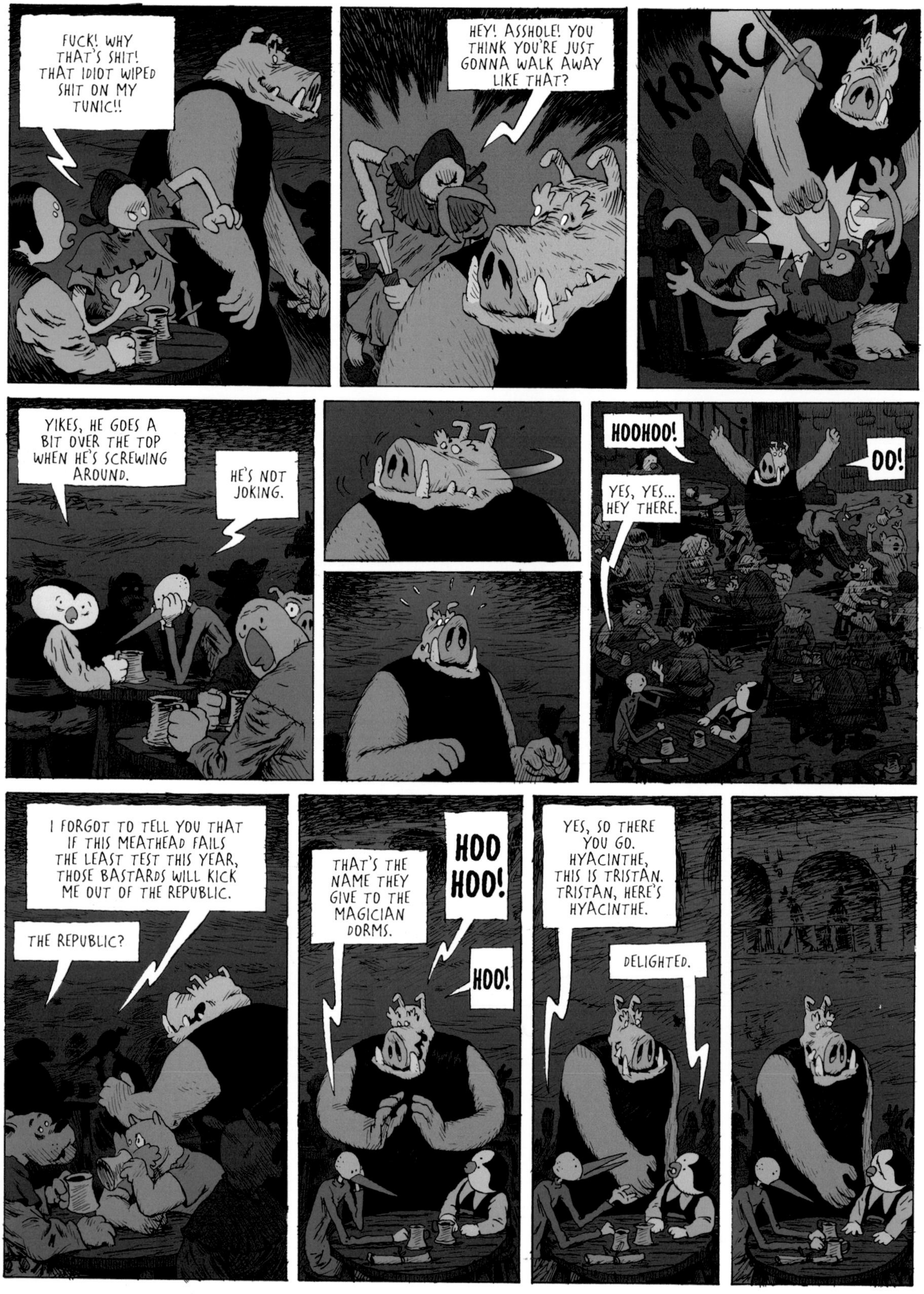
FUCK! WHY THAT'S SHIT! THAT IDIOT WIPED SHIT ON MY TUNIC!!
HEY! ASSHOLE! YOU THINK YOU'RE JUST GONNA WALK AWAY LIKE THAT?
KRAC
YIKES, HE GOES A BIT OVER THE TOP WHEN HE'S SCREWING AROUND.
HE'S NOT JOKING.
HOOHOO!
OO!
YES, YES... HEY THERE.
I FORGOT TO TELL YOU THAT IF THIS MEATHEAD FAILS THE LEAST TEST THIS YEAR, THOSE BASTARDS WILL KICK ME OUT OF THE REPUBLIC.
THE REPUBLIC?
THAT'S THE NAME THEY GIVE TO THE MAGICIAN DORMS.
HOO HOO!
HOO!
YES, SO THERE YOU GO. HYACINTHE, THIS IS TRISTAN. TRISTAN, HERE'S HYACINTHE.
DELIGHTED.

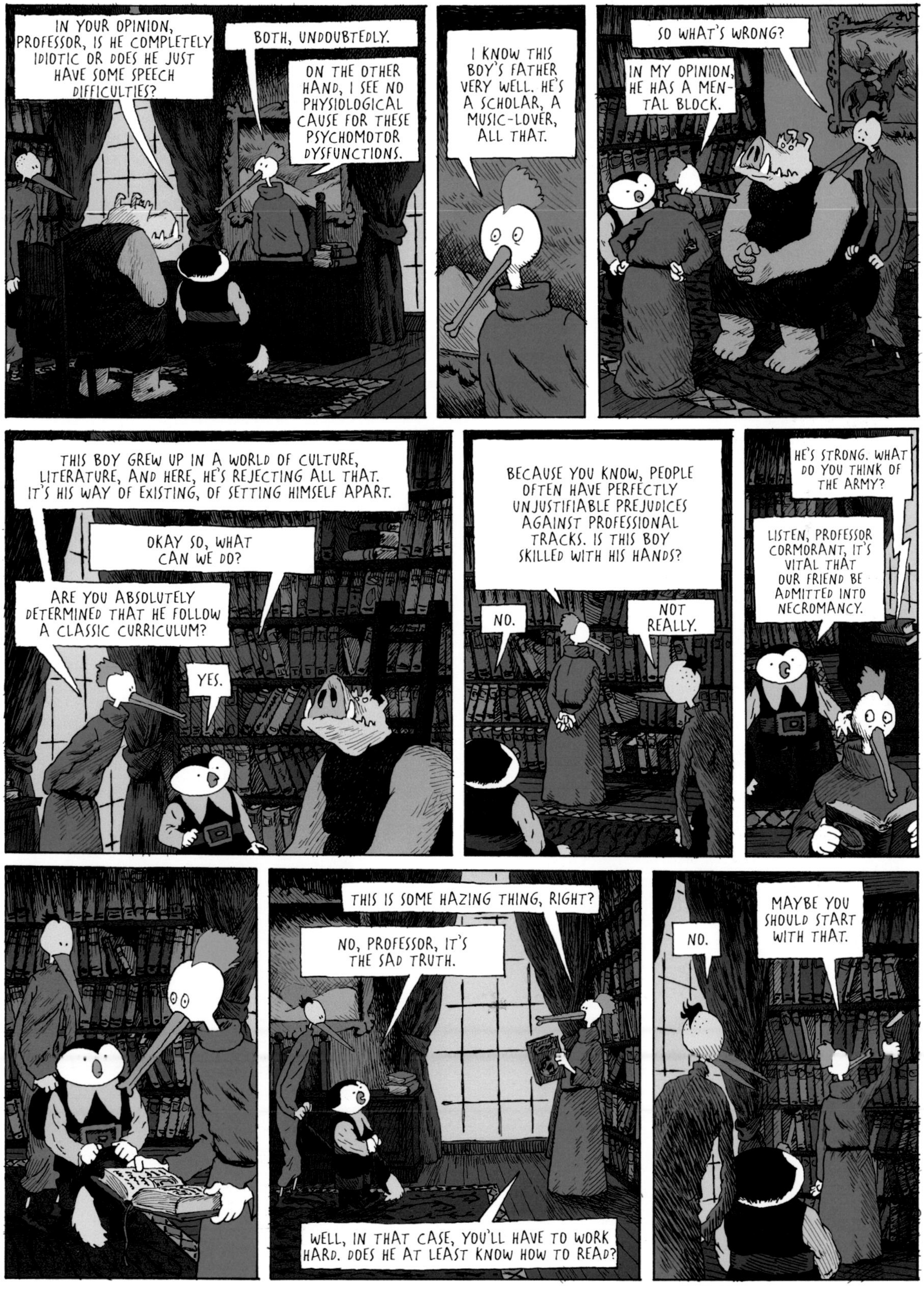
IN YOUR OPINION, PROFESSOR, IS HE COMPLETELY IDIOTIC OR DOES HE JUST HAVE SOME SPEECH DIFFICULTIES?
BOTH, UNDOUBTEDLY.
ON THE OTHER HAND, I SEE NO PHYSIOLOGICAL CAUSE FOR THESE PSYCHOMOTOR DYSFUNCTIONS.
I KNOW THIS BOY'S FATHER VERY WELL. HE'S A SCHOLAR, A MUSIC-LOVER, ALL THAT.
SO WHAT'S WRONG?
IN MY OPINION, HE HAS A MENTAL BLOCK.
THIS BOY GREW UP IN A WORLD OF CULTURE, LITERATURE, AND HERE, HE'S REJECTING ALL THAT. IT'S HIS WAY OF EXISTING, OF SETTING HIMSELF APART.
OKAY SO, WHAT CAN WE DO?
ARE YOU ABSOLUTELY DETERMINED THAT HE FOLLOW A CLASSIC CURRICULUM?
YES.
BECAUSE YOU KNOW, PEOPLE OFTEN HAVE PERFECTLY UNJUSTIFIABLE PREJUDICES AGAINST PROFESSIONAL TRACKS. IS THIS BOY SKILLED WITH HIS HANDS?
NO.
NOT REALLY.
HE'S STRONG. WHAT DO YOU THINK OF THE ARMY?
LISTEN, PROFESSOR CORMORANT, IT'S VITAL THAT OUR FRIEND BE ADMITTED INTO NECROMANCY.
THIS IS SOME HAZING THING, RIGHT?
NO, PROFESSOR, IT'S THE SAD TRUTH.
WELL, IN THAT CASE, YOU'LL HAVE TO WORK HARD. DOES HE AT LEAST KNOW HOW TO READ?
NO.
MAYBE YOU SHOULD START WITH THAT.

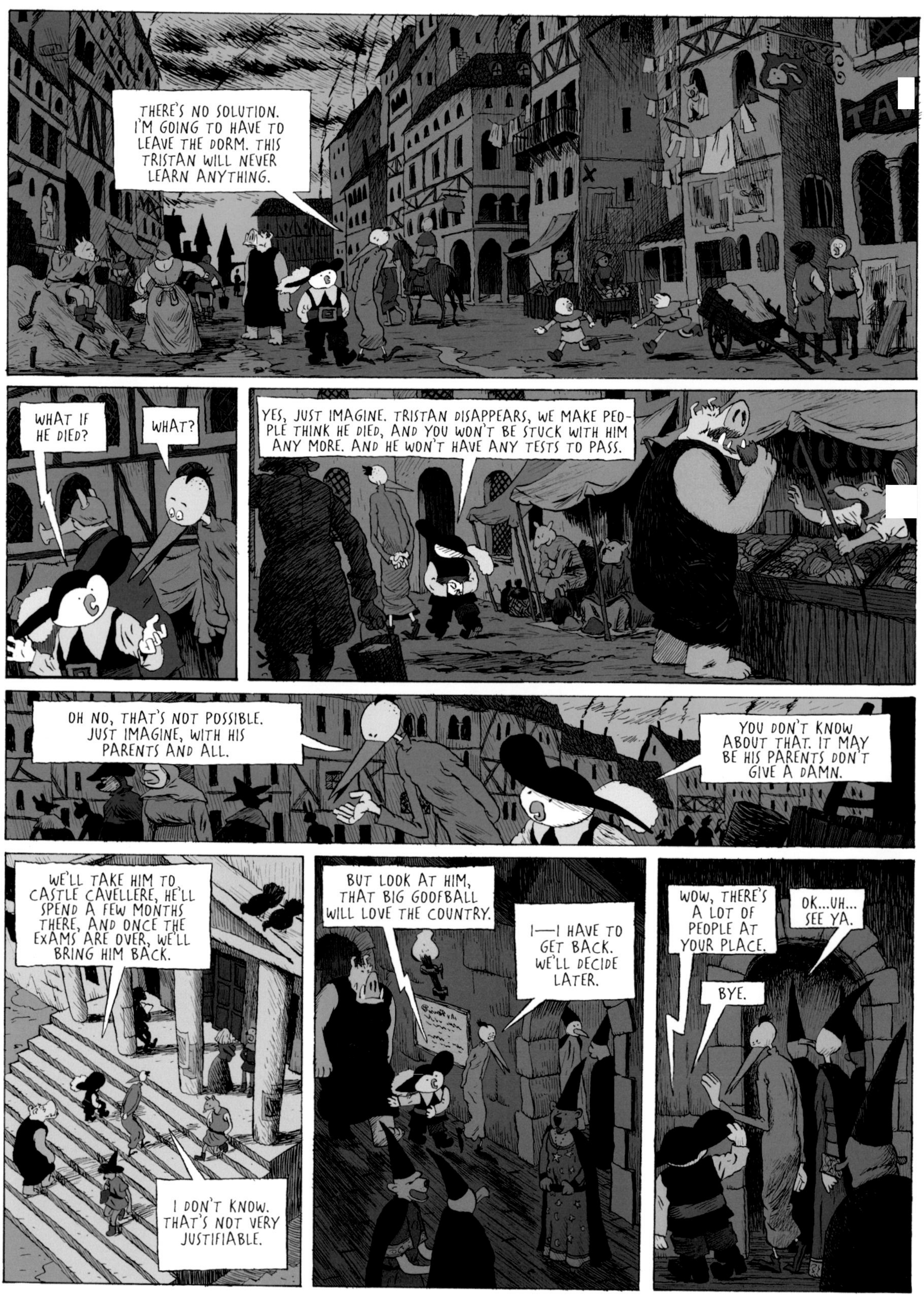
THERE'S NO SOLUTION. I'M GOING TO HAVE TO LEAVE THE DORM. THIS TRISTAN WILL NEVER LEARN ANYTHING.
WHAT IF HE DIED?
WHAT?
YES, JUST IMAGINE. TRISTAN DISAPPEARS, WE MAKE PEOPLE THINK HE DIED, AND YOU WON'T BE STUCK WITH HIM ANY MORE. AND HE WON'T HAVE ANY TESTS TO PASS.
OH NO, THAT'S NOT POSSIBLE. JUST IMAGINE, WITH HIS PARENTS AND ALL.
YOU DON'T KNOW ABOUT THAT. IT MAY BE HIS PARENTS DON'T GIVE A DAMN.
WE'LL TAKE HIM TO CASTLE CAVELLERE, HE'LL SPEND A FEW MONTHS THERE, AND ONCE THE EXAMS ARE OVER, WE'LL BRING HIM BACK.
I DON'T KNOW. THAT'S NOT VERY JUSTIFIABLE.
BUT LOOK AT HIM, THAT BIG GOOFBALL WILL LOVE THE COUNTRY.
I—I HAVE TO GET BACK. WE'LL DECIDE LATER.
WOW, THERE'S A LOT OF PEOPLE AT YOUR PLACE.
OK...UH... SEE YA.
BYE.

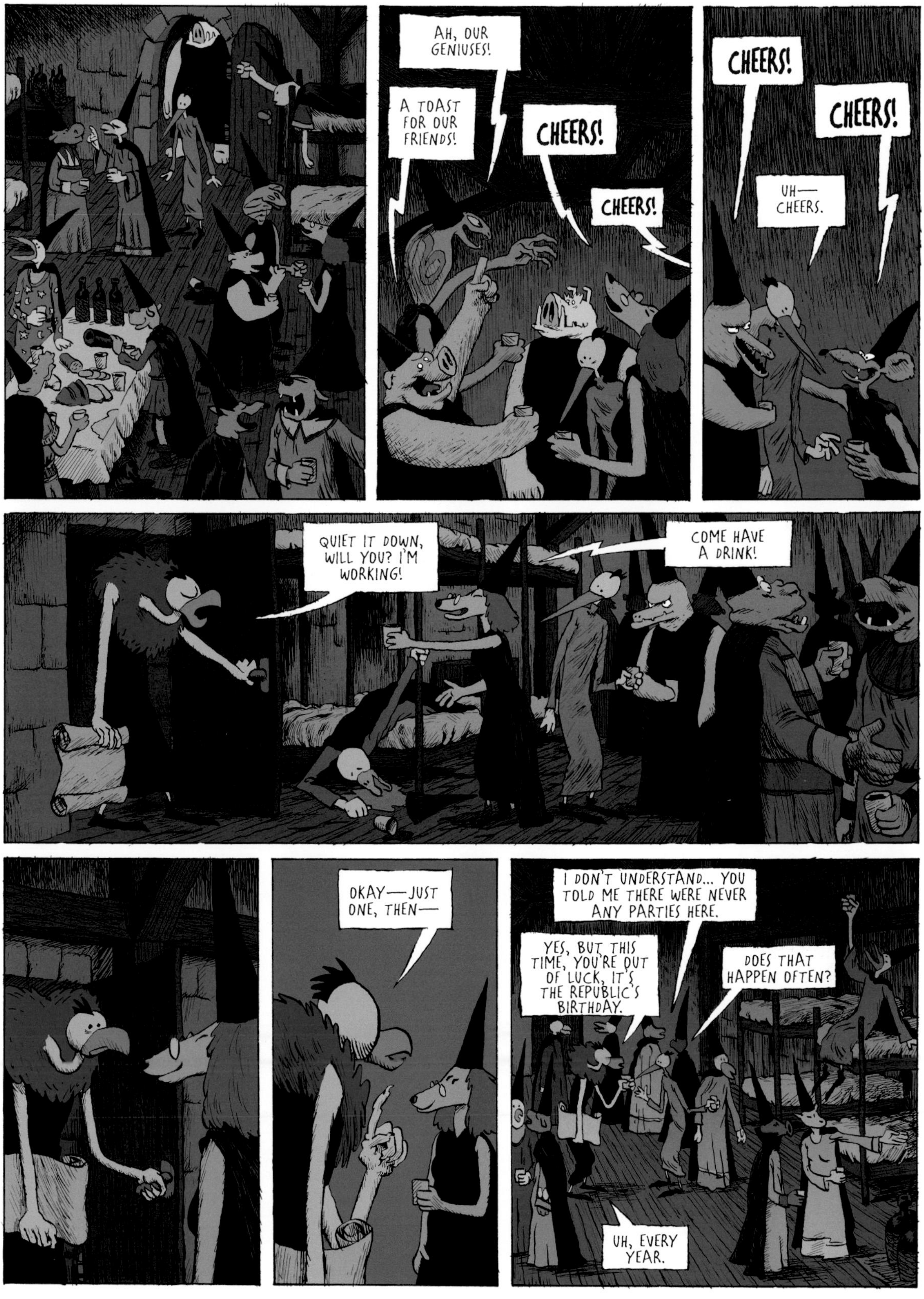
AH, OUR GENIUSES!
A TOAST FOR OUR FRIENDS!
CHEERS!
CHEERS!
CHEERS!
CHEERS!
UH— CHEERS.
QUIET IT DOWN, WILL YOU? I'M WORKING!
COME HAVE A DRINK!
OKAY—JUST ONE, THEN—
I DON'T UNDERSTAND... YOU TOLD ME THERE WERE NEVER ANY PARTIES HERE.
YES, BUT THIS TIME, YOU'RE OUT OF LUCK, IT'S THE REPUBLIC'S BIRTHDAY.
DOES THAT HAPPEN OFTEN?
UH, EVERY YEAR.

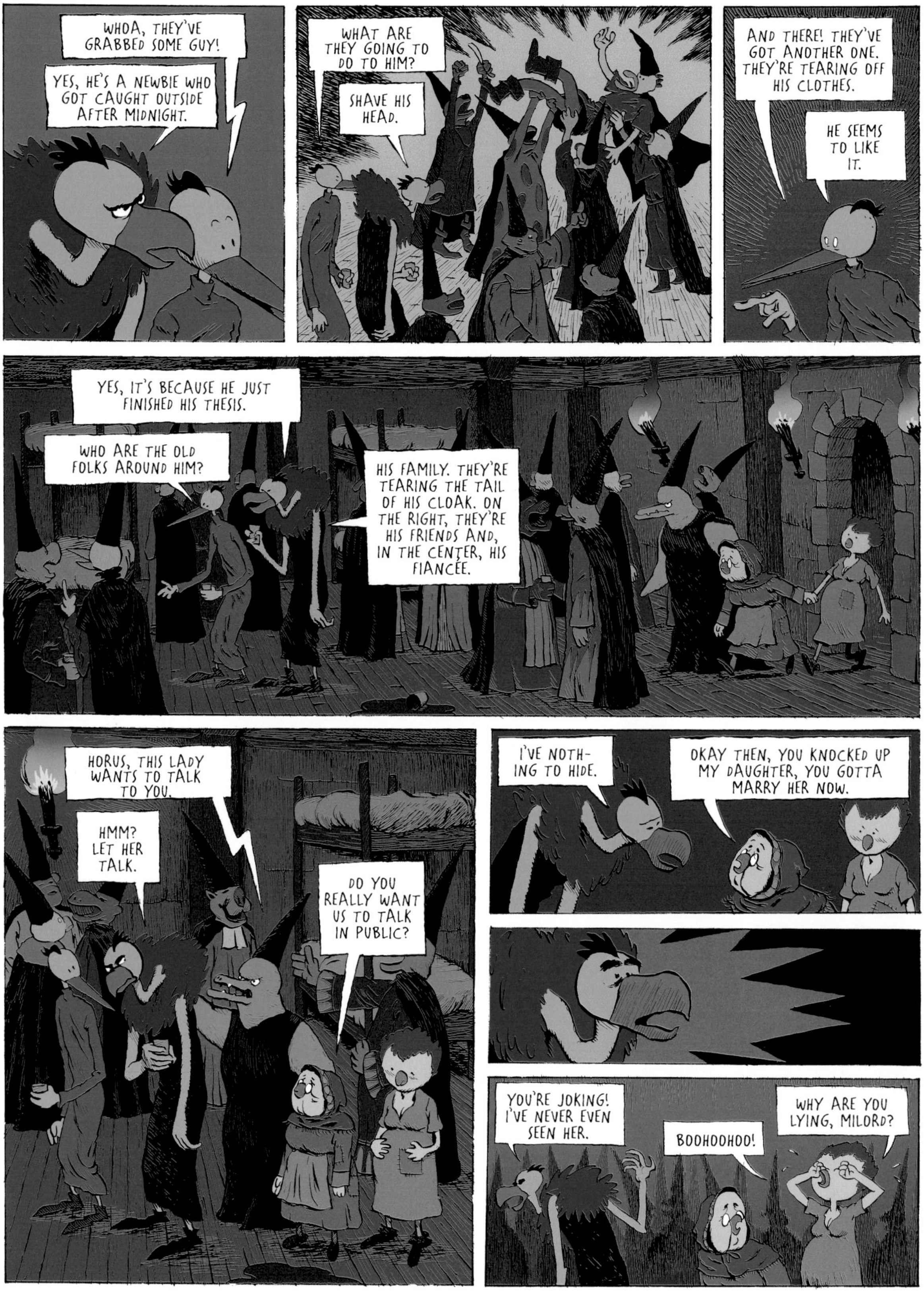
WHOA, THEY'VE GRABBED SOME GUY!
YES, HE'S A NEWBIE WHO GOT CAUGHT OUTSIDE AFTER MIDNIGHT.
WHAT ARE THEY GOING TO DO TO HIM?
SHAVE HIS HEAD.
AND THERE! THEY'VE GOT ANOTHER ONE. THEY'RE TEARING OFF HIS CLOTHES.
HE SEEMS TO LIKE IT.
YES, IT'S BECAUSE HE JUST FINISHED HIS THESIS.
WHO ARE THE OLD FOLKS AROUND HIM?
HIS FAMILY. THEY'RE TEARING THE TAIL OF HIS CLOAK. ON THE RIGHT, THEY'RE HIS FRIENDS AND, IN THE CENTER, HIS FIANCÉE.
HORUS, THIS LADY WANTS TO TALK TO YOU.
HMM? LET HER TALK.
DO YOU REALLY WANT US TO TALK IN PUBLIC?
I'VE NOTH-ING TO HIDE.
OKAY THEN, YOU KNOCKED UP MY DAUGHTER, YOU GOTTA MARRY HER NOW.
YOU'RE JOKING! I'VE NEVER EVEN SEEN HER.
BOOHOOHOO!
WHY ARE YOU LYING, MILORD?

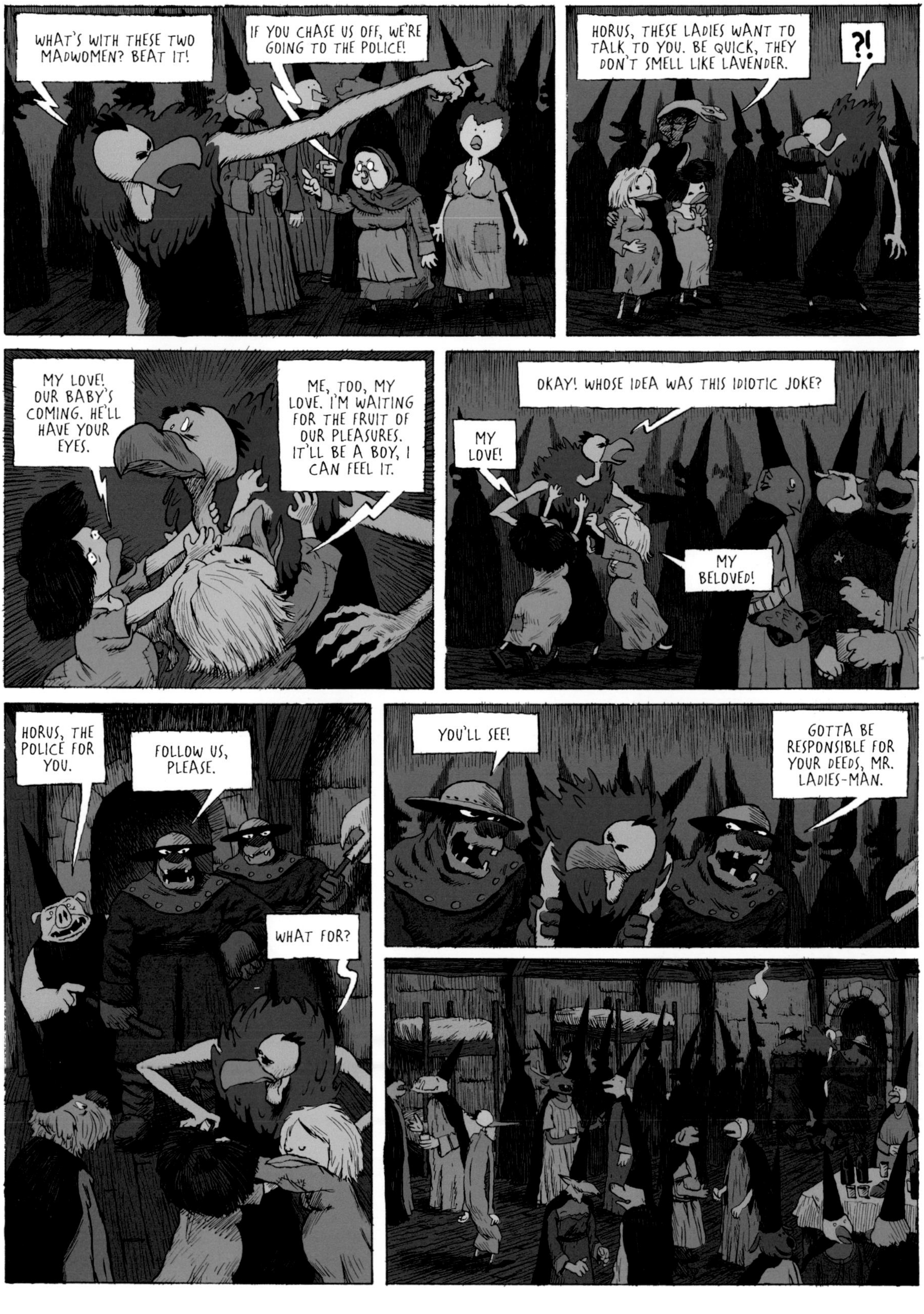
WHAT'S WITH THESE TWO MADWOMEN? BEAT IT!
IF YOU CHASE US OFF, WE'RE GOING TO THE POLICE!
HORUS, THESE LADIES WANT TO TALK TO YOU. BE QUICK, THEY DON'T SMELL LIKE LAVENDER.
?!
MY LOVE! OUR BABY'S COMING. HE'LL HAVE YOUR EYES.
ME, TOO, MY LOVE. I'M WAITING FOR THE FRUIT OF OUR PLEASURES. IT'LL BE A BOY, I CAN FEEL IT.
OKAY! WHOSE IDEA WAS THIS IDIOTIC JOKE?
MY LOVE!
MY BELOVED!
HORUS, THE POLICE FOR YOU.
FOLLOW US, PLEASE.
WHAT FOR?
YOU'LL SEE!
GOTTA BE RESPONSIBLE FOR YOUR DEEDS, MR. LADIES-MAN.

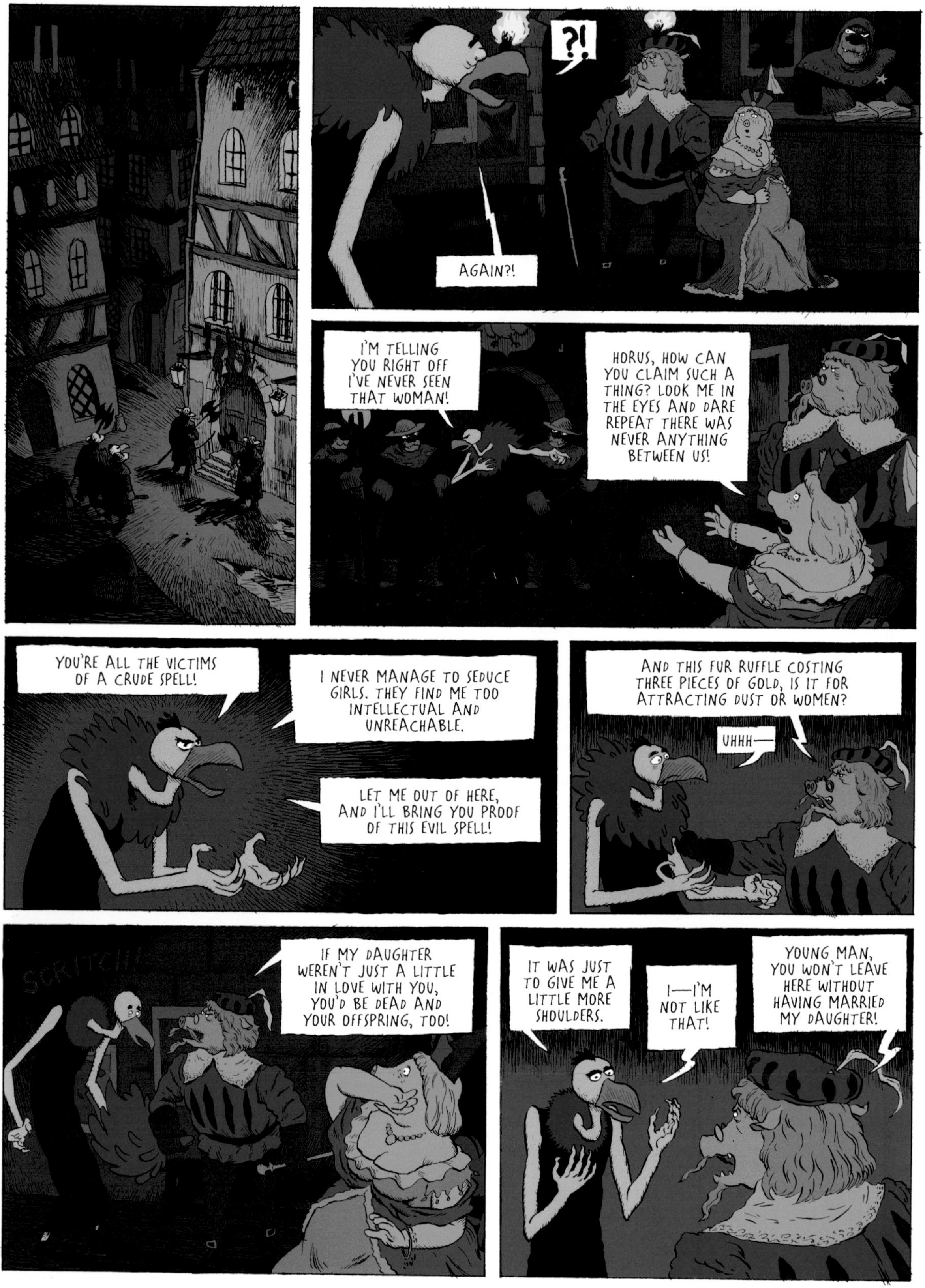
?!
AGAIN?!
I'M TELLING YOU RIGHT OFF I'VE NEVER SEEN THAT WOMAN!
HORUS, HOW CAN YOU CLAIM SUCH A THING? LOOK ME IN THE EYES AND DARE REPEAT THERE WAS NEVER ANYTHING BETWEEN US!
YOU'RE ALL THE VICTIMS OF A CRUDE SPELL!
I NEVER MANAGE TO SEDUCE GIRLS. THEY FIND ME TOO INTELLECTUAL AND UNREACHABLE.
LET ME OUT OF HERE, AND I'LL BRING YOU PROOF OF THIS EVIL SPELL!
AND THIS FUR RUFFLE COSTING THREE PIECES OF GOLD, IS IT FOR ATTRACTING DUST OR WOMEN?
UHHH—
SCRITCH!!
IF MY DAUGHTER WEREN'T JUST A LITTLE IN LOVE WITH YOU, YOU'D BE DEAD AND YOUR OFFSPRING, TOO!
IT WAS JUST TO GIVE ME A LITTLE MORE SHOULDERS.
I—I'M NOT LIKE THAT!
YOUNG MAN, YOU WON'T LEAVE HERE WITHOUT HAVING MARRIED MY DAUGHTER!

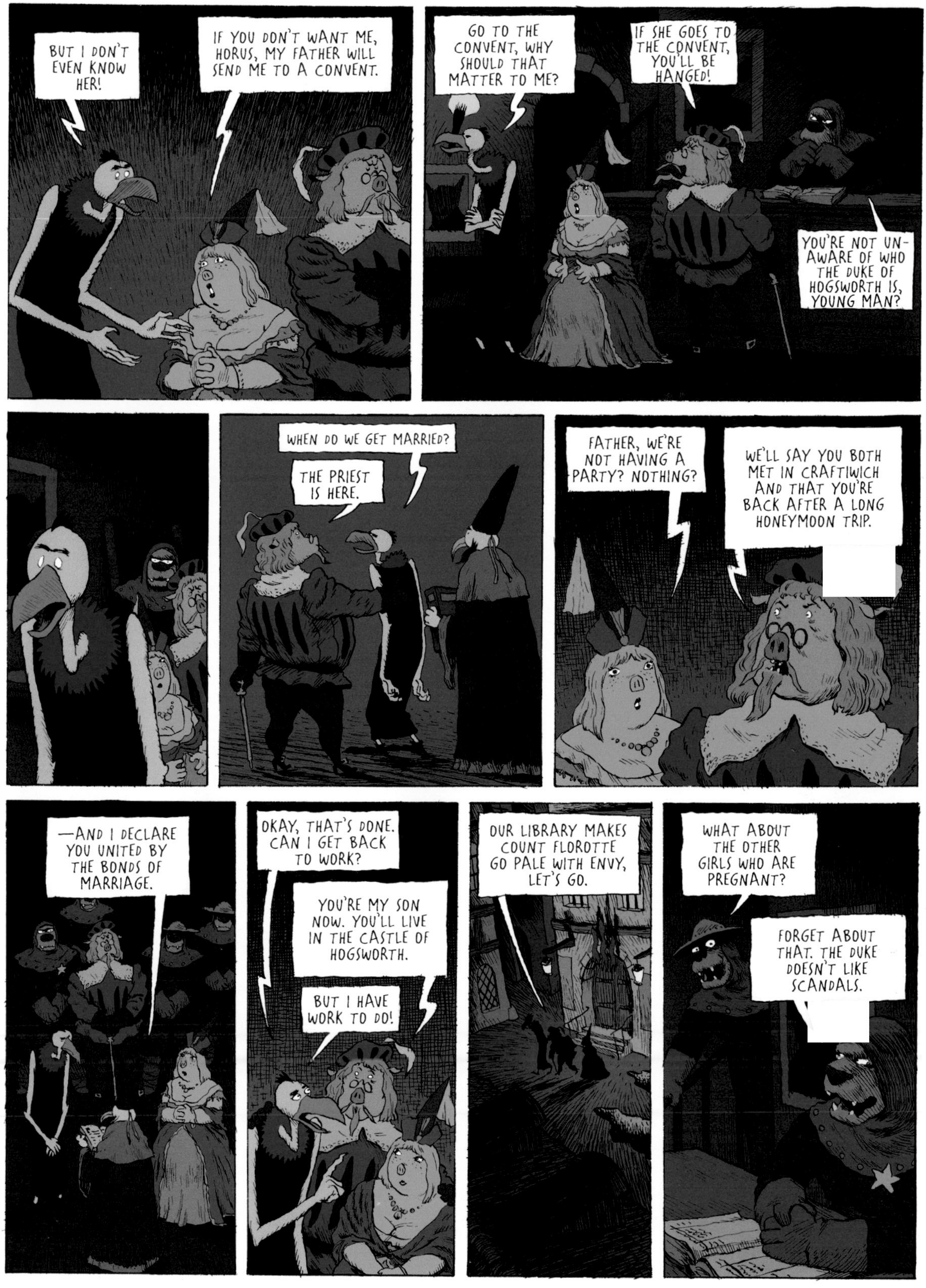
BUT I DON'T EVEN KNOW HER!
IF YOU DON'T WANT ME, HORUS, MY FATHER WILL SEND ME TO A CONVENT.
GO TO THE CONVENT, WHY SHOULD THAT MATTER TO ME?
IF SHE GOES TO THE CONVENT, YOU'LL BE HANGED!
YOU'RE NOT UNAWARE OF WHO THE DUKE OF HOGSWORTH IS, YOUNG MAN?
WHEN DO WE GET MARRIED?
THE PRIEST IS HERE.
FATHER, WE'RE NOT HAVING A PARTY? NOTHING?
WE'LL SAY YOU BOTH MET IN CRAFTIWICH AND THAT YOU'RE BACK AFTER A LONG HONEYMOON TRIP.
—AND I DECLARE YOU UNITED BY THE BONDS OF MARRIAGE.
OKAY, THAT'S DONE. CAN I GET BACK TO WORK?
YOU'RE MY SON NOW. YOU'LL LIVE IN THE CASTLE OF HOGSWORTH.
BUT I HAVE WORK TO DO!
OUR LIBRARY MAKES COUNT FLOROTTE GO PALE WITH ENVY, LET'S GO.
WHAT ABOUT THE OTHER GIRLS WHO ARE PREGNANT?
FORGET ABOUT THAT. THE DUKE DOESN'T LIKE SCANDALS.

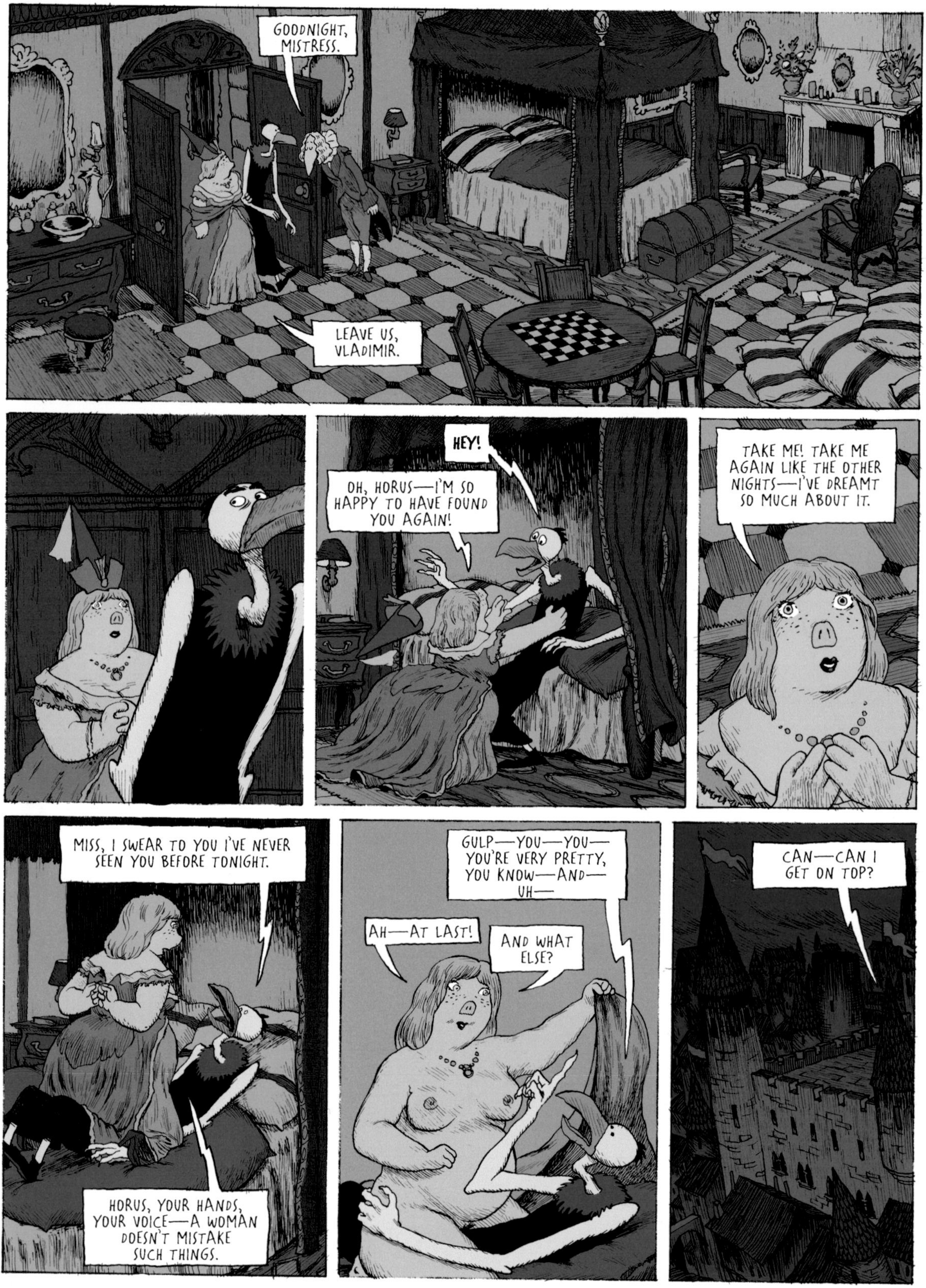
GOODNIGHT, MISTRESS.
LEAVE US, VLADIMIR.
OH, HORUS—I'M SO HAPPY TO HAVE FOUND YOU AGAIN!
HEY!
TAKE ME! TAKE ME AGAIN LIKE THE OTHER NIGHTS—I'VE DREAMT SO MUCH ABOUT IT.
MISS, I SWEAR TO YOU I'VE NEVER SEEN YOU BEFORE TONIGHT.
HORUS, YOUR HANDS, YOUR VOICE—A WOMAN DOESN'T MISTAKE SUCH THINGS.
GULP—YOU—YOU—YOU'RE VERY PRETTY, YOU KNOW—AND—UH—
AH—AT LAST!
AND WHAT ELSE?
CAN—CAN I GET ON TOP?

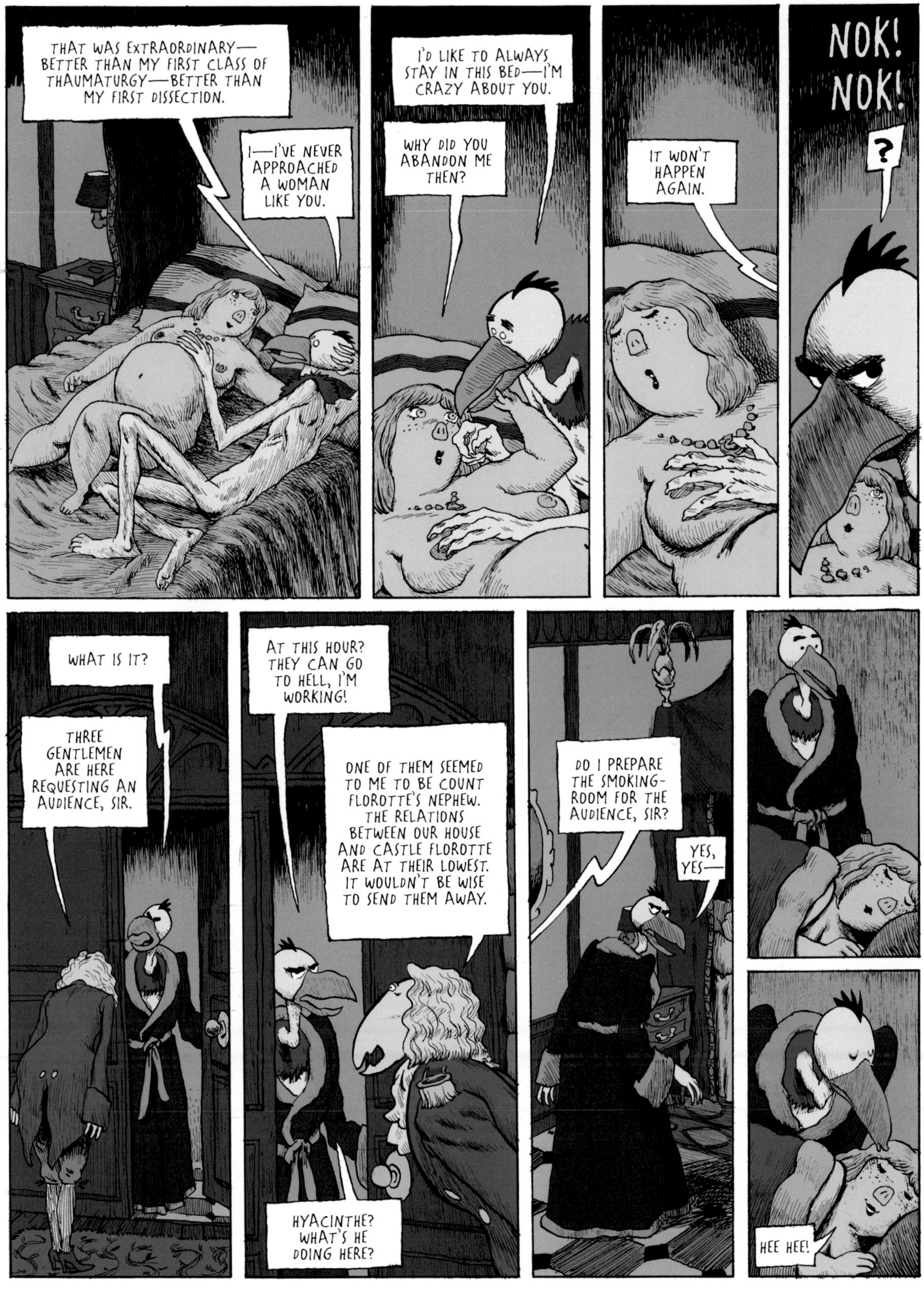
THAT WAS EXTRAORDINARY—BETTER THAN MY FIRST CLASS OF THAUMATURGY—BETTER THAN MY FIRST DISSECTION.
I—I'VE NEVER APPROACHED A WOMAN LIKE YOU.
I'D LIKE TO ALWAYS STAY IN THIS BED—I'M CRAZY ABOUT YOU.
WHY DID YOU ABANDON ME THEN?
IT WON'T HAPPEN AGAIN.
NOK! NOK!
?
WHAT IS IT?
THREE GENTLEMEN ARE HERE REQUESTING AN AUDIENCE, SIR.
AT THIS HOUR? THEY CAN GO TO HELL, I'M WORKING!
ONE OF THEM SEEMED TO ME TO BE COUNT FLOROTTE'S NEPHEW. THE RELATIONS BETWEEN OUR HOUSE AND CASTLE FLOROTTE ARE AT THEIR LOWEST. IT WOULDN'T BE WISE TO SEND THEM AWAY.
HYACINTHE? WHAT'S HE DOING HERE?
DO I PREPARE THE SMOKING-ROOM FOR THE AUDIENCE, SIR?
YES, YES—
HEE HEE!

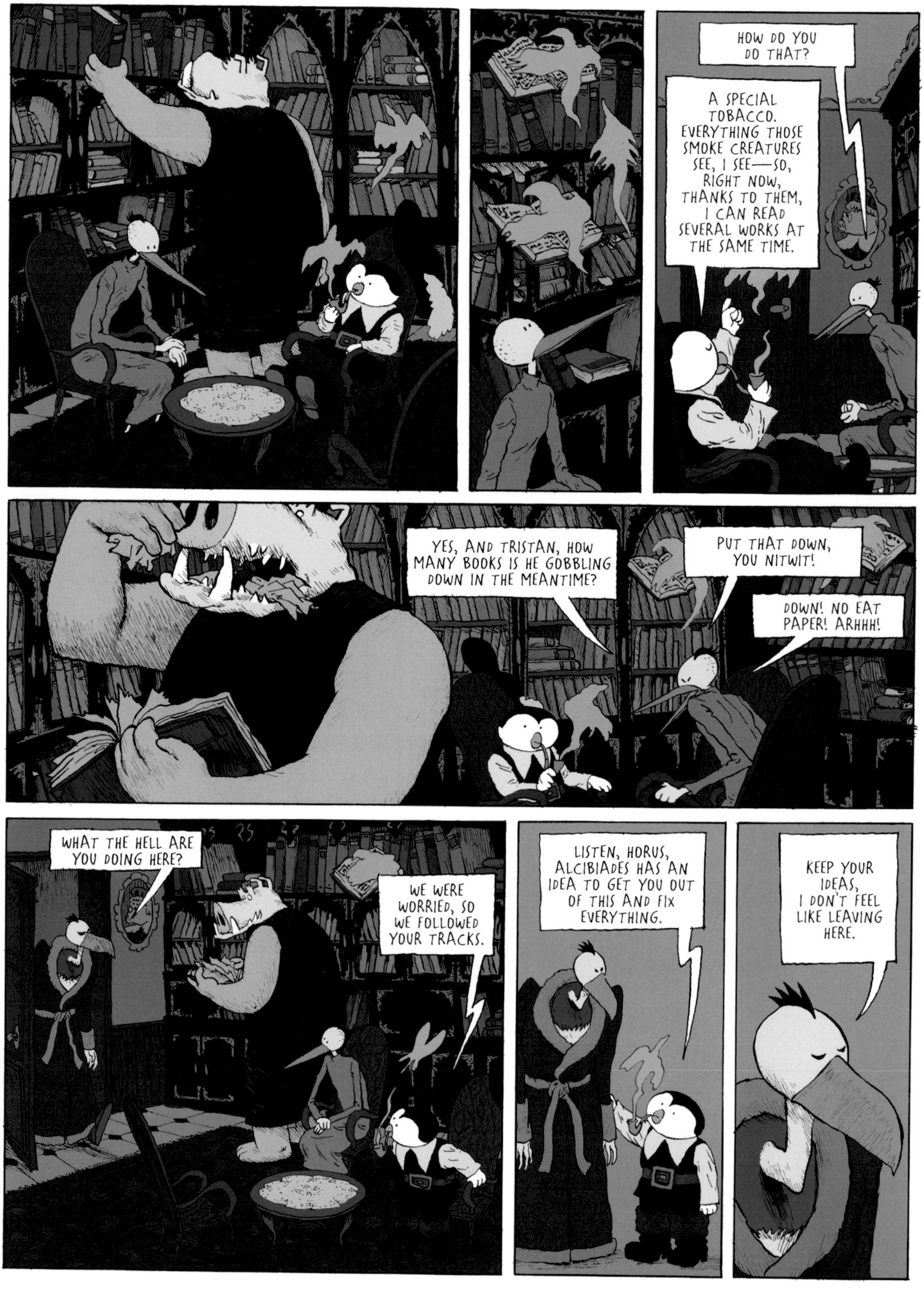
HOW DO YOU DO THAT?
A SPECIAL TOBACCO. EVERYTHING THOSE SMOKE CREATURES SEE, I SEE—SO, RIGHT NOW, THANKS TO THEM, I CAN READ SEVERAL WORKS AT THE SAME TIME.
YES, AND TRISTAN, HOW MANY BOOKS IS HE GOBBLING DOWN IN THE MEANTIME?
PUT THAT DOWN, YOU NITWIT!
DOWN! NO EAT PAPER! ARHHH!
WHAT THE HELL ARE YOU DOING HERE?
WE WERE WORRIED, SO WE FOLLOWED YOUR TRACKS.
LISTEN, HORUS, ALCIBIADES HAS AN IDEA TO GET YOU OUT OF THIS AND FIX EVERYTHING.
KEEP YOUR IDEAS, I DON'T FEEL LIKE LEAVING HERE.

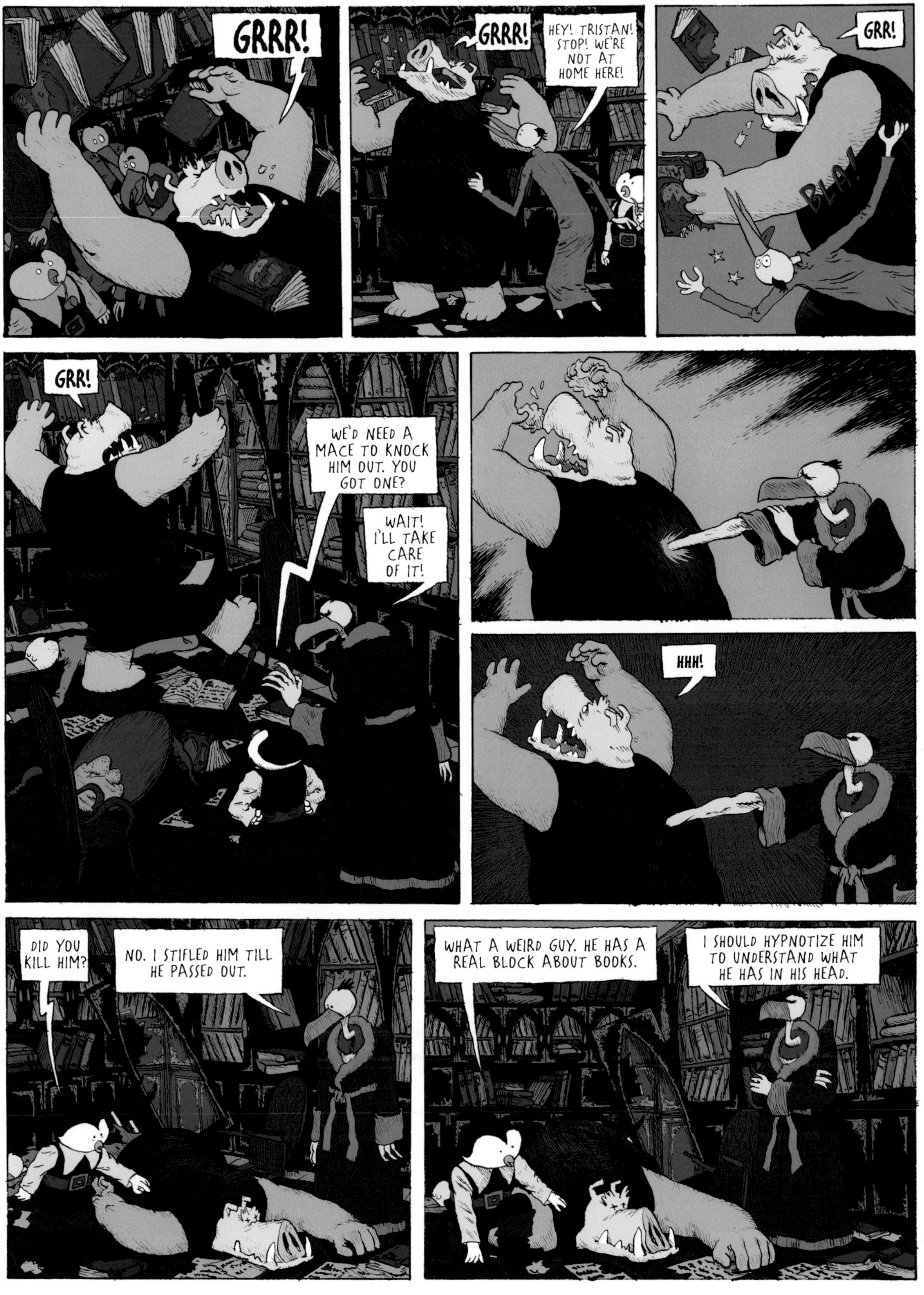
GRRR!
GRRR!
HEY! TRISTAN! STOP! WE'RE NOT AT HOME HERE!
GRR!
BLA!
GRR!
WE'D NEED A MACE TO KNOCK HIM OUT. YOU GOT ONE?
WAIT! I'LL TAKE CARE OF IT!
HHH!
DID YOU KILL HIM?
NO. I STIFLED HIM TILL HE PASSED OUT.
WHAT A WEIRD GUY. HE HAS A REAL BLOCK ABOUT BOOKS.
I SHOULD HYPNOTIZE HIM TO UNDERSTAND WHAT HE HAS IN HIS HEAD.

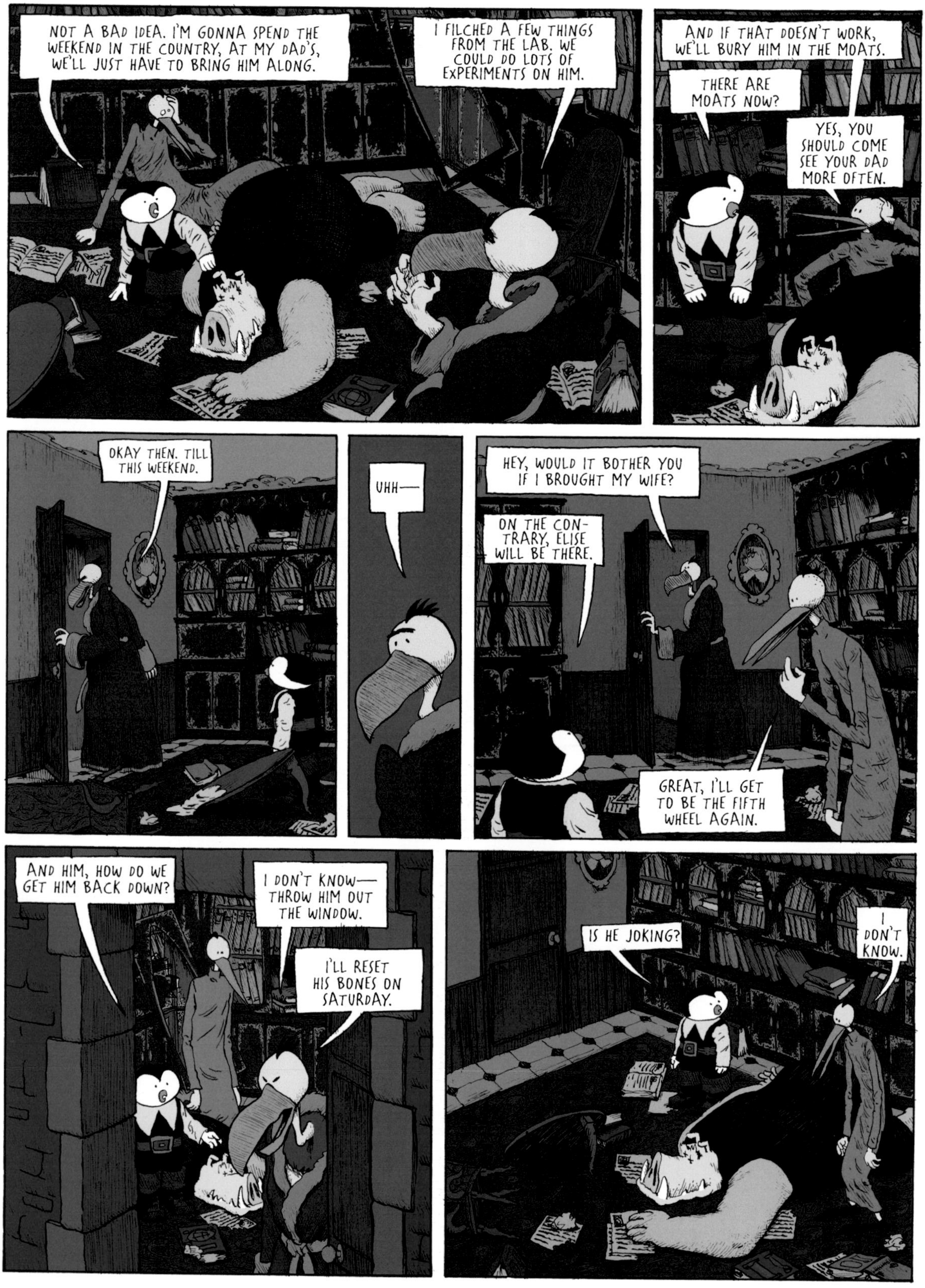
NOT A BAD IDEA. I'M GONNA SPEND THE WEEKEND IN THE COUNTRY, AT MY DAD'S, WE'LL JUST HAVE TO BRING HIM ALONG.
I FILCHED A FEW THINGS FROM THE LAB. WE COULD DO LOTS OF EXPERIMENTS ON HIM.
AND IF THAT DOESN'T WORK, WE'LL BURY HIM IN THE MOATS.
THERE ARE MOATS NOW?
YES, YOU SHOULD COME SEE YOUR DAD MORE OFTEN.
OKAY THEN. TILL THIS WEEKEND.
UHH—
HEY, WOULD IT BOTHER YOU IF I BROUGHT MY WIFE?
ON THE CONTRARY, ELISE WILL BE THERE.
GREAT, I'LL GET TO BE THE FIFTH WHEEL AGAIN.
AND HIM, HOW DO WE GET HIM BACK DOWN?
I DON'T KNOW— THROW HIM OUT THE WINDOW.
I'LL RESET HIS BONES ON SATURDAY.
IS HE JOKING?
I DON'T KNOW.

Panel 1

DID YOU SLEEP POORLY, MY LOVE?

TO TELL THE TRUTH, I DIDN'T SLEEP A WINK.

Panel 2

I'M SORRY, I MUST HAVE SNORED.

NO, IT WAS THE LOVELIEST NIGHT OF MY LIFE. I COULDN'T STOP LOOKING AT YOU. I'M SO AMAZED AT BEING BY YOUR SIDE THAT SLEEPING WOULD BE A WASTE OF TIME.

Panel 3

YOU GROPED ME, DIDN'T YOU, ONCE.

I DIDN'T REALIZE YOU NOTICED.

BAD BOY!

Panel 4

NO! IT WAS A SCIENTIFIC EXPERIMENT. I WAS TRYING TO DETERMINE AT WHAT POINT IN YOUR SLEEP AND TO WHAT EXTENT I COULD FONDLE YOU WITHOUT WAKING YOU.

WELL THEN?

Panel 5

AHA! AT CERTAIN STAGES, I CAN GO PRETTY FAR—

IDIOT! I WAS JUST PRETENDING TO SLEEP.

Panel 6

NOT ALL THE TIME. WHEN YOU'RE SOUND ASLEEP, YOUR MUSCLES UNDERGO REGULAR SPASMS WHICH TRAP MY FINGERS PERIODICALLY. EVEN IF YOU WANTED TO, YOU COULDN'T FAKE THAT SEA ANEMONE-LIKE PALPITATION.

SUCH A ROMANTIC!

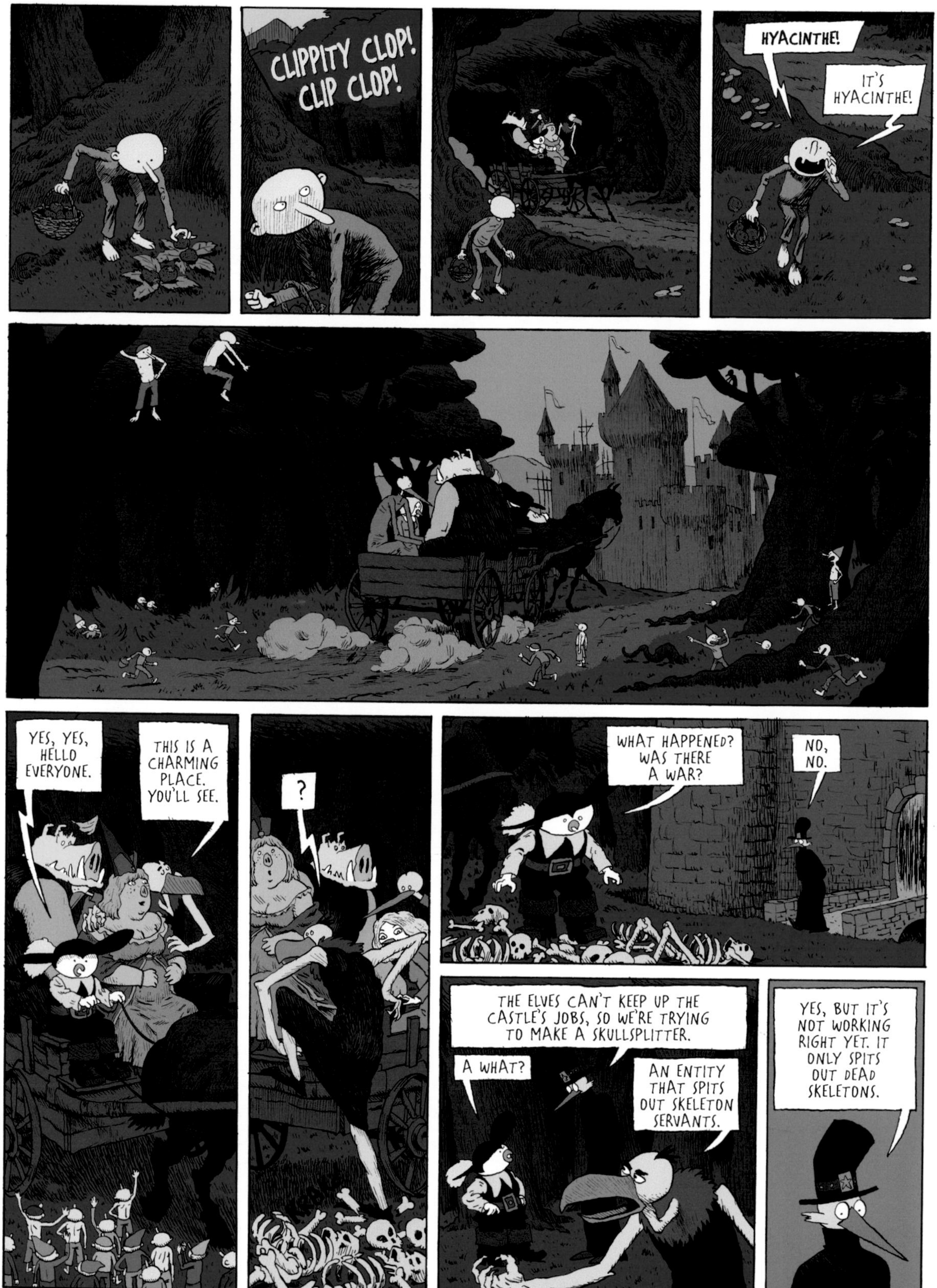
CLIPPITY CLOP!
CLIP CLOP!
HYACINTHE!
IT'S HYACINTHE!
YES, YES, HELLO EVERYONE.
THIS IS A CHARMING PLACE. YOU'LL SEE.
?
WHAT HAPPENED? WAS THERE A WAR?
NO, NO.
THE ELVES CAN'T KEEP UP THE CASTLE'S JOBS, SO WE'RE TRYING TO MAKE A SKULLSPLITTER.
A WHAT?
AN ENTITY THAT SPITS OUT SKELETON SERVANTS.
YES, BUT IT'S NOT WORKING RIGHT YET. IT ONLY SPITS OUT DEAD SKELETONS.

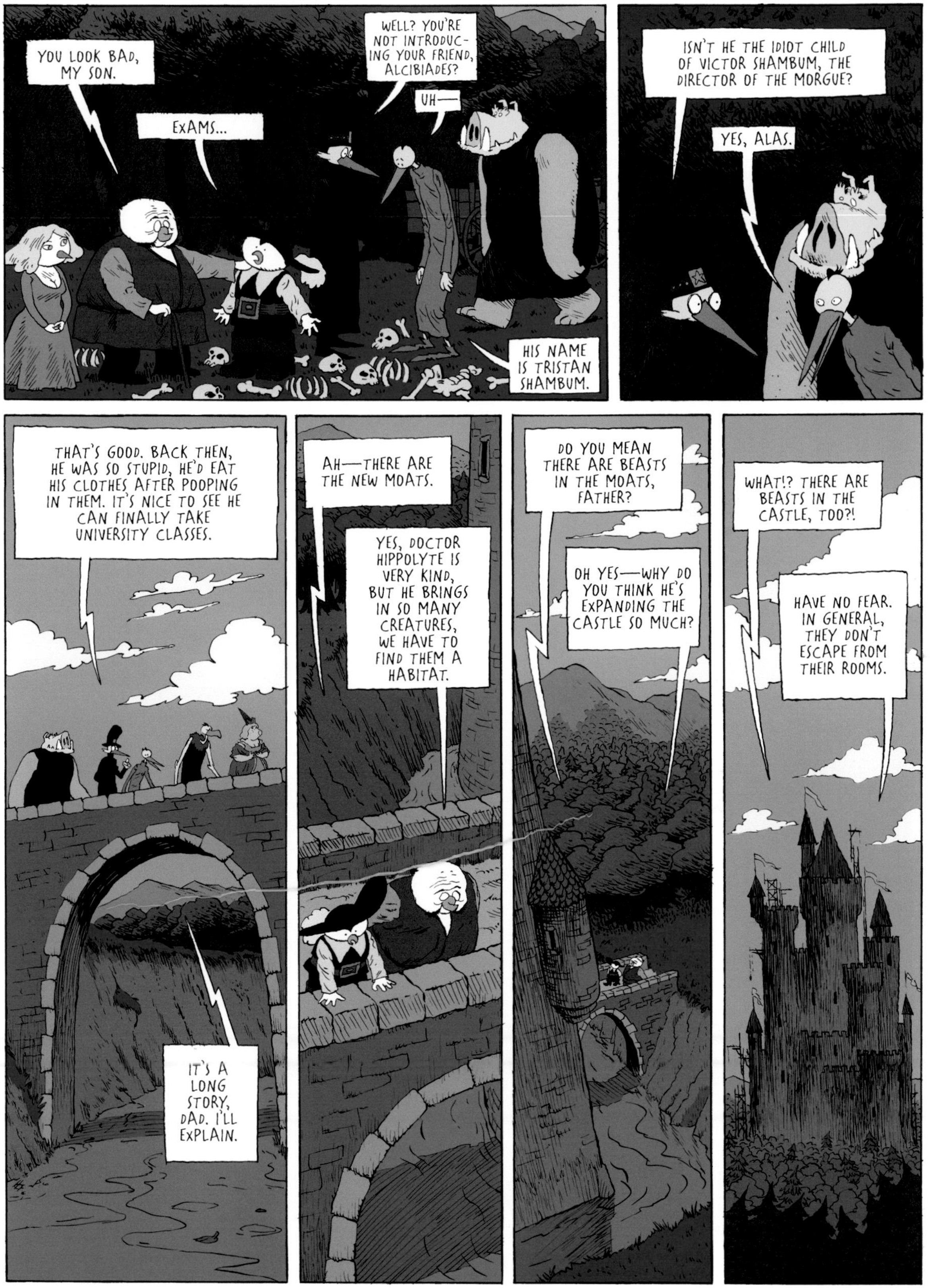
YOU LOOK BAD, MY SON.
EXAMS...
WELL? YOU'RE NOT INTRODUCING YOUR FRIEND, ALCIBIADES?
UH—
HIS NAME IS TRISTAN SHAMBUM.
ISN'T HE THE IDIOT CHILD OF VICTOR SHAMBUM, THE DIRECTOR OF THE MORGUE?
YES, ALAS.
THAT'S GOOD. BACK THEN, HE WAS SO STUPID, HE'D EAT HIS CLOTHES AFTER POOPING IN THEM. IT'S NICE TO SEE HE CAN FINALLY TAKE UNIVERSITY CLASSES.
IT'S A LONG STORY, DAD. I'LL EXPLAIN.
AH—THERE ARE THE NEW MOATS.
YES, DOCTOR HIPPOLYTE IS VERY KIND, BUT HE BRINGS IN SO MANY CREATURES, WE HAVE TO FIND THEM A HABITAT.
DO YOU MEAN THERE ARE BEASTS IN THE MOATS, FATHER?
OH YES—WHY DO YOU THINK HE'S EXPANDING THE CASTLE SO MUCH?
WHAT!? THERE ARE BEASTS IN THE CASTLE, TOO?!
HAVE NO FEAR. IN GENERAL, THEY DON'T ESCAPE FROM THEIR ROOMS.

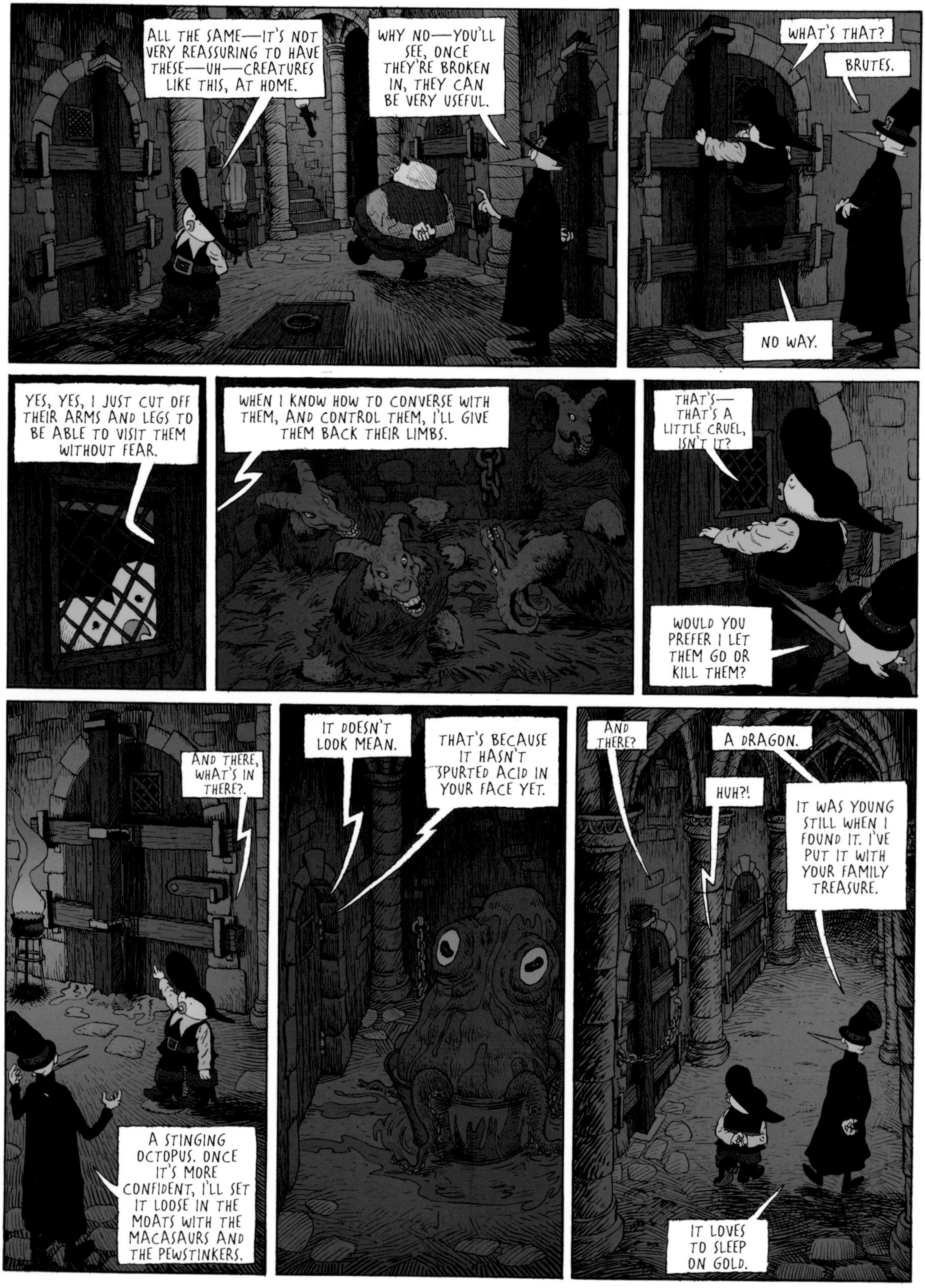
ALL THE SAME—IT'S NOT VERY REASSURING TO HAVE THESE—UH—CREATURES LIKE THIS, AT HOME.
WHY NO—YOU'LL SEE, ONCE THEY'RE BROKEN IN, THEY CAN BE VERY USEFUL.
WHAT'S THAT?
BRUTES.
NO WAY.
YES, YES, I JUST CUT OFF THEIR ARMS AND LEGS TO BE ABLE TO VISIT THEM WITHOUT FEAR.
WHEN I KNOW HOW TO CONVERSE WITH THEM, AND CONTROL THEM, I'LL GIVE THEM BACK THEIR LIMBS.
THAT'S— THAT'S A LITTLE CRUEL, ISN'T IT?
WOULD YOU PREFER I LET THEM GO OR KILL THEM?
AND THERE, WHAT'S IN THERE?.
A STINGING OCTOPUS. ONCE IT'S MORE CONFIDENT, I'LL SET IT LOOSE IN THE MOATS WITH THE MACASAURS AND THE PEWSTINKERS.
IT DOESN'T LOOK MEAN.
THAT'S BECAUSE IT HASN'T SPURTED ACID IN YOUR FACE YET.
AND THERE?
A DRAGON.
HUH?!
IT WAS YOUNG STILL WHEN I FOUND IT. I'VE PUT IT WITH YOUR FAMILY TREASURE.
IT LOVES TO SLEEP ON GOLD.

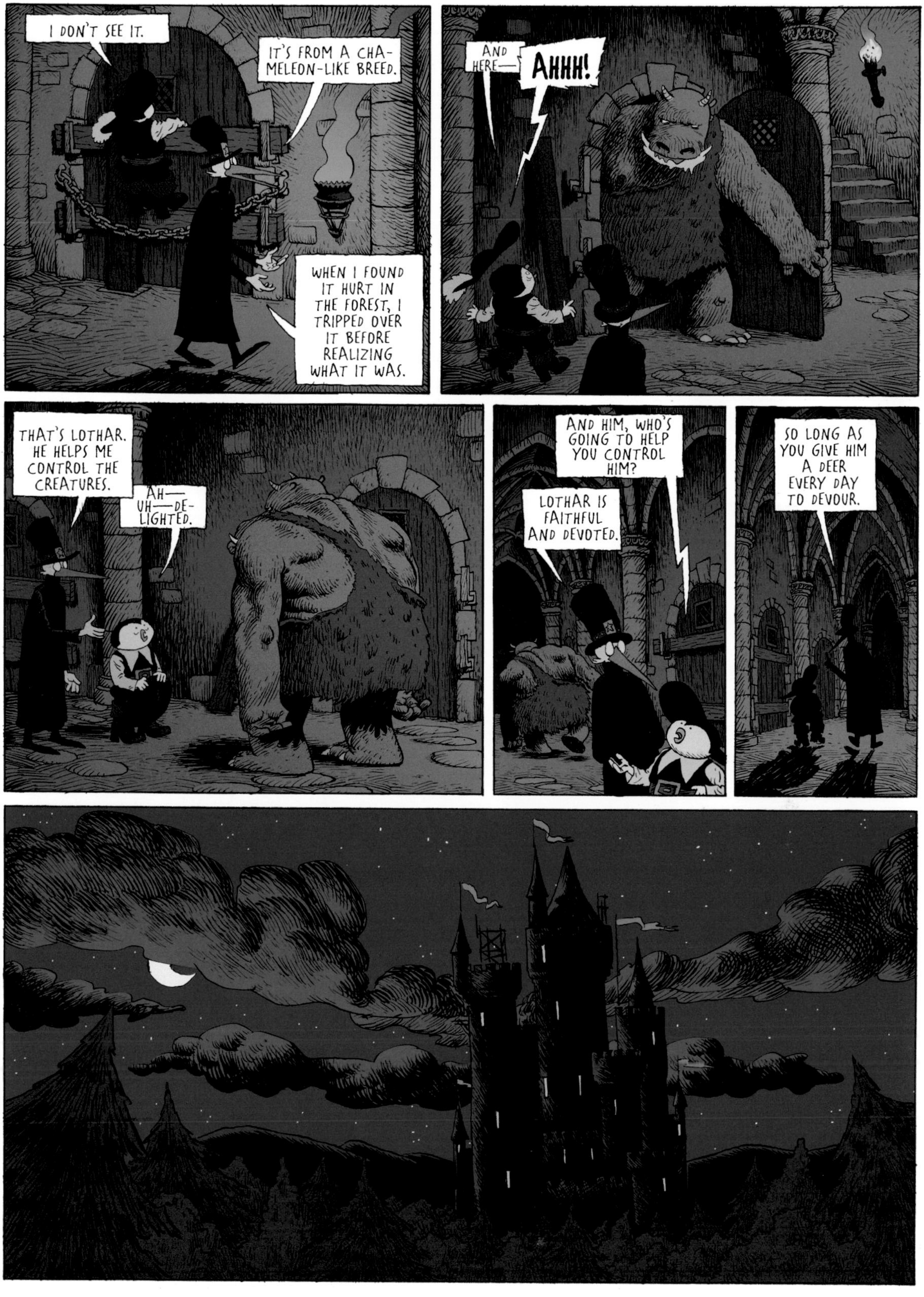
I DON'T SEE IT.
IT'S FROM A CHAMELEON-LIKE BREED.
WHEN I FOUND IT HURT IN THE FOREST, I TRIPPED OVER IT BEFORE REALIZING WHAT IT WAS.
AND HERE—
AHHH!
THAT'S LOTHAR. HE HELPS ME CONTROL THE CREATURES.
AH— UH—DE-LIGHTED.
AND HIM, WHO'S GOING TO HELP YOU CONTROL HIM?
LOTHAR IS FAITHFUL AND DEVOTED.
SO LONG AS YOU GIVE HIM A DEER EVERY DAY TO DEVOUR.

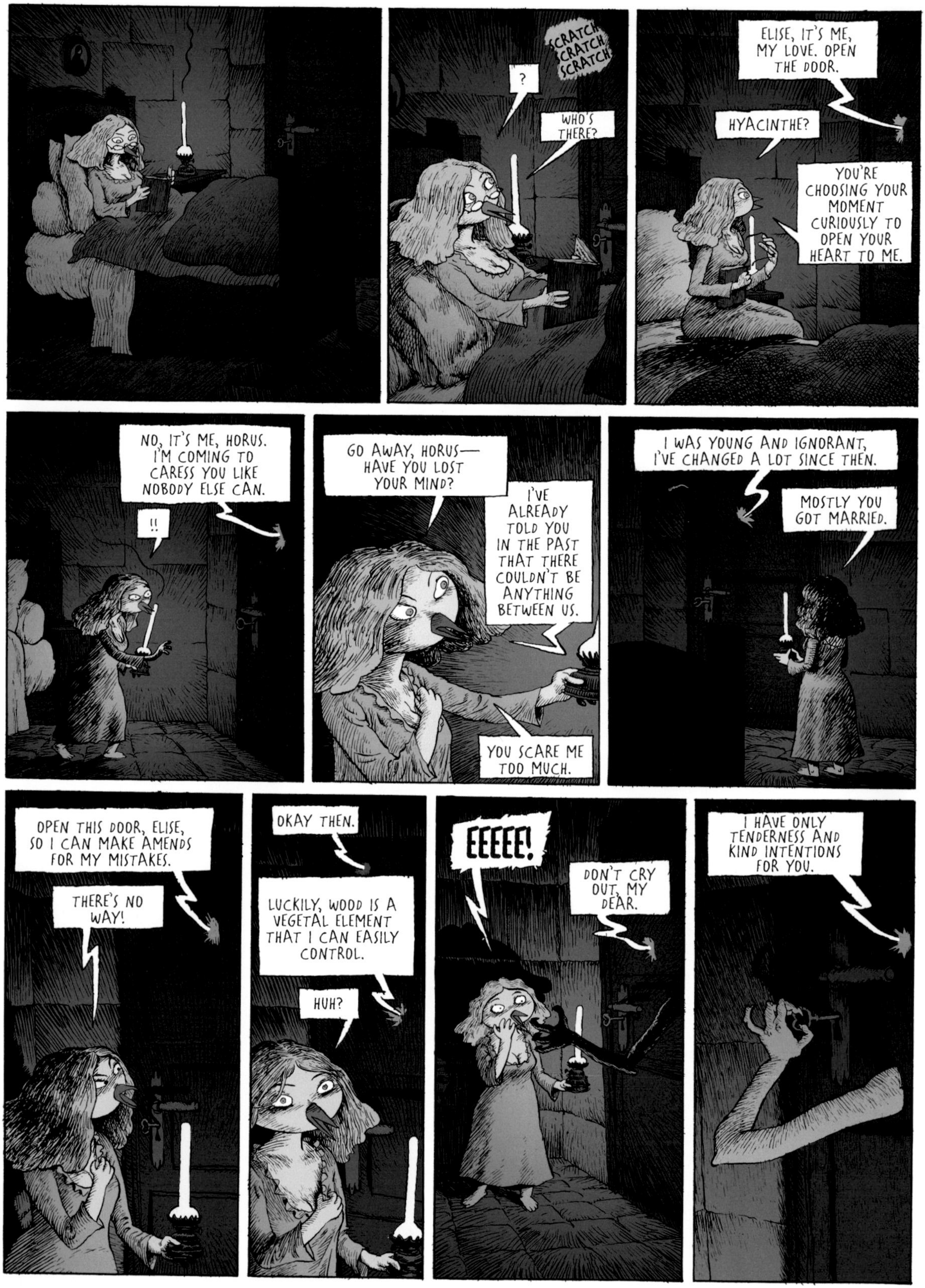
SCRATCH SCRATCH SCRATCH
?
WHO'S THERE?
ELISE, IT'S ME, MY LOVE. OPEN THE DOOR.
HYACINTHE?
YOU'RE CHOOSING YOUR MOMENT CURIOUSLY TO OPEN YOUR HEART TO ME.
NO, IT'S ME, HORUS. I'M COMING TO CARESS YOU LIKE NOBODY ELSE CAN.
!!
GO AWAY, HORUS— HAVE YOU LOST YOUR MIND?
I'VE ALREADY TOLD YOU IN THE PAST THAT THERE COULDN'T BE ANYTHING BETWEEN US.
YOU SCARE ME TOO MUCH.
I WAS YOUNG AND IGNORANT, I'VE CHANGED A LOT SINCE THEN.
MOSTLY YOU GOT MARRIED.
OPEN THIS DOOR, ELISE, SO I CAN MAKE AMENDS FOR MY MISTAKES.
THERE'S NO WAY!
OKAY THEN.
LUCKILY, WOOD IS A VEGETAL ELEMENT THAT I CAN EASILY CONTROL.
HUH?
EEEEE!
DON'T CRY OUT, MY DEAR.
I HAVE ONLY TENDERNESS AND KIND INTENTIONS FOR YOU.

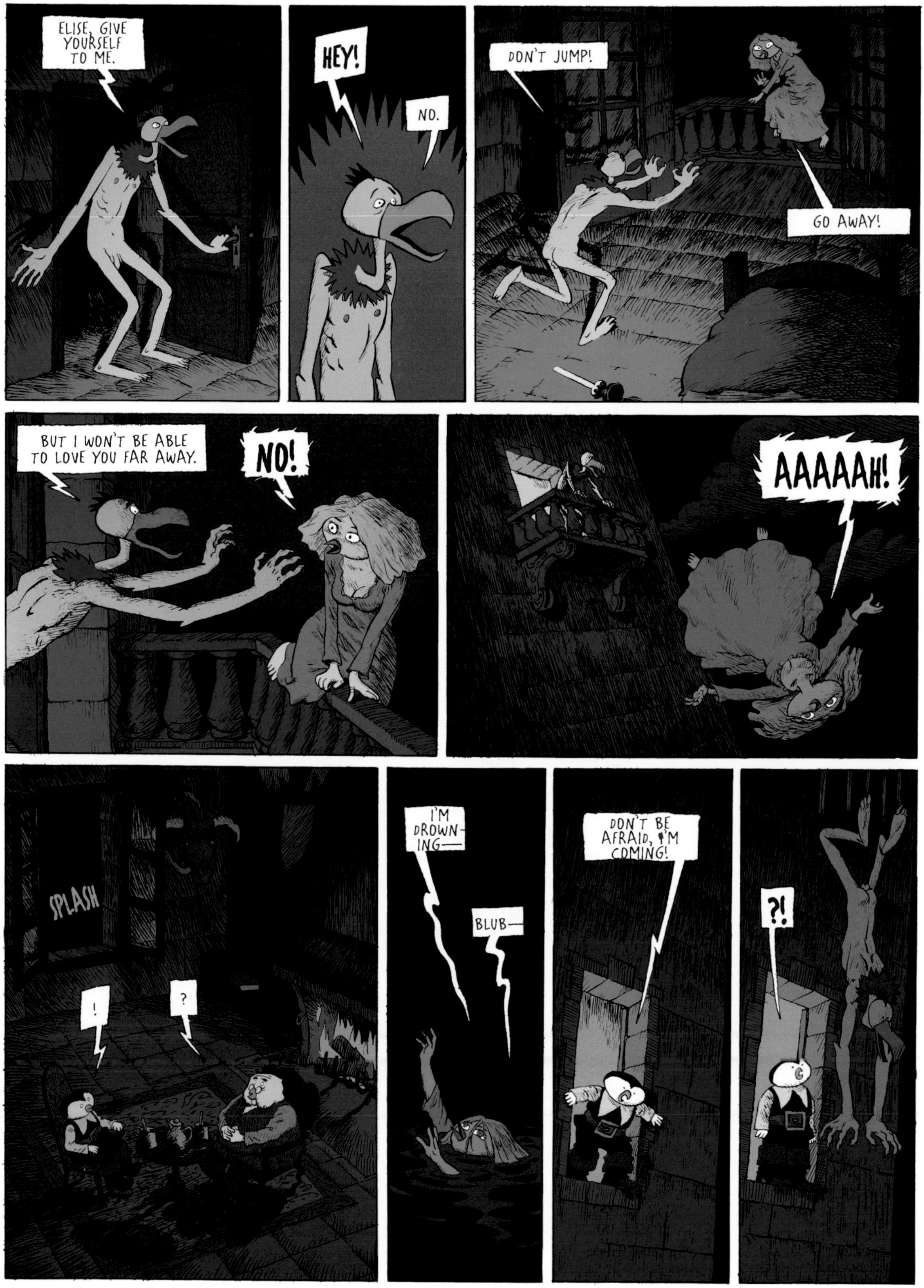

ELISE, GIVE YOURSELF TO ME.
HEY!
NO.
DON'T JUMP!
GO AWAY!
BUT I WON'T BE ABLE TO LOVE YOU FAR AWAY.
NO!
AAAAAH!
SPLASH
!
?
I'M DROWN- ING—
BLUB—
DON'T BE AFRAID, I'M COMING!
?!

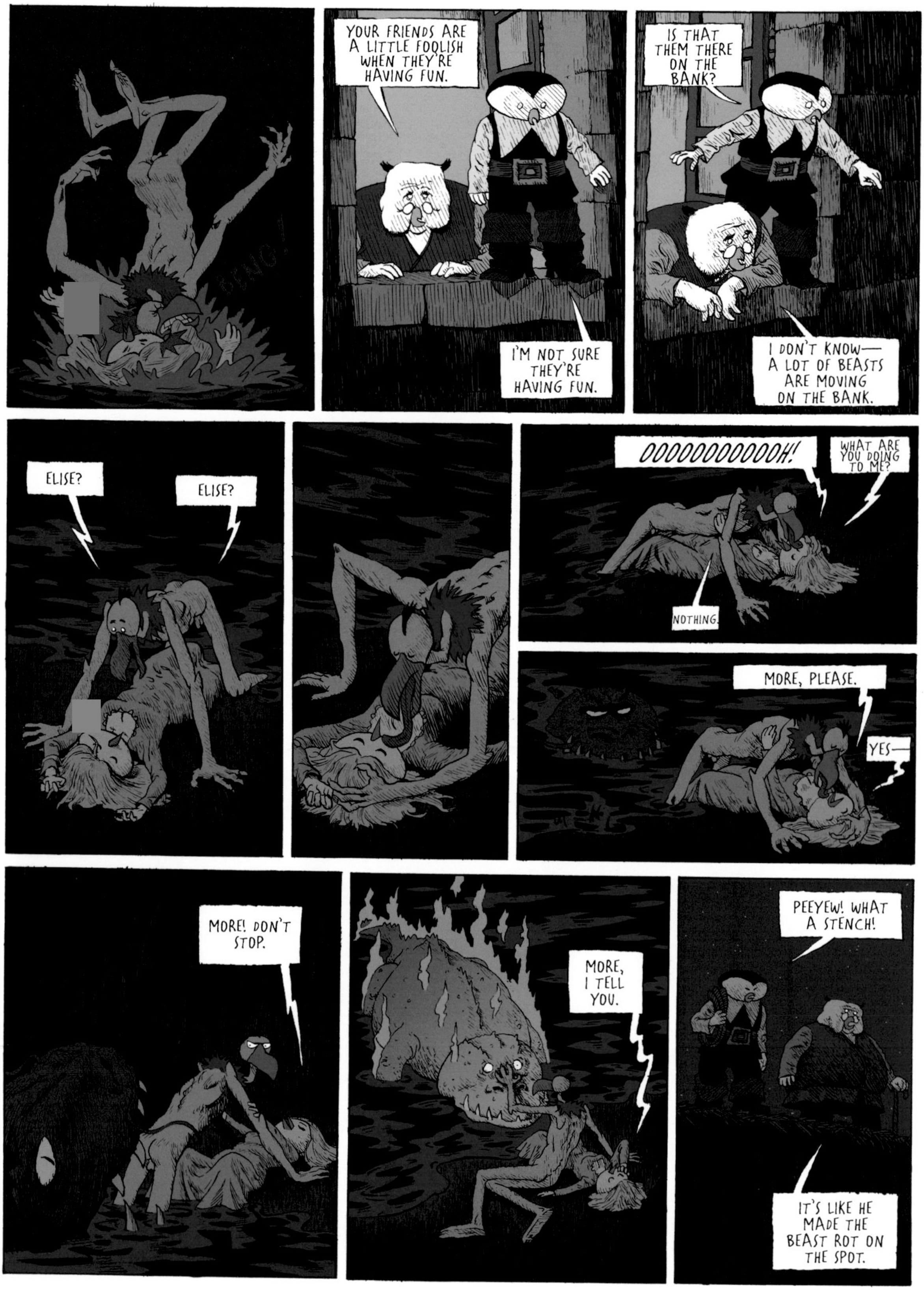
BENG!
YOUR FRIENDS ARE A LITTLE FOOLISH WHEN THEY'RE HAVING FUN.
I'M NOT SURE THEY'RE HAVING FUN.
IS THAT THEM THERE ON THE BANK?
I DON'T KNOW— A LOT OF BEASTS ARE MOVING ON THE BANK.
ELISE?
ELISE?
OOOOOOOOOOOOH!
WHAT ARE YOU DOING TO ME?
NOTHING.
MORE, PLEASE.
YES—
MORE! DON'T STOP.
MORE, I TELL YOU.
PEEYEW! WHAT A STENCH!
IT'S LIKE HE MADE THE BEAST ROT ON THE SPOT.

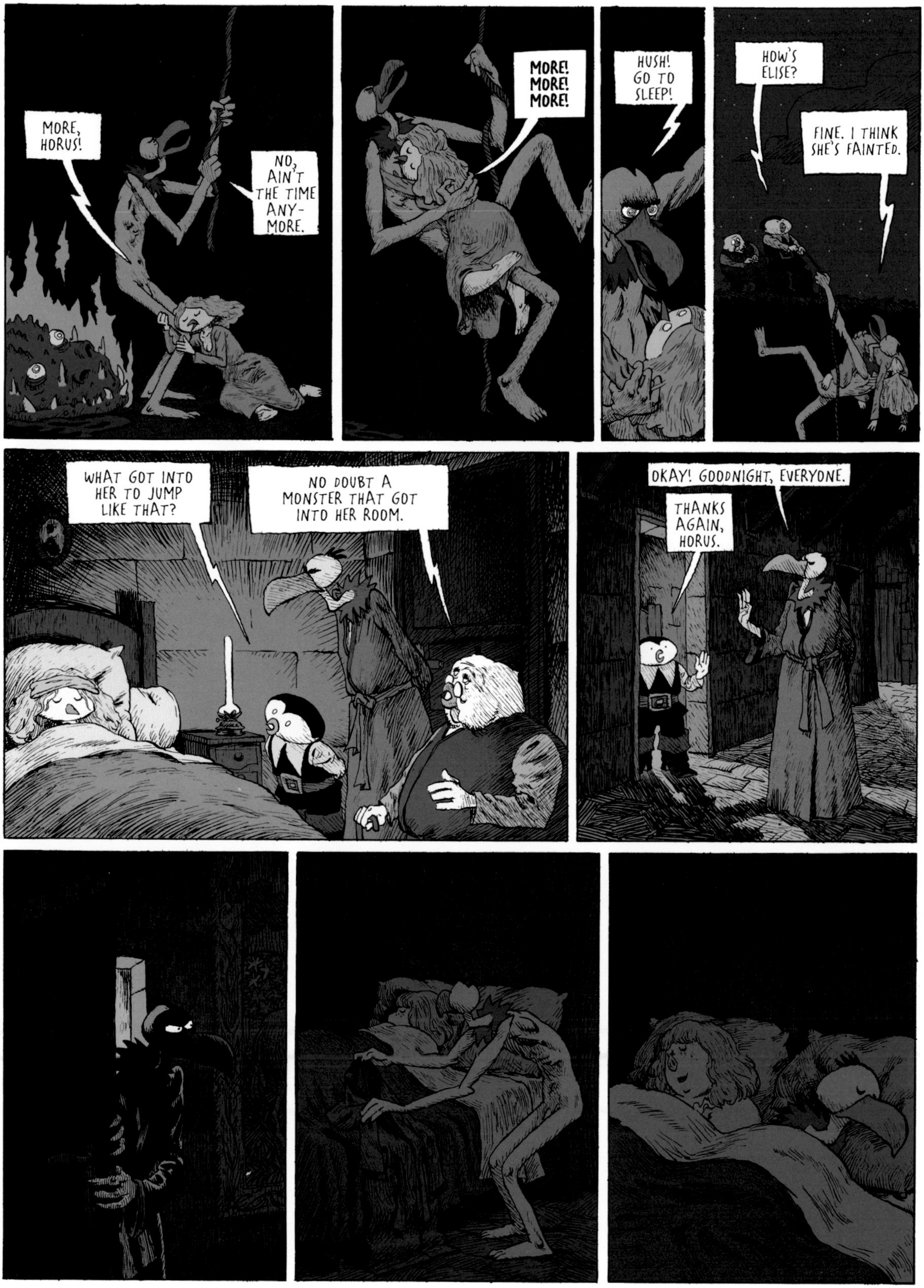

MORE, HORUS!
NO, AIN'T THE TIME ANYMORE.
MORE! MORE! MORE!
HUSH! GO TO SLEEP!
HOW'S ELISE?
FINE. I THINK SHE'S FAINTED.
WHAT GOT INTO HER TO JUMP LIKE THAT?
NO DOUBT A MONSTER THAT GOT INTO HER ROOM.
OKAY! GOODNIGHT, EVERYONE.
THANKS AGAIN, HORUS.

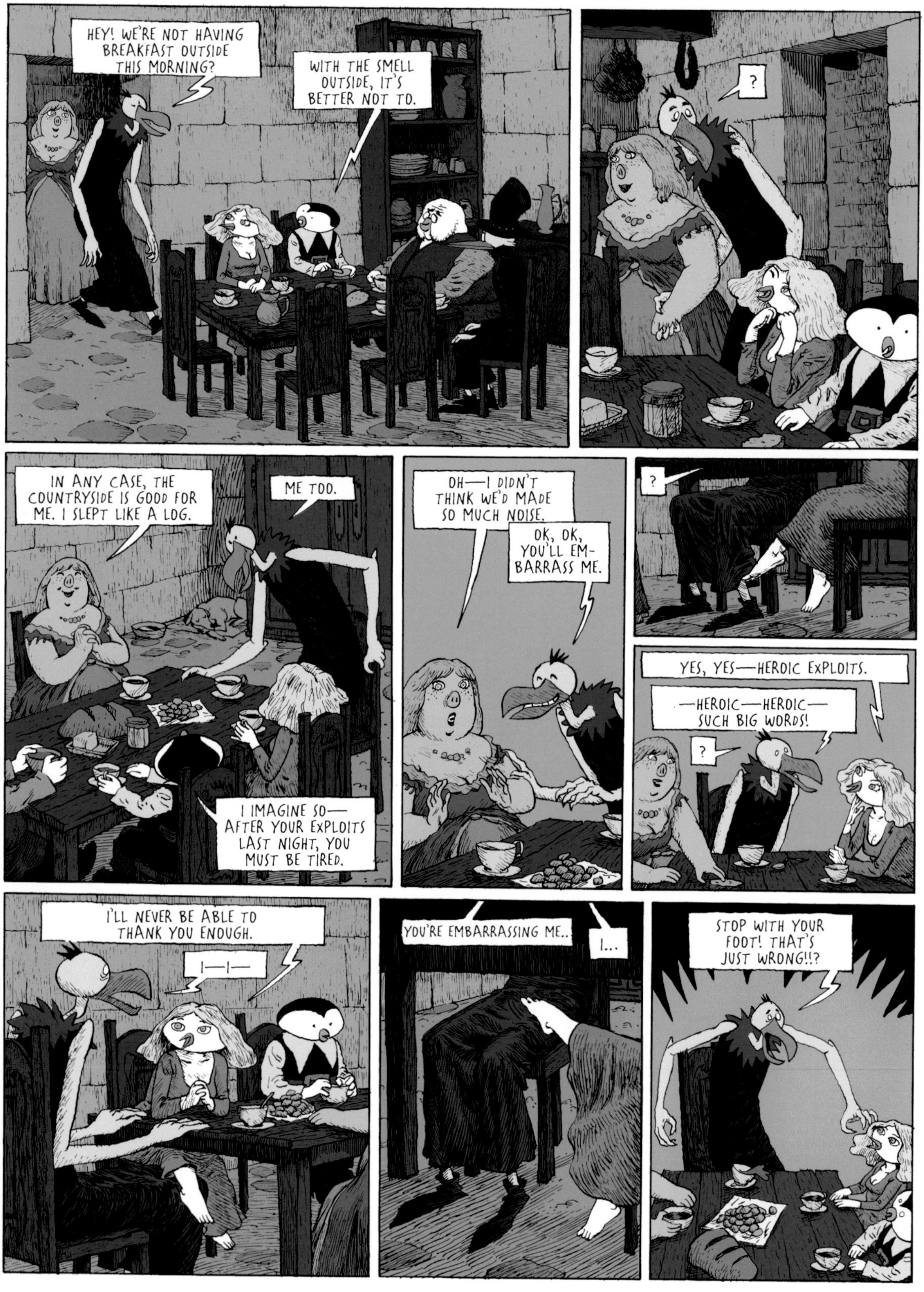
HEY! WE'RE NOT HAVING BREAKFAST OUTSIDE THIS MORNING?
WITH THE SMELL OUTSIDE, IT'S BETTER NOT TO.
?
IN ANY CASE, THE COUNTRYSIDE IS GOOD FOR ME. I SLEPT LIKE A LOG.
ME TOO.
I IMAGINE SO— AFTER YOUR EXPLOITS LAST NIGHT, YOU MUST BE TIRED.
OH—I DIDN'T THINK WE'D MADE SO MUCH NOISE.
OK, OK, YOU'LL EM-BARRASS ME.
?
YES, YES—HEROIC EXPLOITS.
—HEROIC—HEROIC— SUCH BIG WORDS!
?
I'LL NEVER BE ABLE TO THANK YOU ENOUGH.
I—I—
YOU'RE EMBARRASSING ME..
I...
STOP WITH YOUR FOOT! THAT'S JUST WRONG!!?

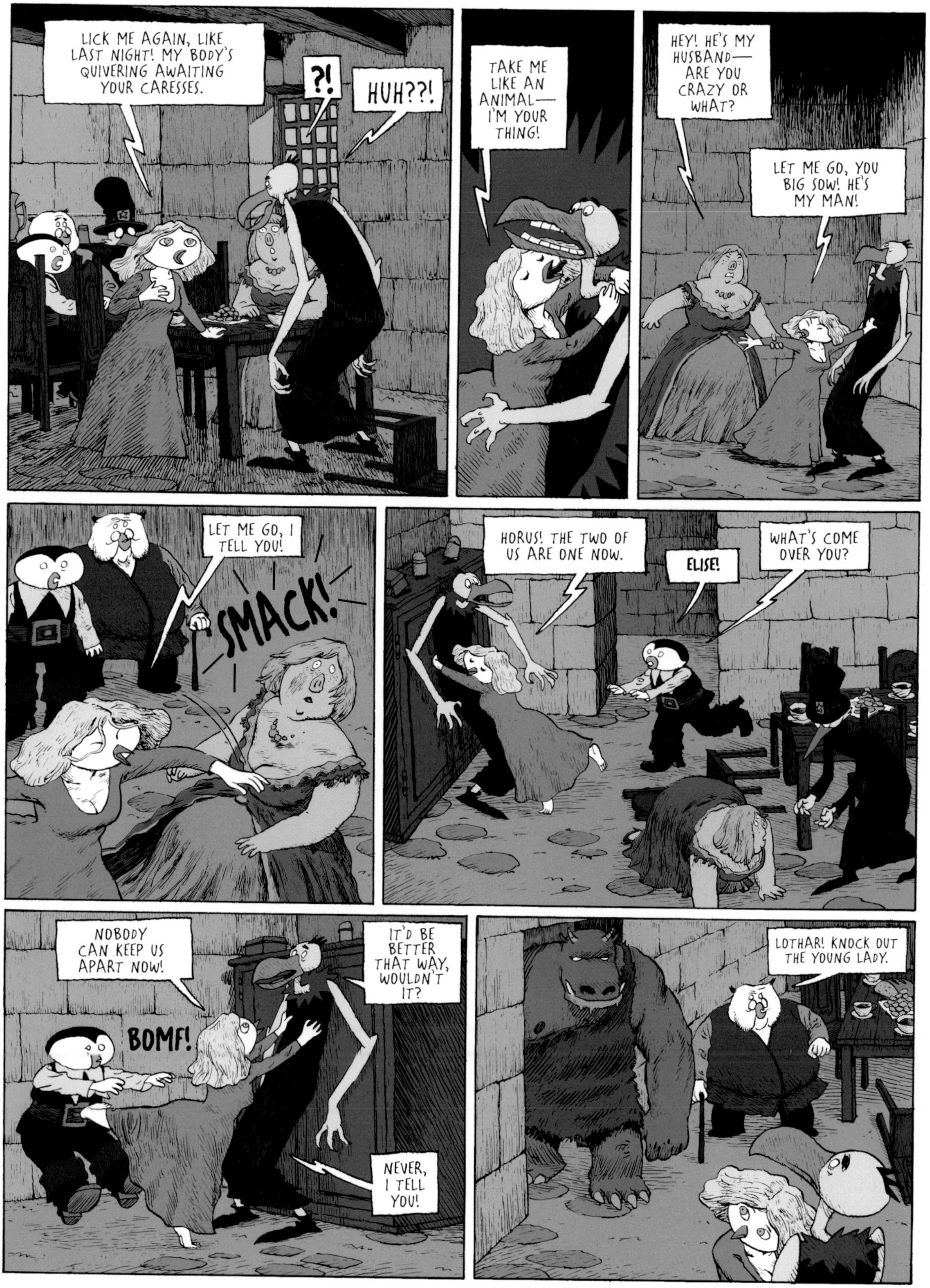
LICK ME AGAIN, LIKE LAST NIGHT! MY BODY'S QUIVERING AWAITING YOUR CARESSES.
?!
HUH??!
TAKE ME LIKE AN ANIMAL— I'M YOUR THING!
HEY! HE'S MY HUSBAND— ARE YOU CRAZY OR WHAT?
LET ME GO, YOU BIG SOW! HE'S MY MAN!
LET ME GO, I TELL YOU!
SMACK!
HORUS! THE TWO OF US ARE ONE NOW.
ELISE!
WHAT'S COME OVER YOU?
NOBODY CAN KEEP US APART NOW!
BOMF!
IT'D BE BETTER THAT WAY, WOULDN'T IT?
NEVER, I TELL YOU!
LOTHAR! KNOCK OUT THE YOUNG LADY.

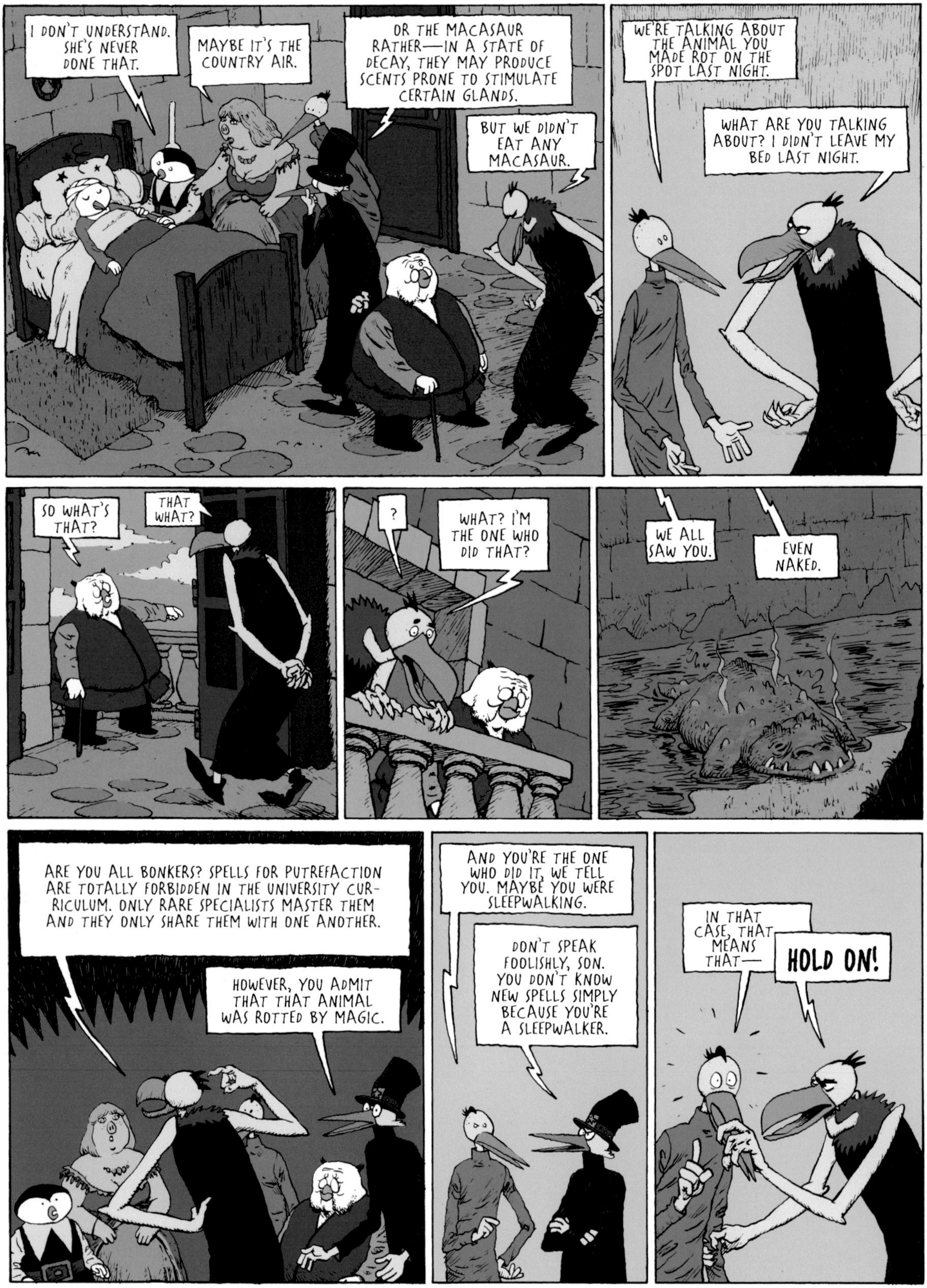
I DON'T UNDERSTAND. SHE'S NEVER DONE THAT.
MAYBE IT'S THE COUNTRY AIR.
OR THE MACASAUR RATHER—IN A STATE OF DECAY, THEY MAY PRODUCE SCENTS PRONE TO STIMULATE CERTAIN GLANDS.
BUT WE DIDN'T EAT ANY MACASAUR.
WE'RE TALKING ABOUT THE ANIMAL YOU MADE ROT ON THE SPOT LAST NIGHT.
WHAT ARE YOU TALKING ABOUT? I DIDN'T LEAVE MY BED LAST NIGHT.
SO WHAT'S THAT?
THAT WHAT?
?
WHAT? I'M THE ONE WHO DID THAT?
WE ALL SAW YOU.
EVEN NAKED.
ARE YOU ALL BONKERS? SPELLS FOR PUTREFACTION ARE TOTALLY FORBIDDEN IN THE UNIVERSITY CURRICULUM. ONLY RARE SPECIALISTS MASTER THEM AND THEY ONLY SHARE THEM WITH ONE ANOTHER.
HOWEVER, YOU ADMIT THAT THAT ANIMAL WAS ROTTED BY MAGIC.
AND YOU'RE THE ONE WHO DID IT, WE TELL YOU. MAYBE YOU WERE SLEEPWALKING.
DON'T SPEAK FOOLISHLY, SON. YOU DON'T KNOW NEW SPELLS SIMPLY BECAUSE YOU'RE A SLEEPWALKER.
IN THAT CASE, THAT MEANS THAT—
HOLD ON!

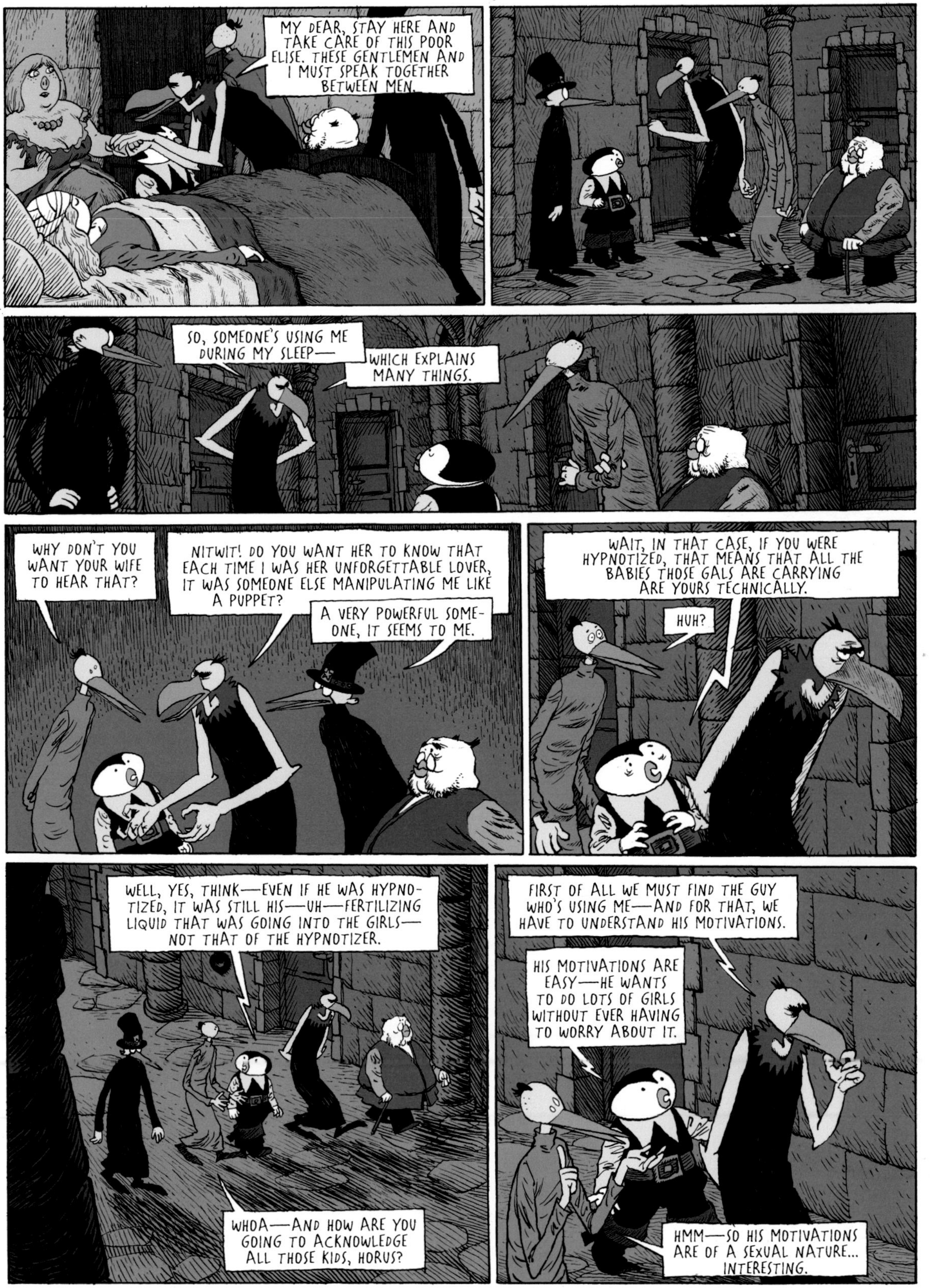
MY DEAR, STAY HERE AND TAKE CARE OF THIS POOR ELISE. THESE GENTLEMEN AND I MUST SPEAK TOGETHER BETWEEN MEN.
SO, SOMEONE'S USING ME DURING MY SLEEP—
WHICH EXPLAINS MANY THINGS.
WHY DON'T YOU WANT YOUR WIFE TO HEAR THAT?
NITWIT! DO YOU WANT HER TO KNOW THAT EACH TIME I WAS HER UNFORGETTABLE LOVER, IT WAS SOMEONE ELSE MANIPULATING ME LIKE A PUPPET?
A VERY POWERFUL SOME-ONE, IT SEEMS TO ME.
WAIT, IN THAT CASE, IF YOU WERE HYPNOTIZED, THAT MEANS THAT ALL THE BABIES THOSE GALS ARE CARRYING ARE YOURS TECHNICALLY.
HUH?
WELL, YES, THINK—EVEN IF HE WAS HYPNO-TIZED, IT WAS STILL HIS—UH—FERTILIZING LIQUID THAT WAS GOING INTO THE GIRLS—NOT THAT OF THE HYPNOTIZER.
WHOA—AND HOW ARE YOU GOING TO ACKNOWLEDGE ALL THOSE KIDS, HORUS?
FIRST OF ALL WE MUST FIND THE GUY WHO'S USING ME—AND FOR THAT, WE HAVE TO UNDERSTAND HIS MOTIVATIONS.
HIS MOTIVATIONS ARE EASY—HE WANTS TO DO LOTS OF GIRLS WITHOUT EVER HAVING TO WORRY ABOUT IT.
HMM—SO HIS MOTIVATIONS ARE OF A SEXUAL NATURE... INTERESTING.

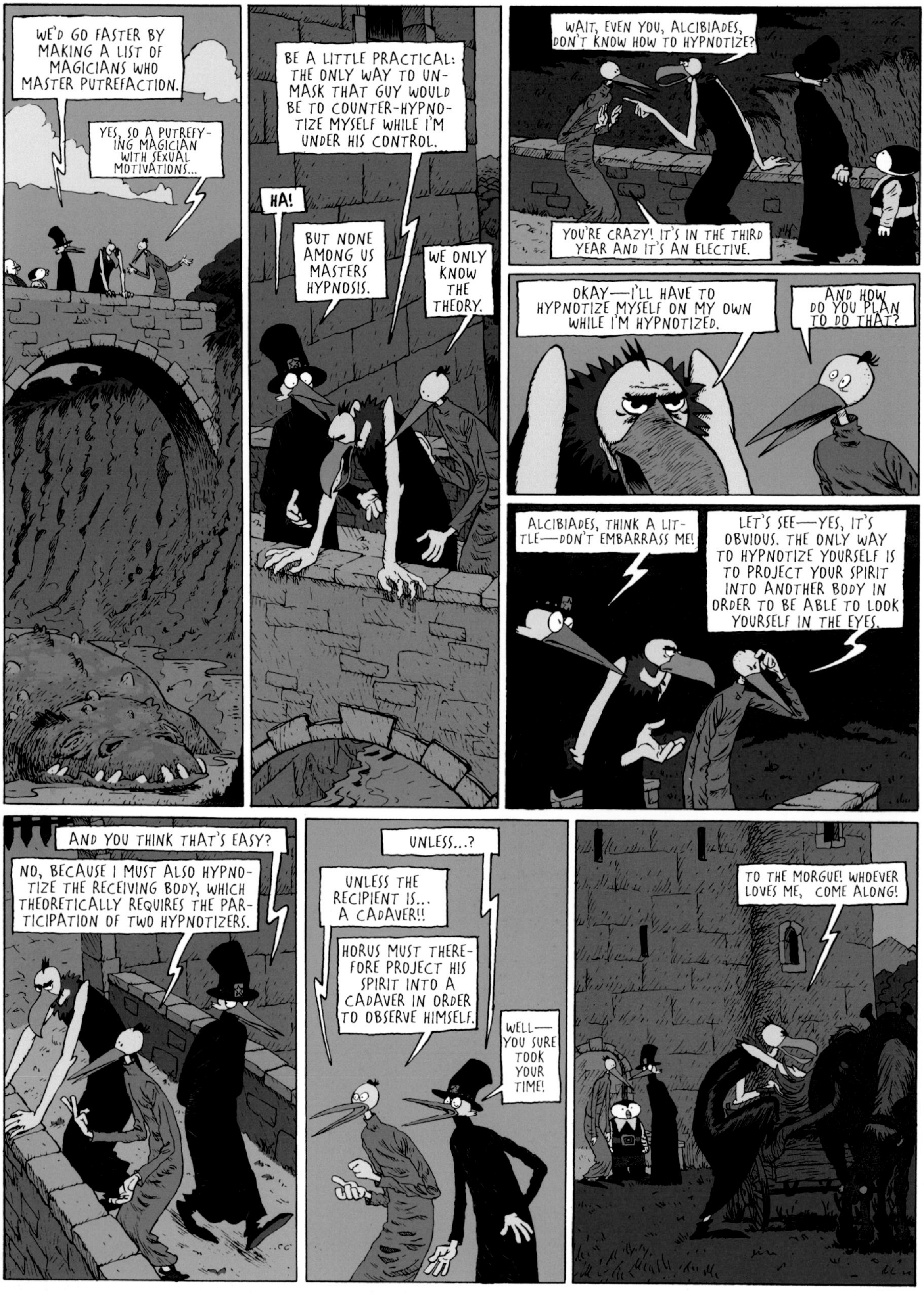

WE'D GO FASTER BY MAKING A LIST OF MAGICIANS WHO MASTER PUTREFACTION.
YES, SO A PUTREFYING MAGICIAN WITH SEXUAL MOTIVATIONS...
BE A LITTLE PRACTICAL: THE ONLY WAY TO UNMASK THAT GUY WOULD BE TO COUNTER-HYPNOTIZE MYSELF WHILE I'M UNDER HIS CONTROL.
HA!
BUT NONE AMONG US MASTERS HYPNOSIS.
WE ONLY KNOW THE THEORY.
WAIT, EVEN YOU, ALCIBIADES, DON'T KNOW HOW TO HYPNOTIZE?
YOU'RE CRAZY! IT'S IN THE THIRD YEAR AND IT'S AN ELECTIVE.
OKAY—I'LL HAVE TO HYPNOTIZE MYSELF ON MY OWN WHILE I'M HYPNOTIZED.
AND HOW DO YOU PLAN TO DO THAT?
ALCIBIADES, THINK A LITTLE—DON'T EMBARRASS ME!
LET'S SEE—YES, IT'S OBVIOUS. THE ONLY WAY TO HYPNOTIZE YOURSELF IS TO PROJECT YOUR SPIRIT INTO ANOTHER BODY IN ORDER TO BE ABLE TO LOOK YOURSELF IN THE EYES.
AND YOU THINK THAT'S EASY?
NO, BECAUSE I MUST ALSO HYPNOTIZE THE RECEIVING BODY, WHICH THEORETICALLY REQUIRES THE PARTICIPATION OF TWO HYPNOTIZERS.
UNLESS...?
UNLESS THE RECIPIENT IS... A CADAVER!!
HORUS MUST THEREFORE PROJECT HIS SPIRIT INTO A CADAVER IN ORDER TO OBSERVE HIMSELF.
WELL—YOU SURE TOOK YOUR TIME!
TO THE MORGUE! WHOEVER LOVES ME, COME ALONG!

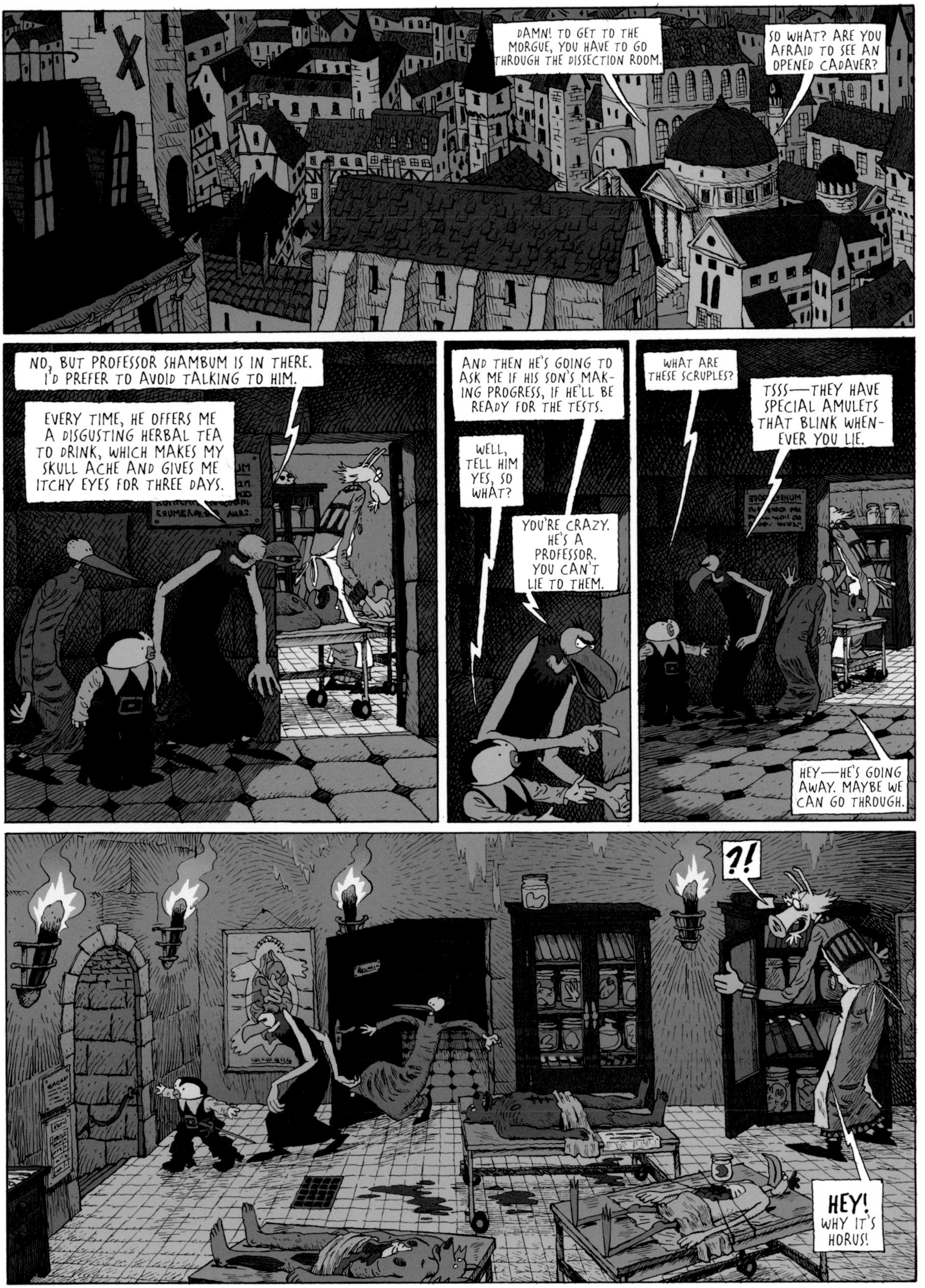
DAMN! TO GET TO THE MORGUE, YOU HAVE TO GO THROUGH THE DISSECTION ROOM.
SO WHAT? ARE YOU AFRAID TO SEE AN OPENED CADAVER?
NO, BUT PROFESSOR SHAMBUM IS IN THERE. I'D PREFER TO AVOID TALKING TO HIM.
EVERY TIME, HE OFFERS ME A DISGUSTING HERBAL TEA TO DRINK, WHICH MAKES MY SKULL ACHE AND GIVES ME ITCHY EYES FOR THREE DAYS.
AND THEN HE'S GOING TO ASK ME IF HIS SON'S MAKING PROGRESS, IF HE'LL BE READY FOR THE TESTS.
WELL, TELL HIM YES, SO WHAT?
YOU'RE CRAZY. HE'S A PROFESSOR. YOU CAN'T LIE TO THEM.
WHAT ARE THESE SCRUPLES?
TSSS—THEY HAVE SPECIAL AMULETS THAT BLINK WHENEVER YOU LIE.
HEY—HE'S GOING AWAY. MAYBE WE CAN GO THROUGH.
?!
HEY! WHY IT'S HORUS!

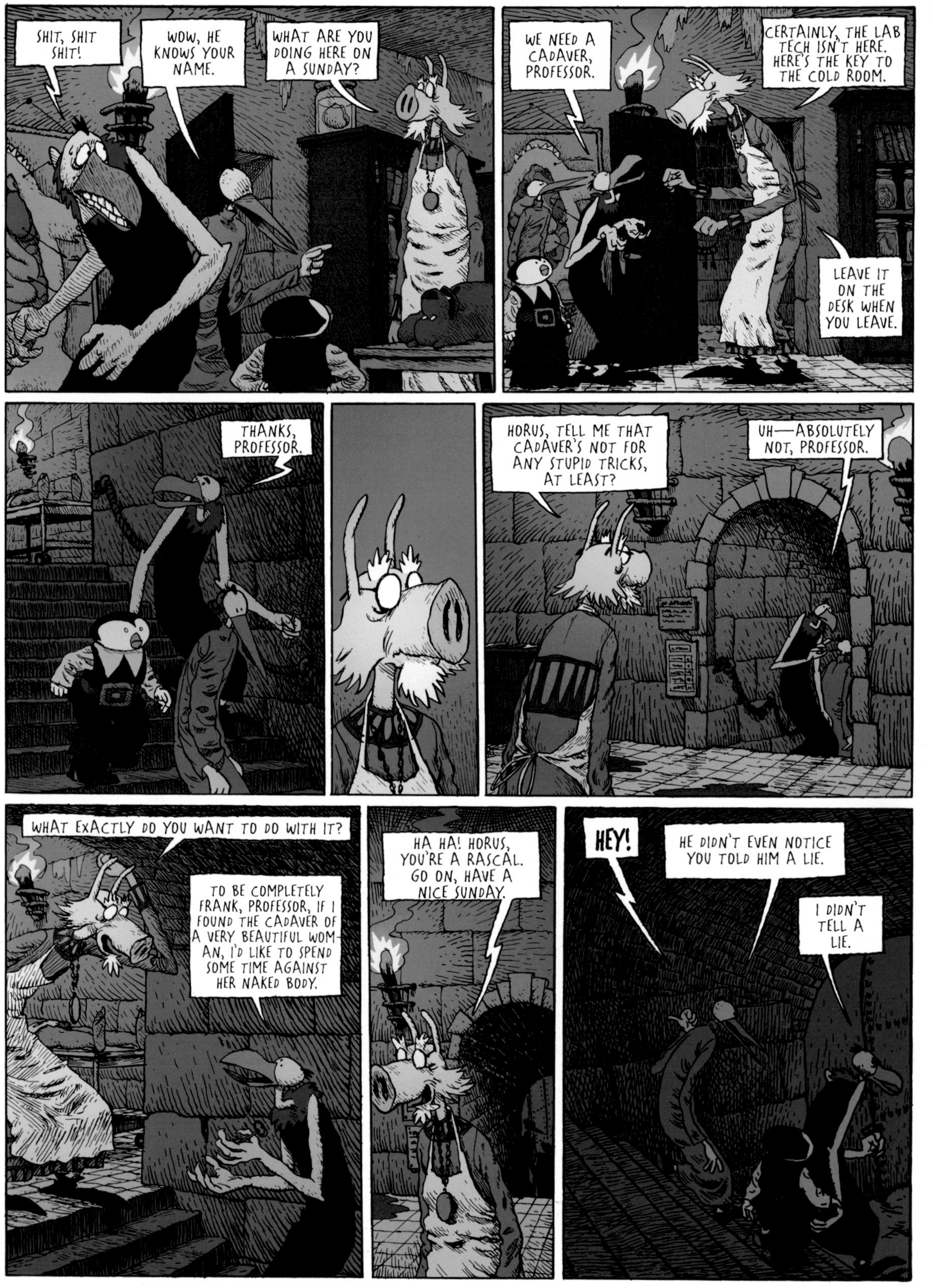
SHIT, SHIT SHIT!
WOW, HE KNOWS YOUR NAME.
WHAT ARE YOU DOING HERE ON A SUNDAY?
WE NEED A CADAVER, PROFESSOR.
CERTAINLY, THE LAB TECH ISN'T HERE. HERE'S THE KEY TO THE COLD ROOM.
LEAVE IT ON THE DESK WHEN YOU LEAVE.
THANKS, PROFESSOR.
HORUS, TELL ME THAT CADAVER'S NOT FOR ANY STUPID TRICKS, AT LEAST?
UH—ABSOLUTELY NOT, PROFESSOR.
WHAT EXACTLY DO YOU WANT TO DO WITH IT?
TO BE COMPLETELY FRANK, PROFESSOR, IF I FOUND THE CADAVER OF A VERY BEAUTIFUL WOMAN, I'D LIKE TO SPEND SOME TIME AGAINST HER NAKED BODY.
HA HA! HORUS, YOU'RE A RASCAL. GO ON, HAVE A NICE SUNDAY.
HEY!
HE DIDN'T EVEN NOTICE YOU TOLD HIM A LIE.
I DIDN'T TELL A LIE.

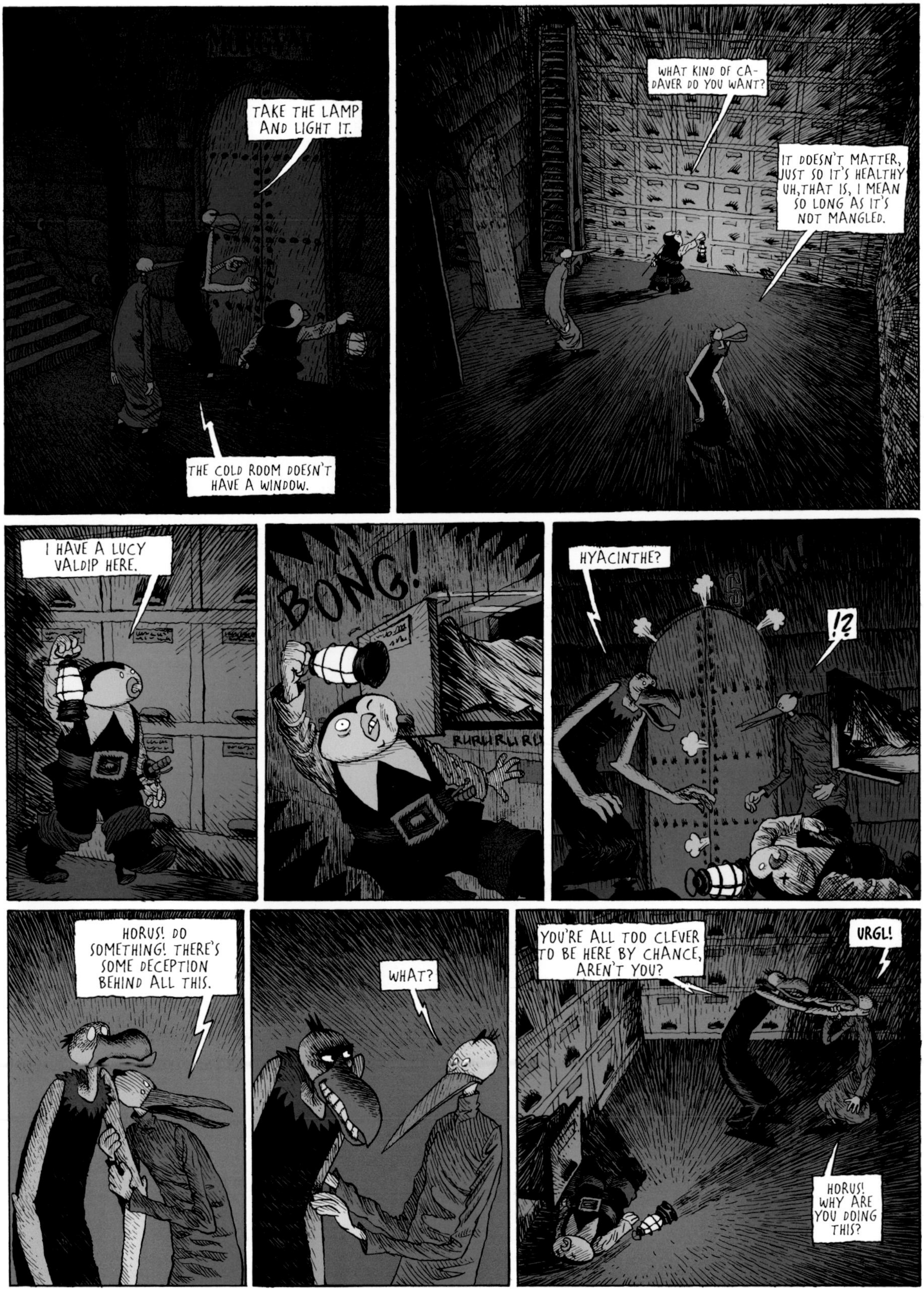

TAKE THE LAMP AND LIGHT IT.
THE COLD ROOM DOESN'T HAVE A WINDOW.
WHAT KIND OF CA-DAVER DO YOU WANT?
IT DOESN'T MATTER, JUST SO IT'S HEALTHY UH, THAT IS, I MEAN SO LONG AS IT'S NOT MANGLED.
I HAVE A LUCY VALDIP HERE.
BONG!
RURURURU
HYACINTHE?
SLAM!
!?
HORUS! DO SOMETHING! THERE'S SOME DECEPTION BEHIND ALL THIS.
WHAT?
YOU'RE ALL TOO CLEVER TO BE HERE BY CHANCE, AREN'T YOU?
URGL!
HORUS! WHY ARE YOU DOING THIS?

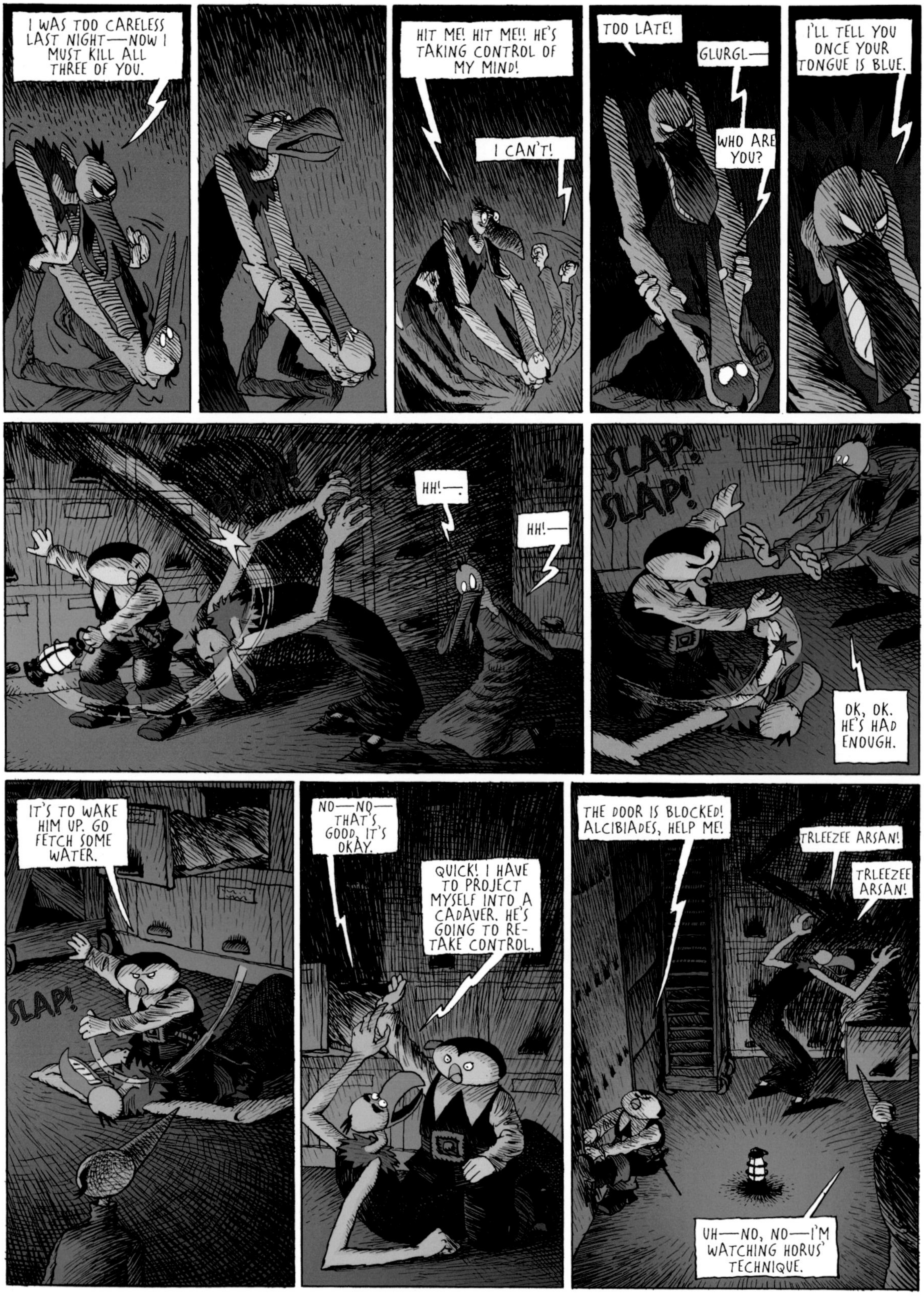
I WAS TOO CARELESS LAST NIGHT—NOW I MUST KILL ALL THREE OF YOU.
HIT ME! HIT ME!! HE'S TAKING CONTROL OF MY MIND!
I CAN'T!
TOO LATE!
GLURGL—
WHO ARE YOU?
I'LL TELL YOU ONCE YOUR TONGUE IS BLUE.
HH!—.
HH!—
SLAP! SLAP!
OK, OK. HE'S HAD ENOUGH.
IT'S TO WAKE HIM UP. GO FETCH SOME WATER.
SLAP!
NO—NO—THAT'S GOOD, IT'S OKAY.
QUICK! I HAVE TO PROJECT MYSELF INTO A CADAVER. HE'S GOING TO RE-TAKE CONTROL.
THE DOOR IS BLOCKED! ALCIBIADES, HELP ME!
TRLEEZEE ARSAN!
TRLEEZEE ARSAN!
UH—NO, NO—I'M WATCHING HORUS' TECHNIQUE.

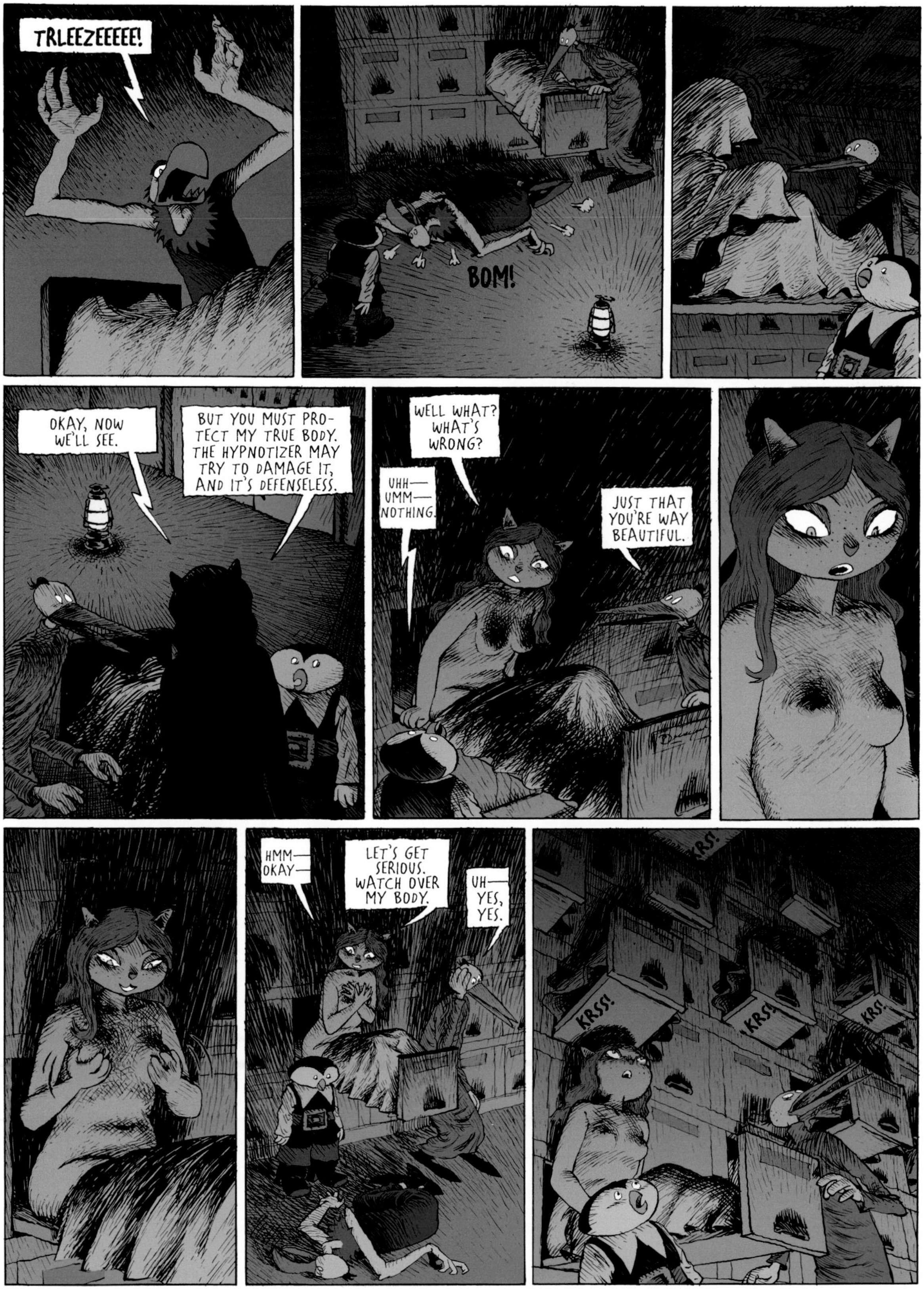

TRLEEZEEEEE!
BOM!
OKAY, NOW WE'LL SEE.
BUT YOU MUST PROTECT MY TRUE BODY. THE HYPNOTIZER MAY TRY TO DAMAGE IT, AND IT'S DEFENSELESS.
WELL WHAT? WHAT'S WRONG?
UHH— UMM— NOTHING.
JUST THAT YOU'RE WAY BEAUTIFUL.
HMM— OKAY—
LET'S GET SERIOUS. WATCH OVER MY BODY.
UH— YES, YES.
KRS!
KRSS!
KRS!
KRS!

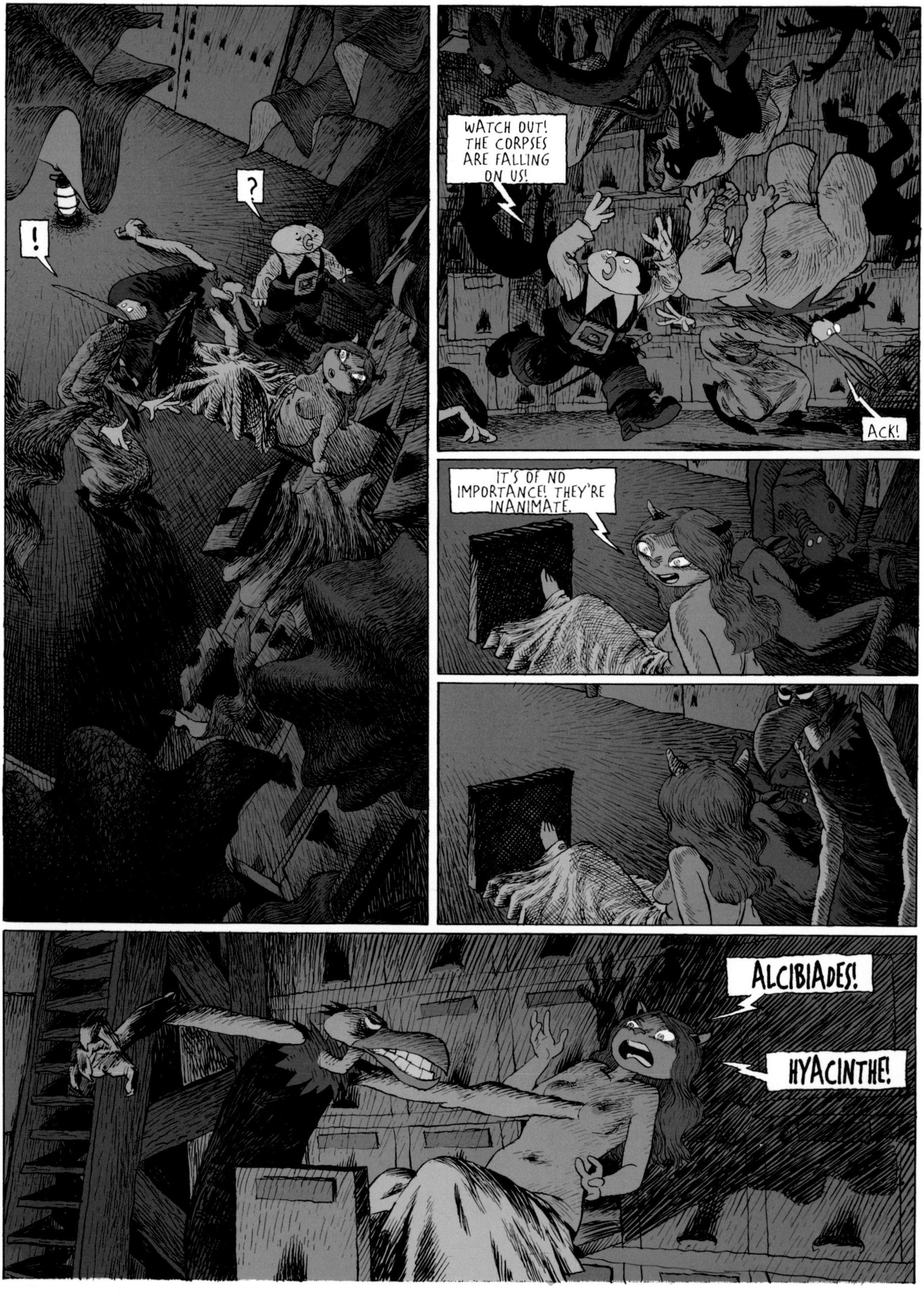
!
?
WATCH OUT! THE CORPSES ARE FALLING ON US!
ACK!
IT'S OF NO IMPORTANCE! THEY'RE INANIMATE.
ALCIBIADES!
HYACINTHE!

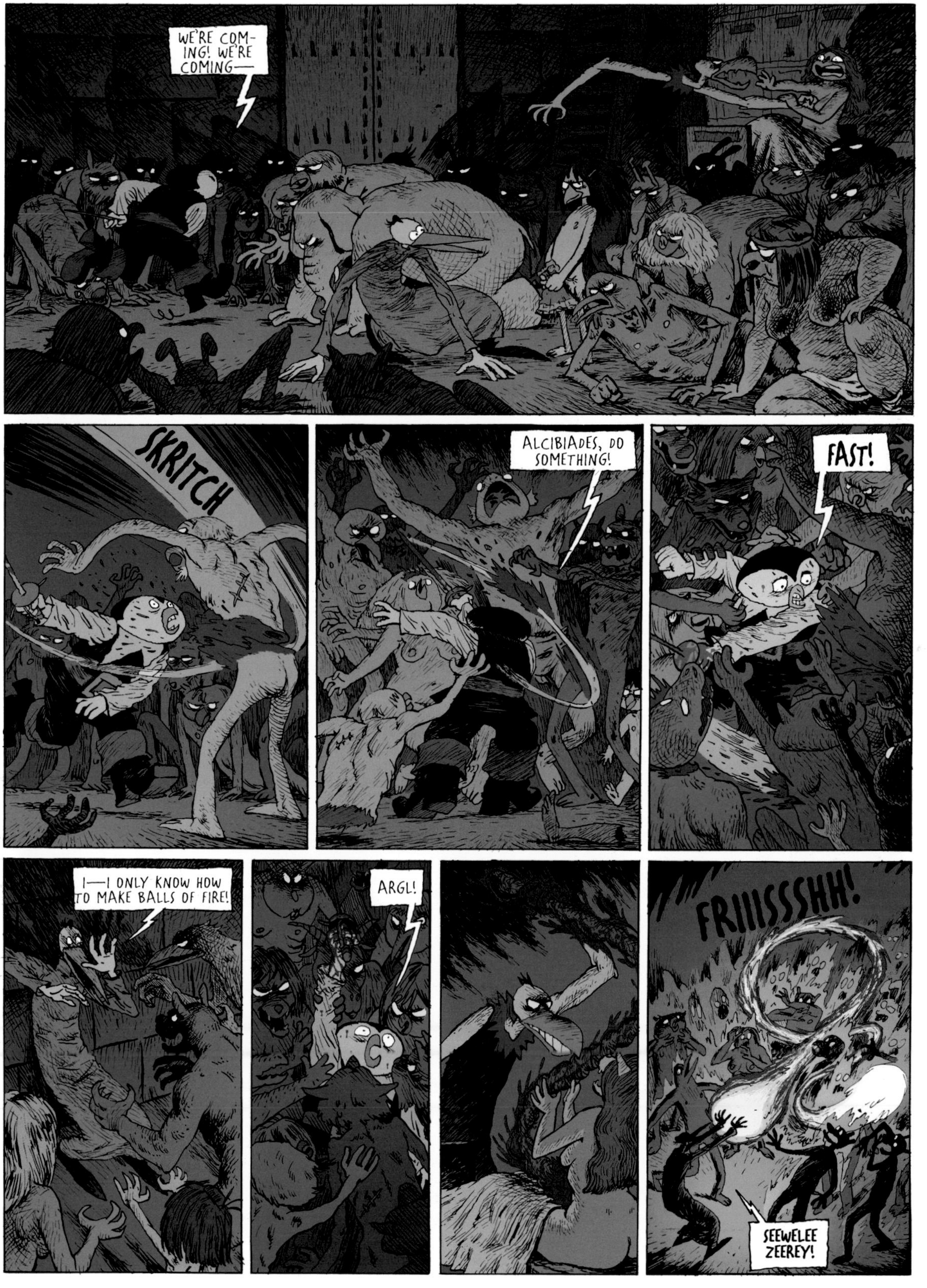
WE'RE COMING! WE'RE COMING—
SKRITCH
ALCIBIADES, DO SOMETHING!
FAST!
I—I ONLY KNOW HOW TO MAKE BALLS OF FIRE!
ARGL!
FRIIISSSHH!
SEEWELEE ZEEREY!

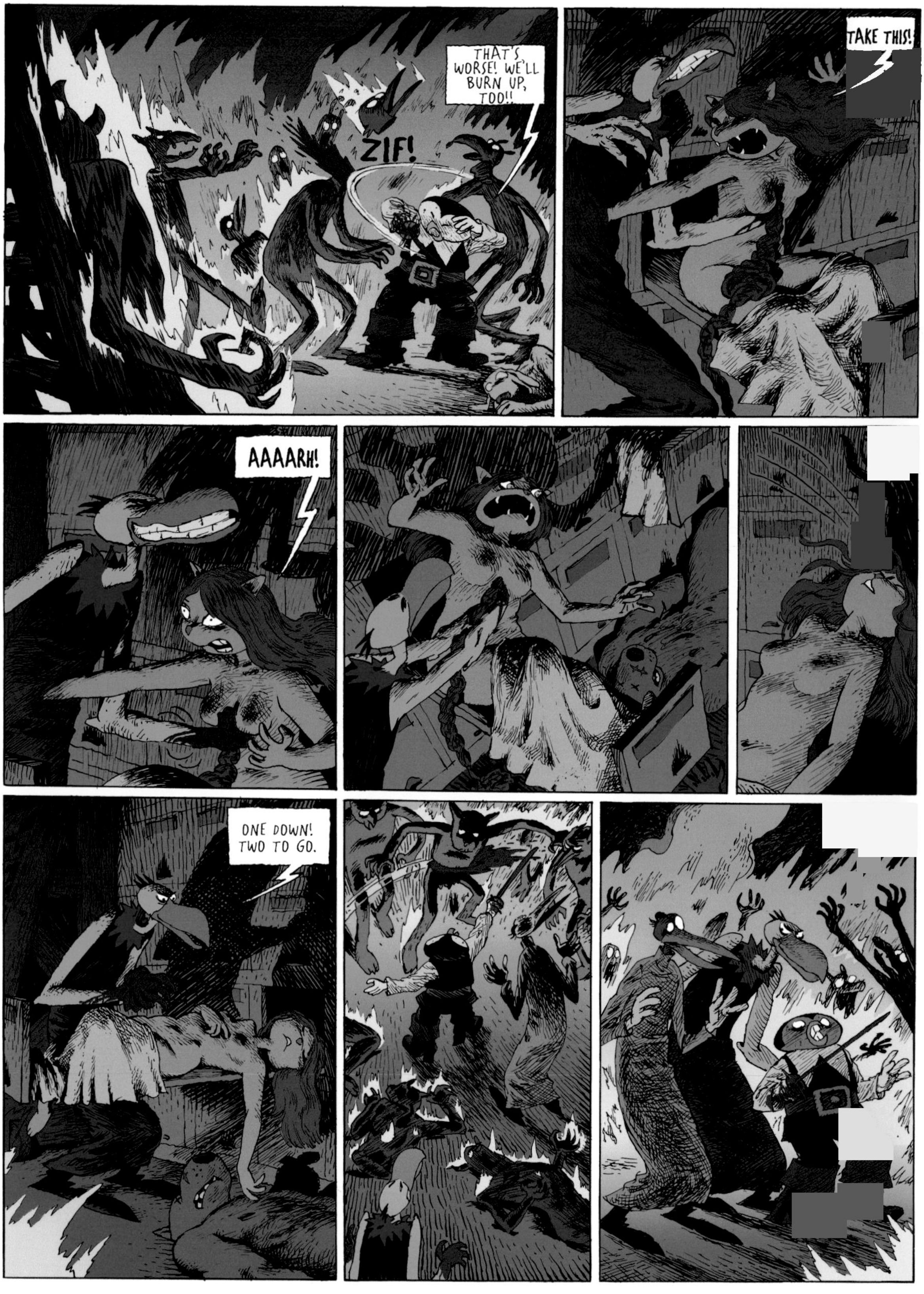
THAT'S WORSE! WE'LL BURN UP, TOO!!
ZIF!
TAKE THIS!
AAAARH!
ONE DOWN! TWO TO GO.

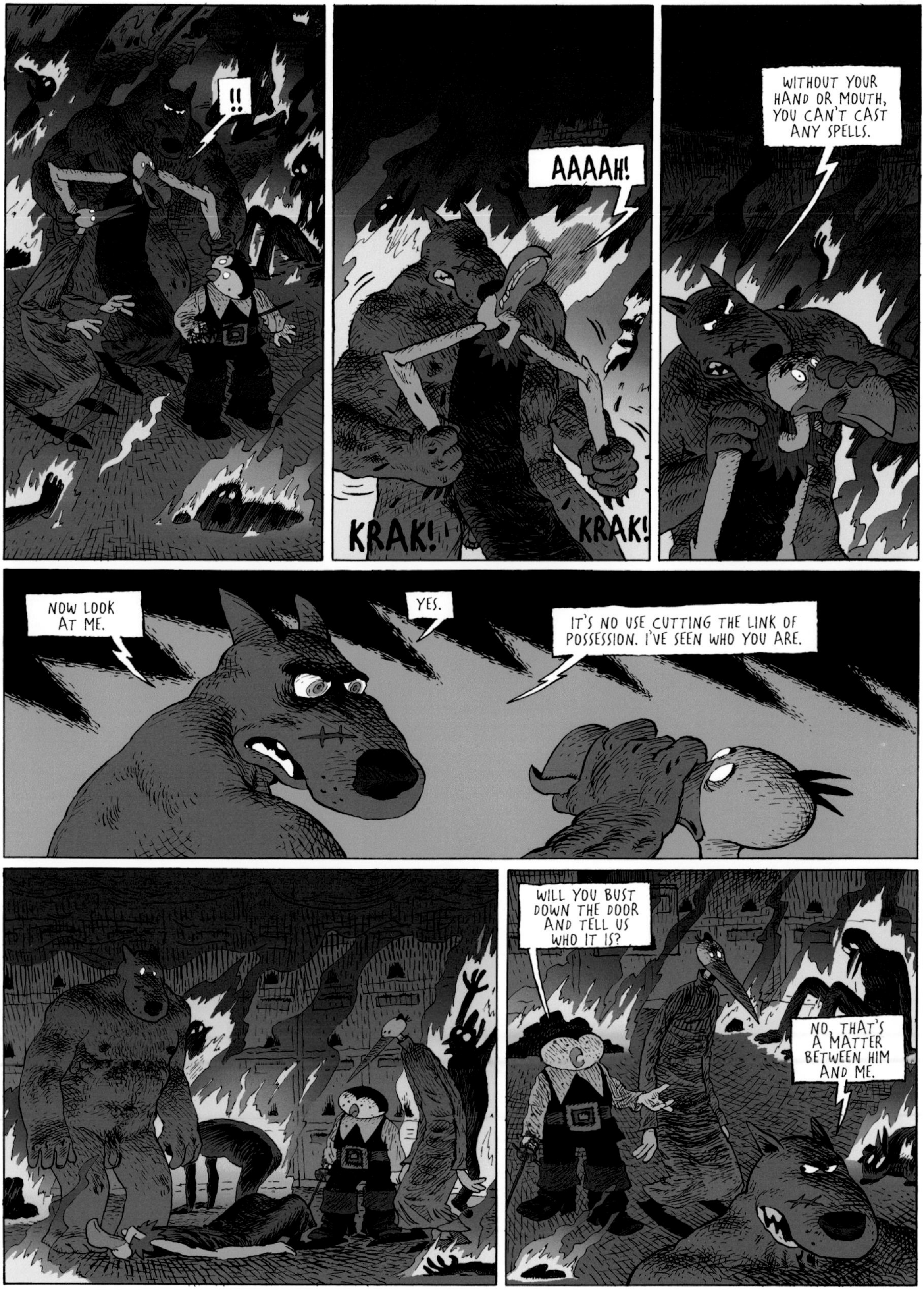
!!
AAAAH!
KRAK!
KRAK!
WITHOUT YOUR HAND OR MOUTH, YOU CAN'T CAST ANY SPELLS.
NOW LOOK AT ME.
YES.
IT'S NO USE CUTTING THE LINK OF POSSESSION. I'VE SEEN WHO YOU ARE.
WILL YOU BUST DOWN THE DOOR AND TELL US WHO IT IS?
NO, THAT'S A MATTER BETWEEN HIM AND ME.

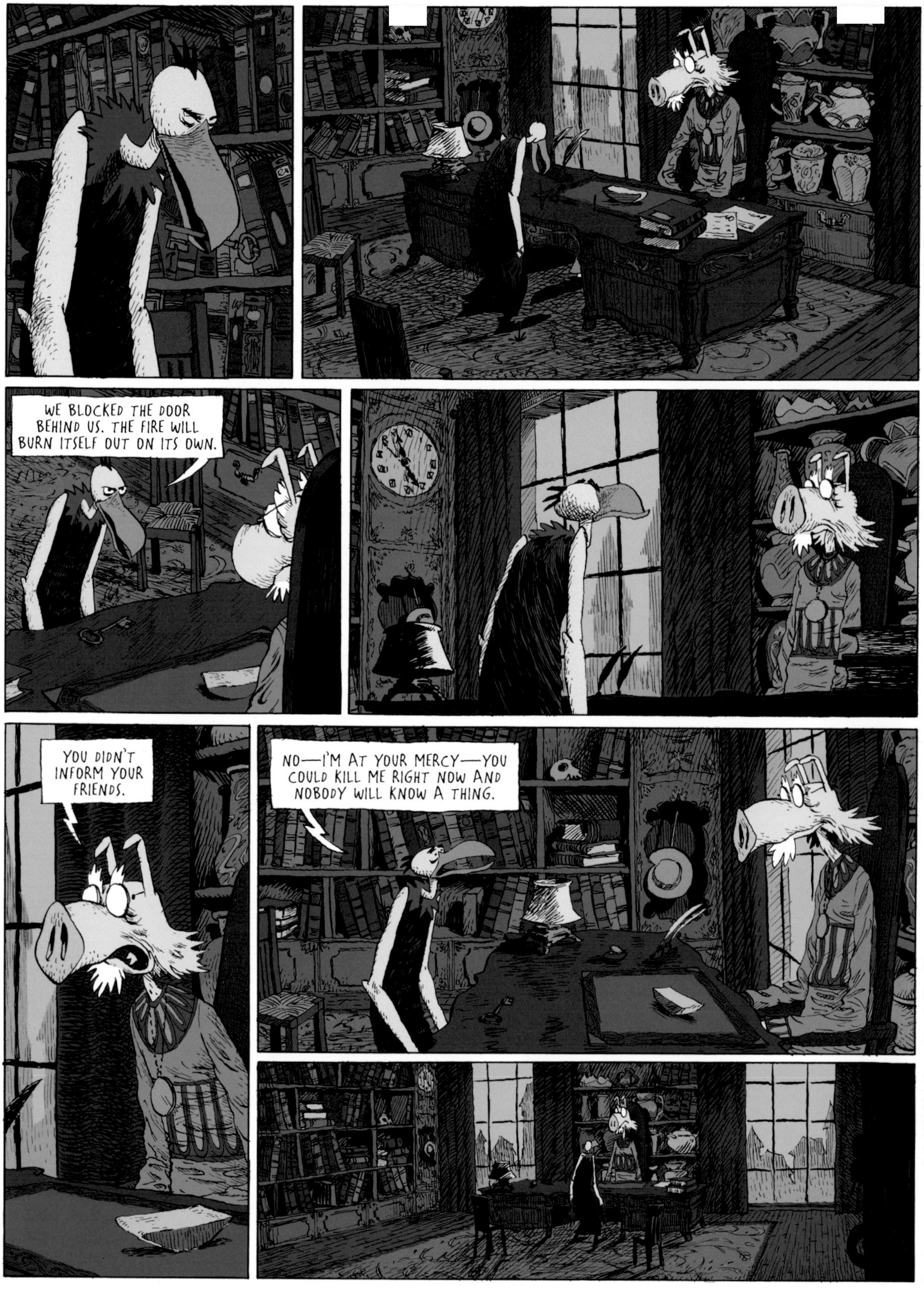
WE BLOCKED THE DOOR BEHIND US. THE FIRE WILL BURN ITSELF OUT ON ITS OWN.
YOU DIDN'T INFORM YOUR FRIENDS.
NO—I'M AT YOUR MERCY—YOU COULD KILL ME RIGHT NOW AND NOBODY WILL KNOW A THING.

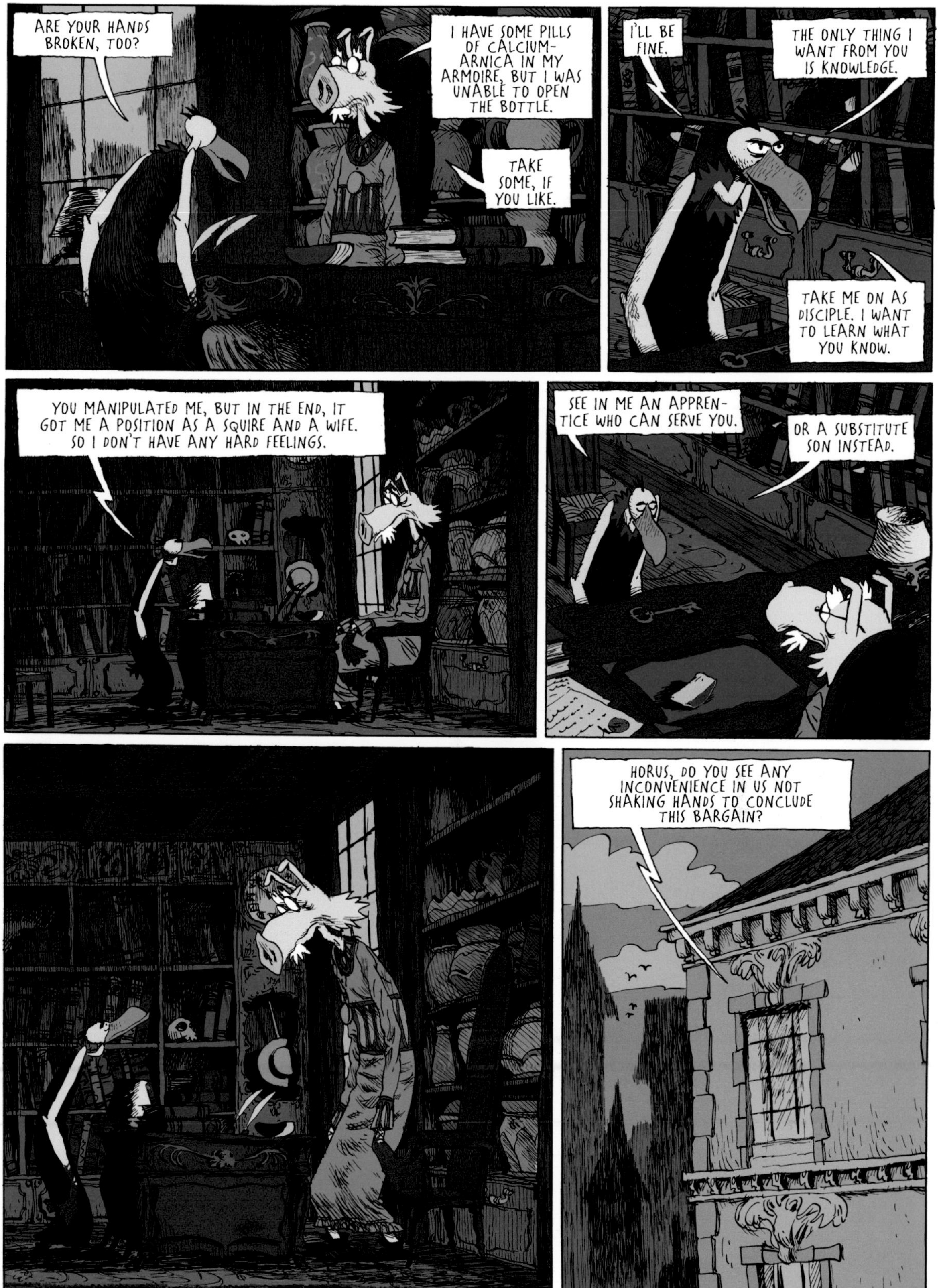
ARE YOUR HANDS BROKEN, TOO?
I HAVE SOME PILLS OF CALCIUM-ARNICA IN MY ARMOIRE, BUT I WAS UNABLE TO OPEN THE BOTTLE.
TAKE SOME, IF YOU LIKE.
I'LL BE FINE.
THE ONLY THING I WANT FROM YOU IS KNOWLEDGE.
TAKE ME ON AS DISCIPLE. I WANT TO LEARN WHAT YOU KNOW.
YOU MANIPULATED ME, BUT IN THE END, IT GOT ME A POSITION AS A SQUIRE AND A WIFE. SO I DON'T HAVE ANY HARD FEELINGS.
SEE IN ME AN APPRENTICE WHO CAN SERVE YOU.
OR A SUBSTITUTE SON INSTEAD.
HORUS, DO YOU SEE ANY INCONVENIENCE IN US NOT SHAKING HANDS TO CONCLUDE THIS BARGAIN?

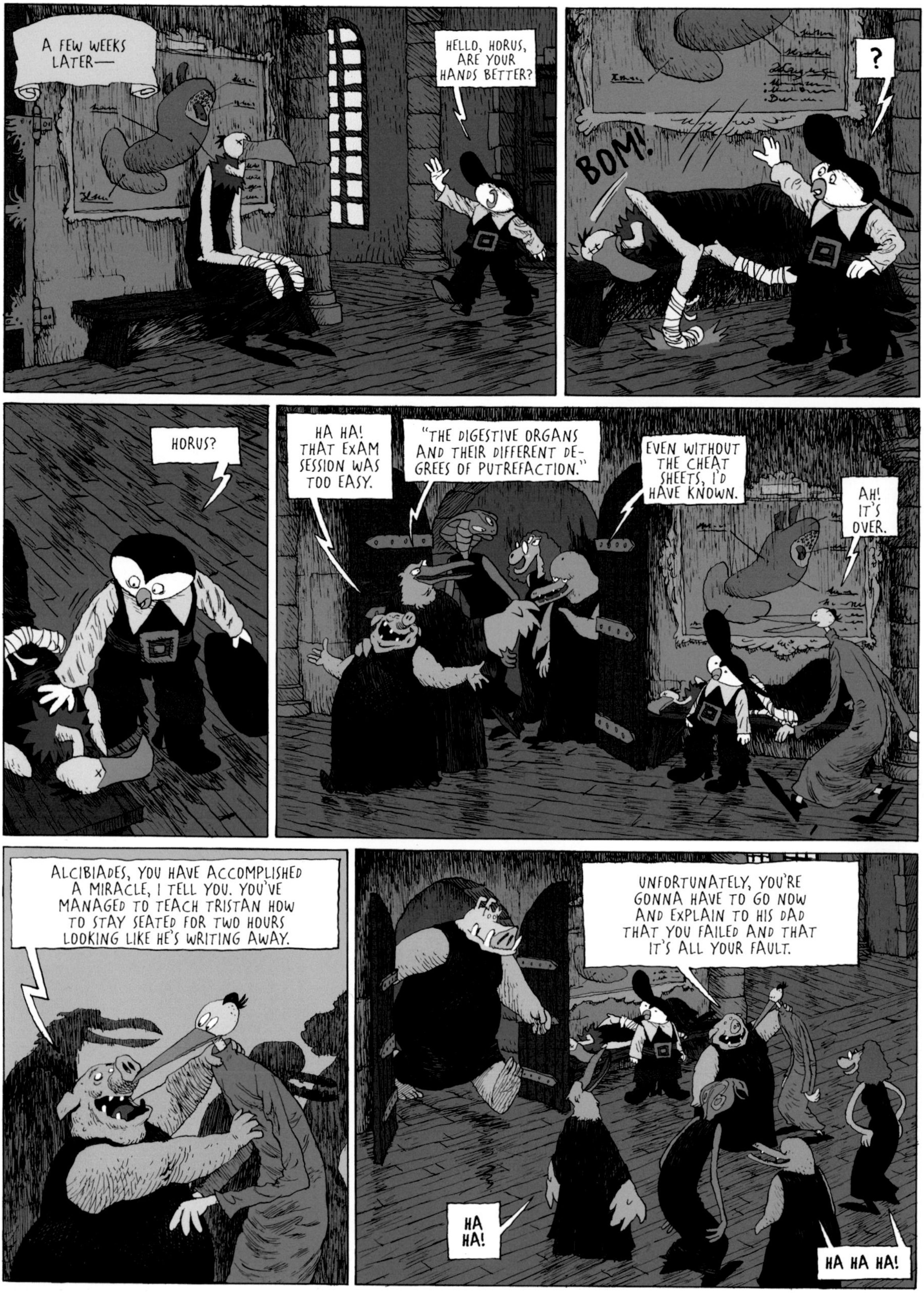

A FEW WEEKS LATER—
HELLO, HORUS, ARE YOUR HANDS BETTER?
BOM!
?
HORUS?
HA HA! THAT EXAM SESSION WAS TOO EASY.
"THE DIGESTIVE ORGANS AND THEIR DIFFERENT DEGREES OF PUTREFACTION."
EVEN WITHOUT THE CHEAT SHEETS, I'D HAVE KNOWN.
AH! IT'S OVER.
ALCIBIADES, YOU HAVE ACCOMPLISHED A MIRACLE, I TELL YOU. YOU'VE MANAGED TO TEACH TRISTAN HOW TO STAY SEATED FOR TWO HOURS LOOKING LIKE HE'S WRITING AWAY.
UNFORTUNATELY, YOU'RE GONNA HAVE TO GO NOW AND EXPLAIN TO HIS DAD THAT YOU FAILED AND THAT IT'S ALL YOUR FAULT.
HA HA!
HA HA HA!

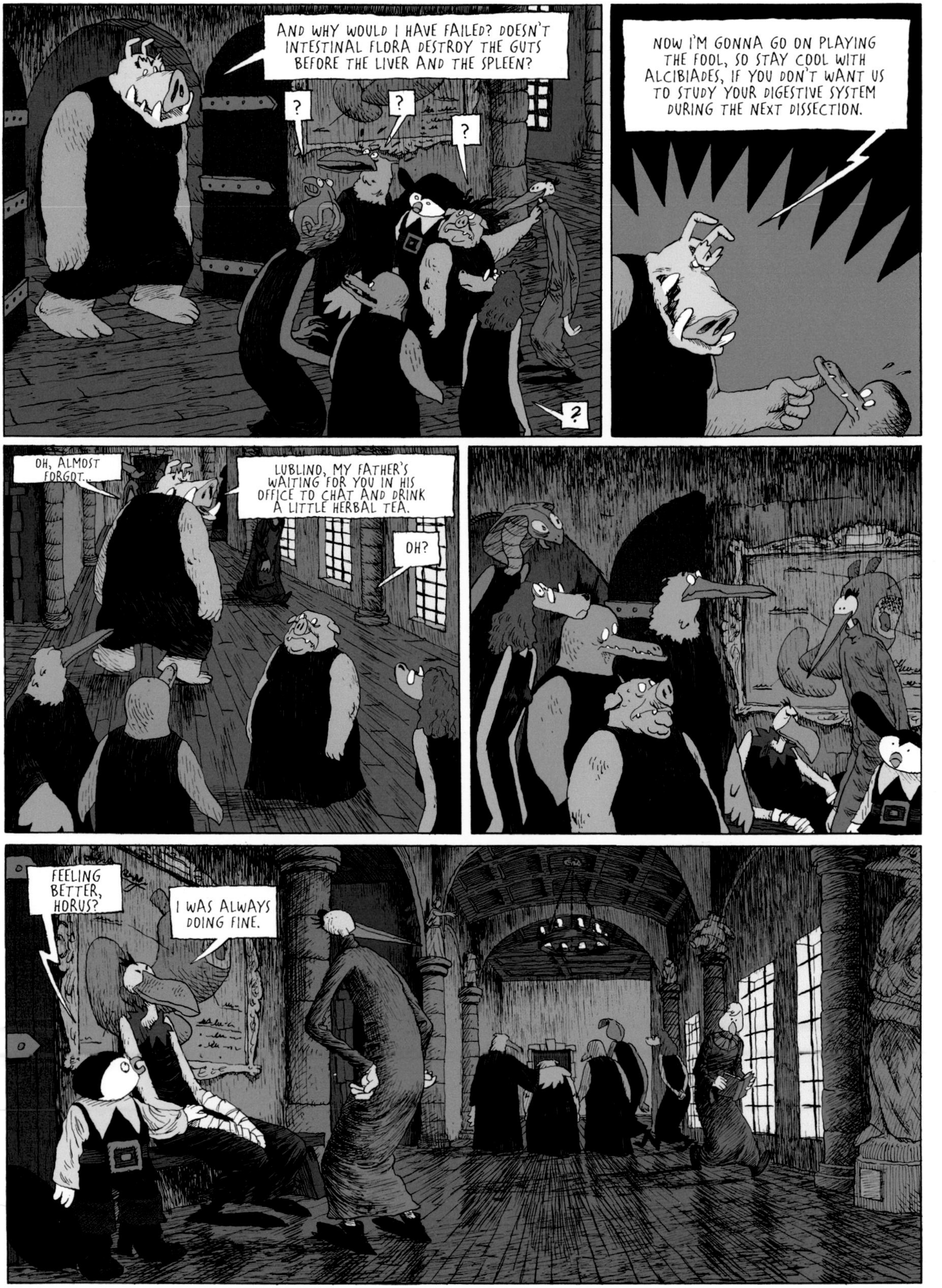

AND WHY WOULD I HAVE FAILED? DOESN'T INTESTINAL FLORA DESTROY THE GUTS BEFORE THE LIVER AND THE SPLEEN?
?
?
?
?
NOW I'M GONNA GO ON PLAYING THE FOOL, SO STAY COOL WITH ALCIBIADES, IF YOU DON'T WANT US TO STUDY YOUR DIGESTIVE SYSTEM DURING THE NEXT DISSECTION.
OH, ALMOST FORGOT...
LUBLIND, MY FATHER'S WAITING FOR YOU IN HIS OFFICE TO CHAT AND DRINK A LITTLE HERBAL TEA.
OH?
FEELING BETTER, HORUS?
I WAS ALWAYS DOING FINE.

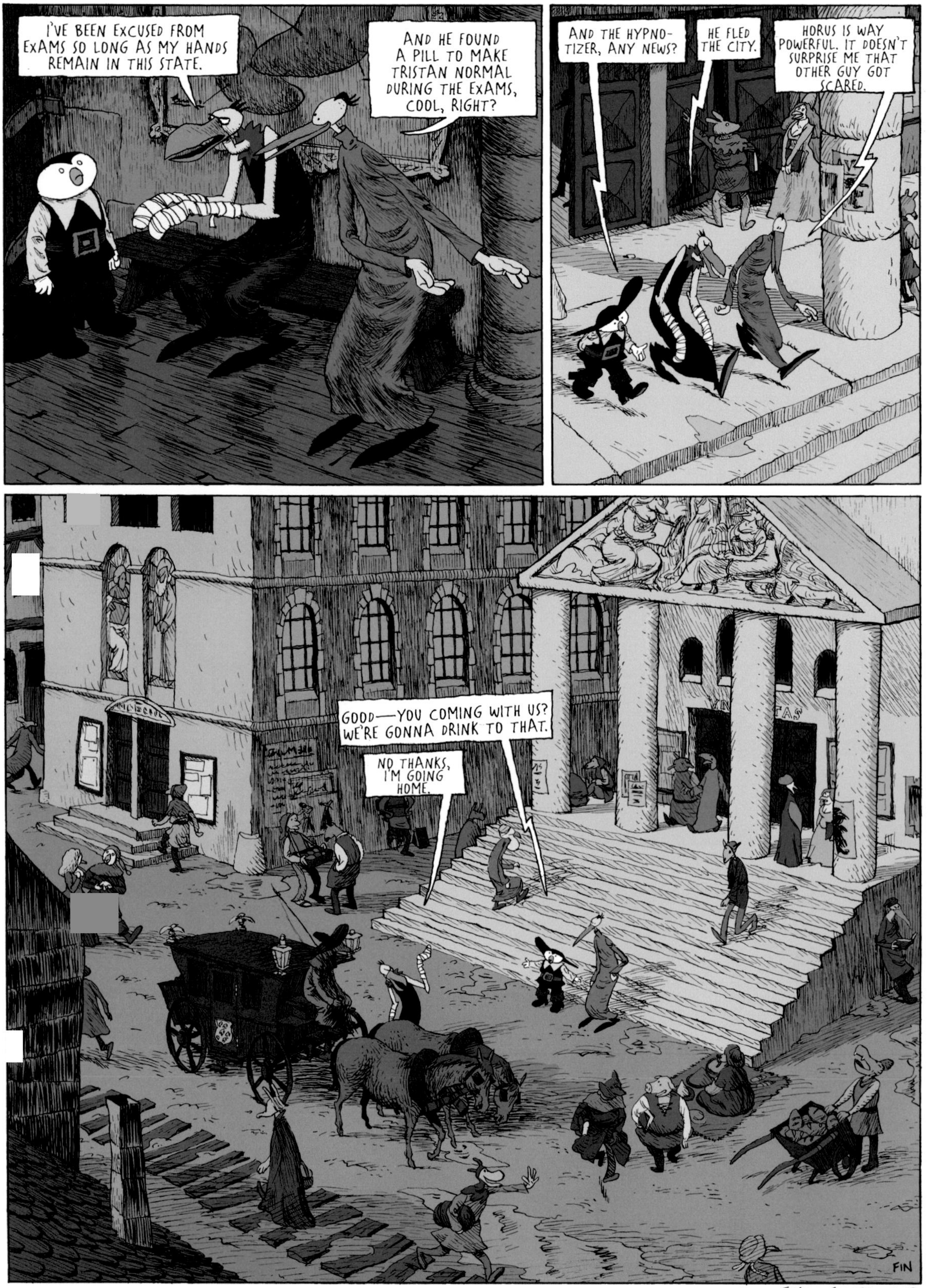
I'VE BEEN EXCUSED FROM EXAMS SO LONG AS MY HANDS REMAIN IN THIS STATE.
AND HE FOUND A PILL TO MAKE TRISTAN NORMAL DURING THE EXAMS, COOL, RIGHT?
AND THE HYPNOTIZER, ANY NEWS?
HE FLED THE CITY.
HORUS IS WAY POWERFUL. IT DOESN'T SURPRISE ME THAT OTHER GUY GOT SCARED.
GOOD—YOU COMING WITH US? WE'RE GONNA DRINK TO THAT.
NO THANKS, I'M GOING HOME.
FIN

Joann Sfar & Trondheim J-E Vermot-Desroches

RUCKUS AT THE BREWERS

Joann SfAR • Lewis TRONDHEIM

Art and Colors: YOANN

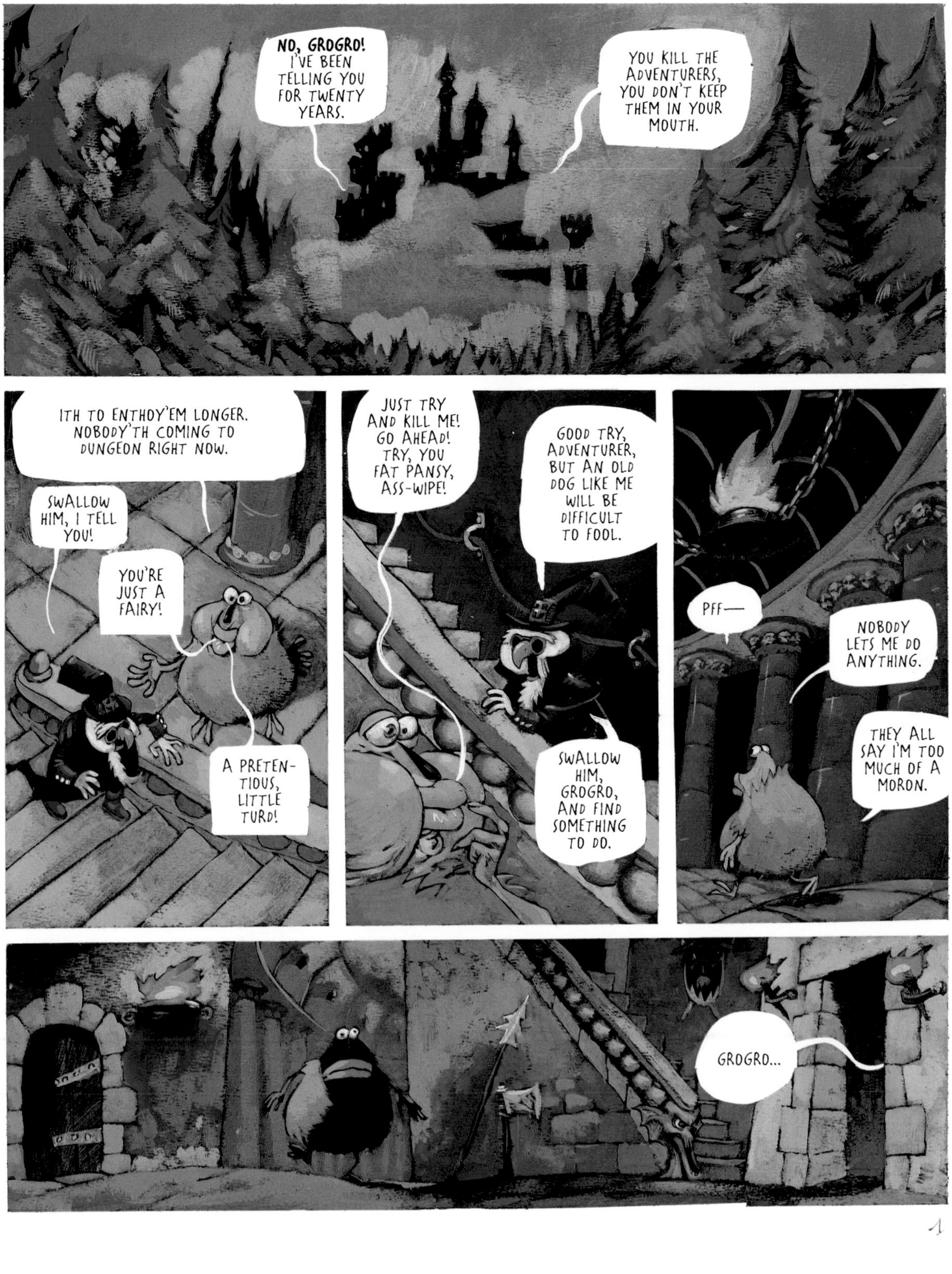
NO, GROGRO! I'VE BEEN TELLING YOU FOR TWENTY YEARS.
YOU KILL THE ADVENTURERS, YOU DON'T KEEP THEM IN YOUR MOUTH.
ITH TO ENTHOY'EM LONGER. NOBODY'TH COMING TO DUNGEON RIGHT NOW.
SWALLOW HIM, I TELL YOU!
YOU'RE JUST A FAIRY!
A PRETEN-TIOUS, LITTLE TURD!
JUST TRY AND KILL ME! GO AHEAD! TRY, YOU FAT PANSY, ASS-WIPE!
GOOD TRY, ADVENTURER, BUT AN OLD DOG LIKE ME WILL BE DIFFICULT TO FOOL.
SWALLOW HIM, GROGRO, AND FIND SOMETHING TO DO.
PFF—
NOBODY LETS ME DO ANYTHING.
THEY ALL SAY I'M TOO MUCH OF A MORON.
GROGRO...

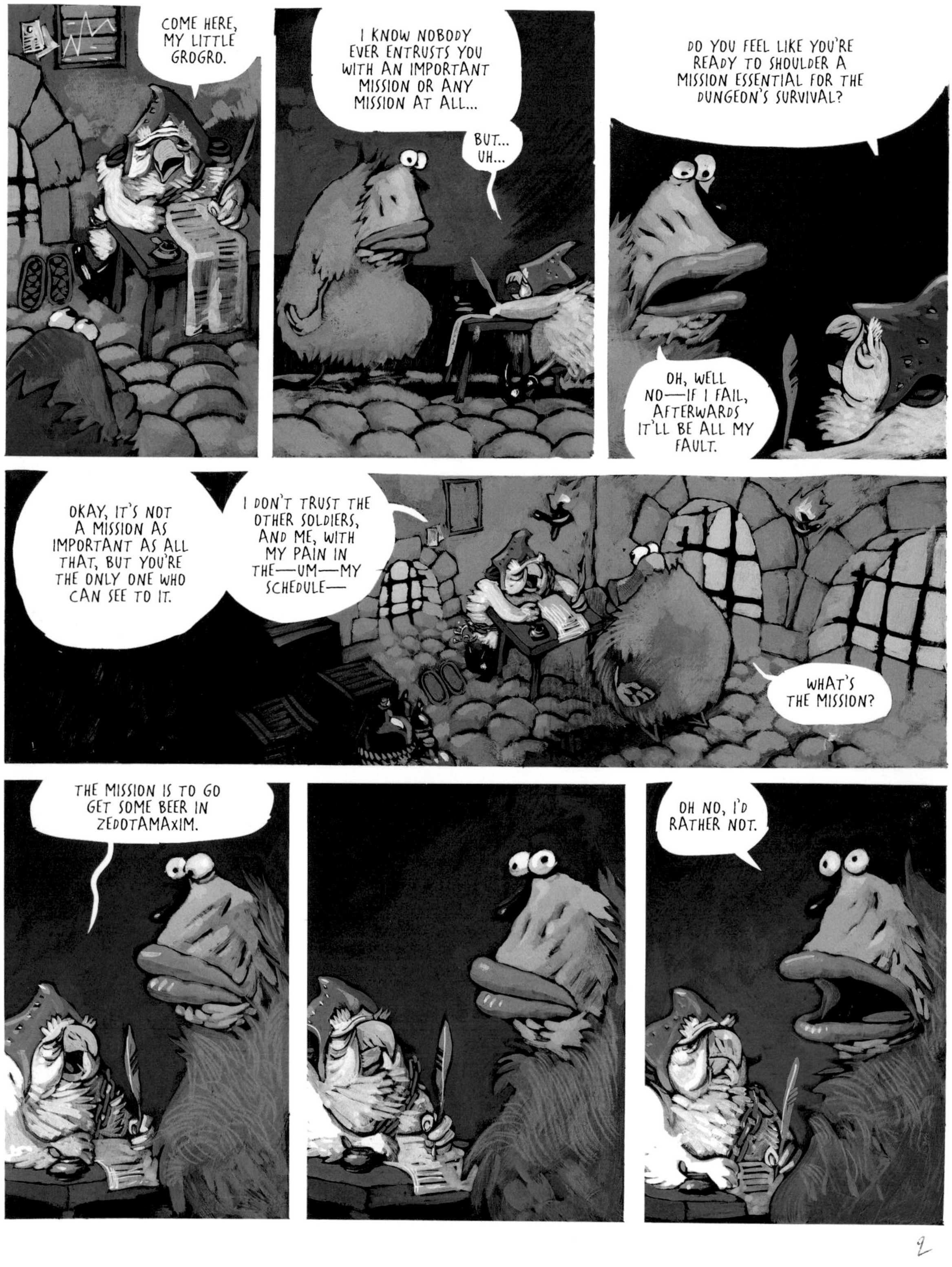
COME HERE, MY LITTLE GROGRO.
I KNOW NOBODY EVER ENTRUSTS YOU WITH AN IMPORTANT MISSION OR ANY MISSION AT ALL...
BUT... UH...
DO YOU FEEL LIKE YOU'RE READY TO SHOULDER A MISSION ESSENTIAL FOR THE DUNGEON'S SURVIVAL?
OH, WELL NO—IF I FAIL, AFTERWARDS IT'LL BE ALL MY FAULT.
OKAY, IT'S NOT A MISSION AS IMPORTANT AS ALL THAT, BUT YOU'RE THE ONLY ONE WHO CAN SEE TO IT.
I DON'T TRUST THE OTHER SOLDIERS, AND ME, WITH MY PAIN IN THE—UM—MY SCHEDULE—
WHAT'S THE MISSION?
THE MISSION IS TO GO GET SOME BEER IN ZEDOTAMAXIM.
OH NO, I'D RATHER NOT.

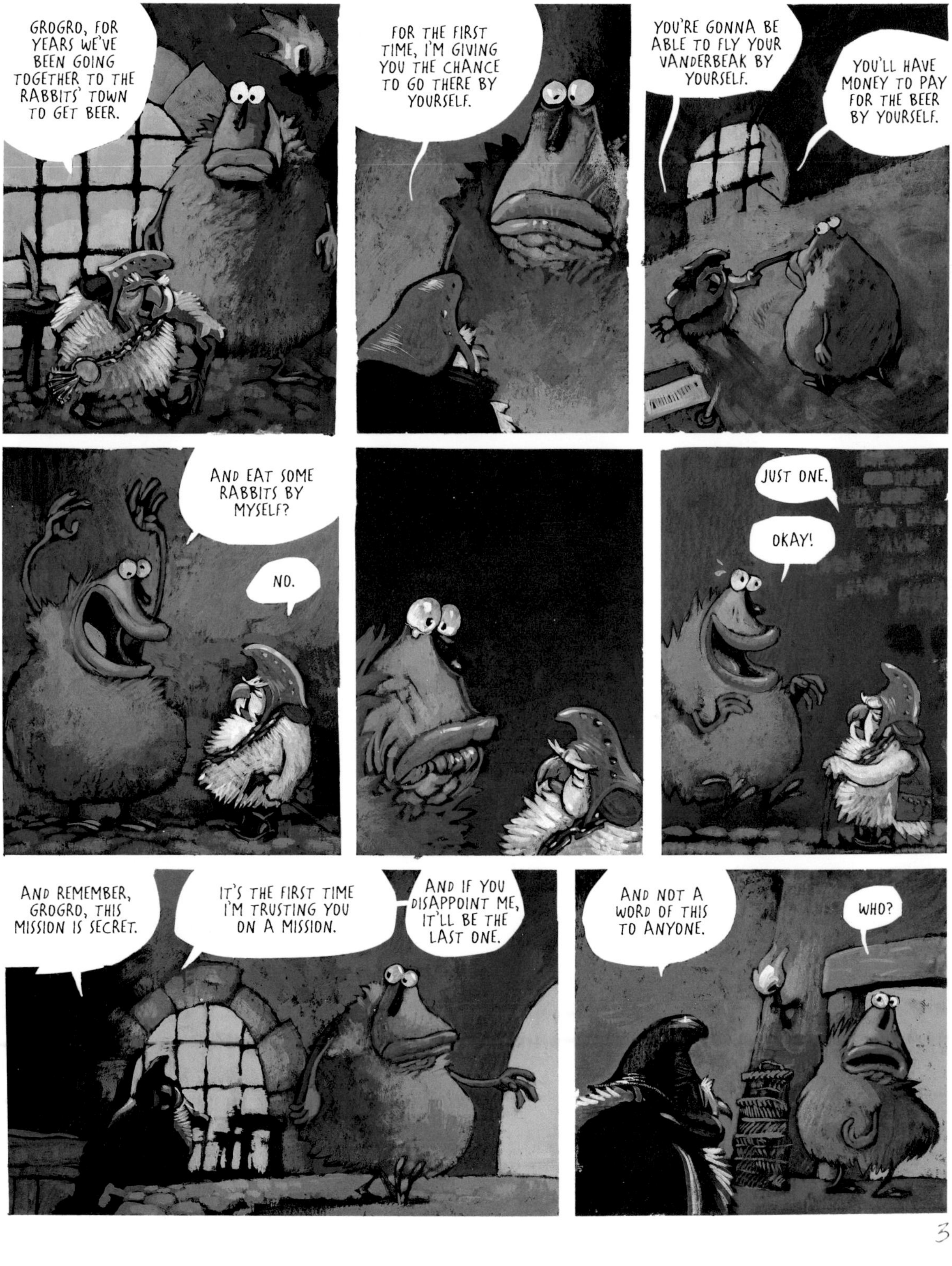
GROGRO, FOR YEARS WE'VE BEEN GOING TOGETHER TO THE RABBITS' TOWN TO GET BEER.
FOR THE FIRST TIME, I'M GIVING YOU THE CHANCE TO GO THERE BY YOURSELF.
YOU'RE GONNA BE ABLE TO FLY YOUR VANDERBEAK BY YOURSELF.
YOU'LL HAVE MONEY TO PAY FOR THE BEER BY YOURSELF.
AND EAT SOME RABBITS BY MYSELF?
NO.
JUST ONE.
OKAY!
AND REMEMBER, GROGRO, THIS MISSION IS SECRET.
IT'S THE FIRST TIME I'M TRUSTING YOU ON A MISSION.
AND IF YOU DISAPPOINT ME, IT'LL BE THE LAST ONE.
AND NOT A WORD OF THIS TO ANYONE.
WHO?

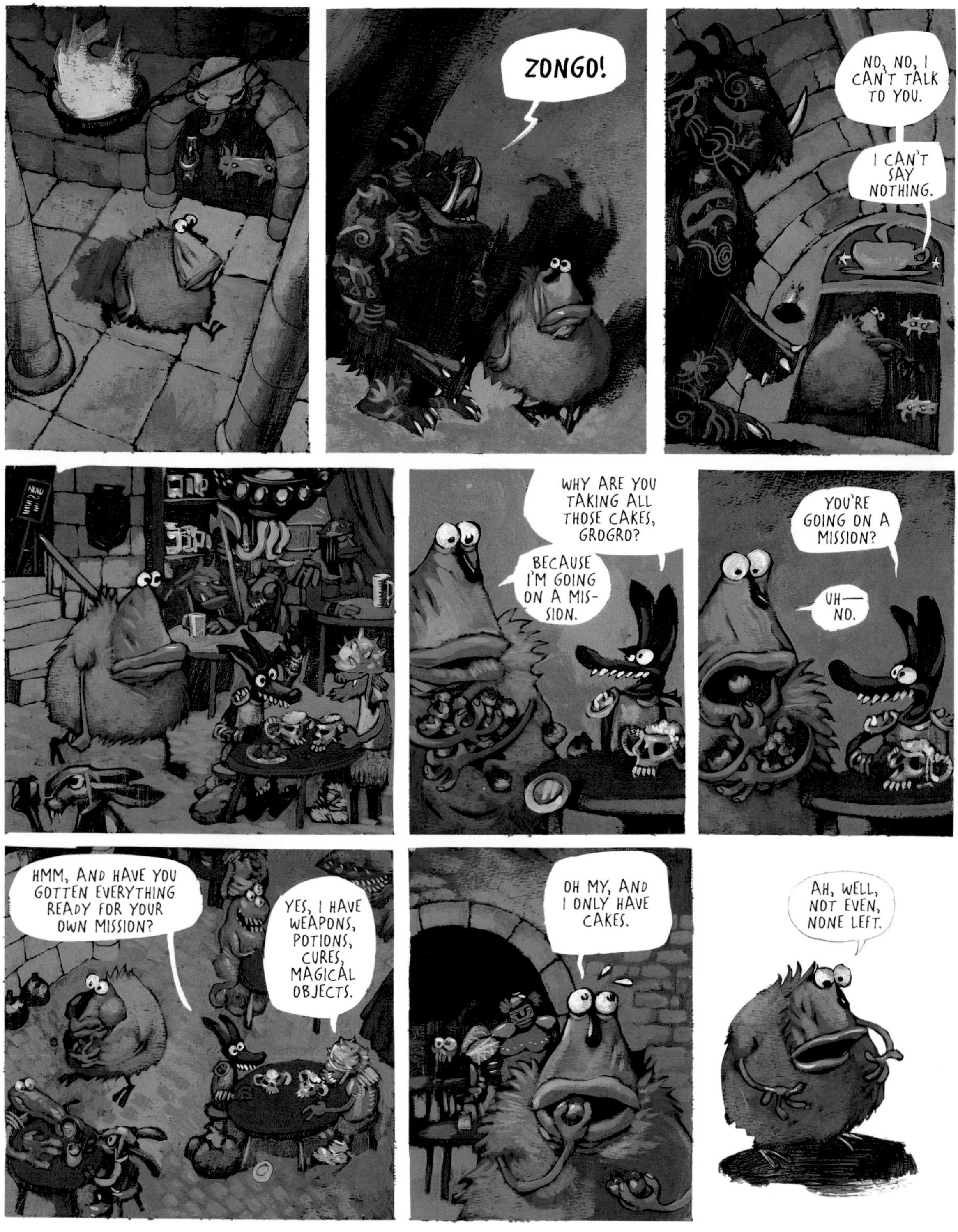
ZONGO!
NO, NO, I CAN'T TALK TO YOU.
I CAN'T SAY NOTHING.
MENU
WHY ARE YOU TAKING ALL THOSE CAKES, GROGRO?
BECAUSE I'M GOING ON A MIS- SION.
YOU'RE GOING ON A MISSION?
UH— NO.
HMM, AND HAVE YOU GOTTEN EVERYTHING READY FOR YOUR OWN MISSION?
YES, I HAVE WEAPONS, POTIONS, CURES, MAGICAL OBJECTS.
OH MY, AND I ONLY HAVE CAKES.
AH, WELL, NOT EVEN, NONE LEFT.

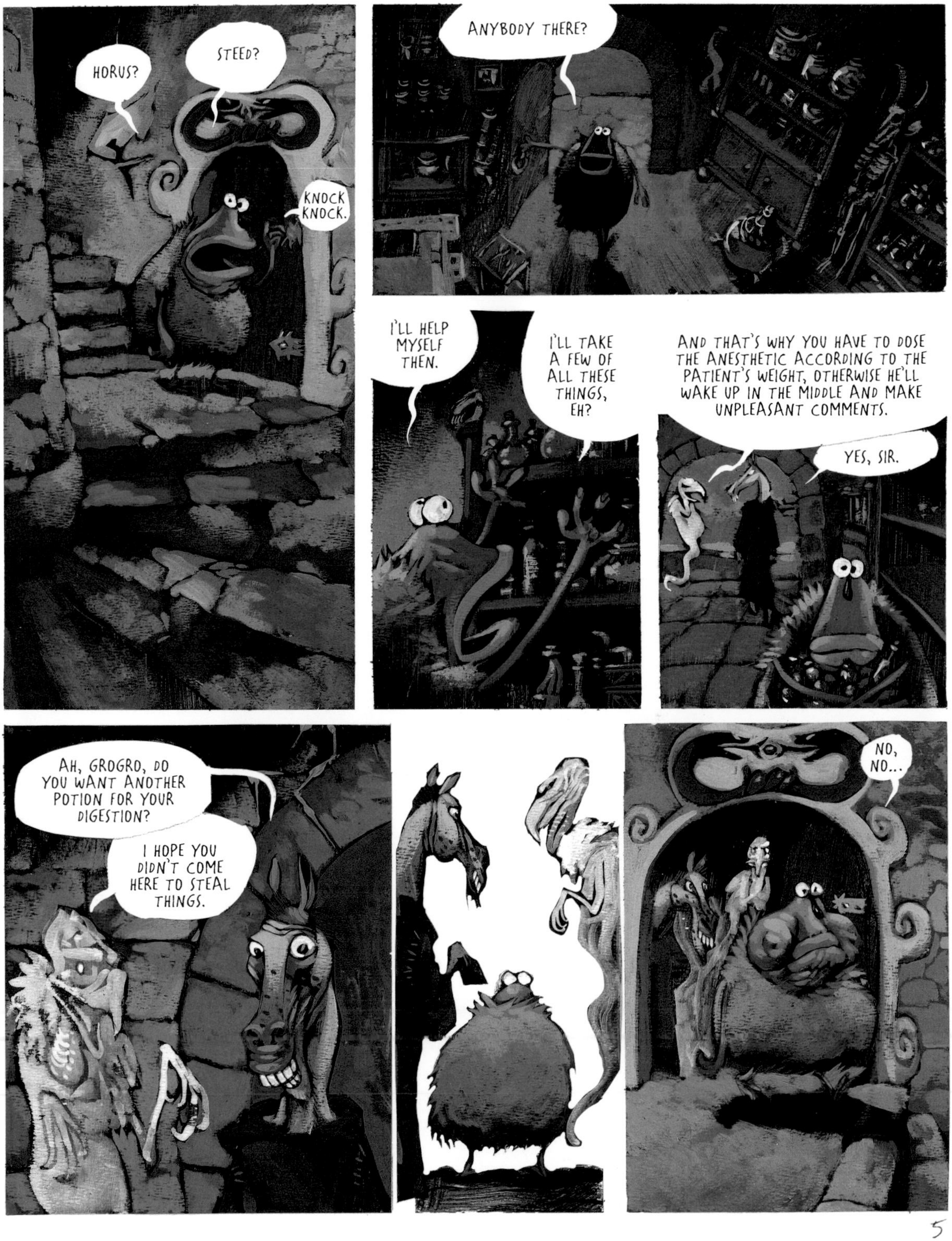
HORUS?
STEED?
KNOCK KNOCK.
ANYBODY THERE?
I'LL HELP MYSELF THEN.
I'LL TAKE A FEW OF ALL THESE THINGS, EH?
AND THAT'S WHY YOU HAVE TO DOSE THE ANESTHETIC ACCORDING TO THE PATIENT'S WEIGHT, OTHERWISE HE'LL WAKE UP IN THE MIDDLE AND MAKE UNPLEASANT COMMENTS.
YES, SIR.
AH, GROGRO, DO YOU WANT ANOTHER POTION FOR YOUR DIGESTION?
I HOPE YOU DIDN'T COME HERE TO STEAL THINGS.
NO, NO...

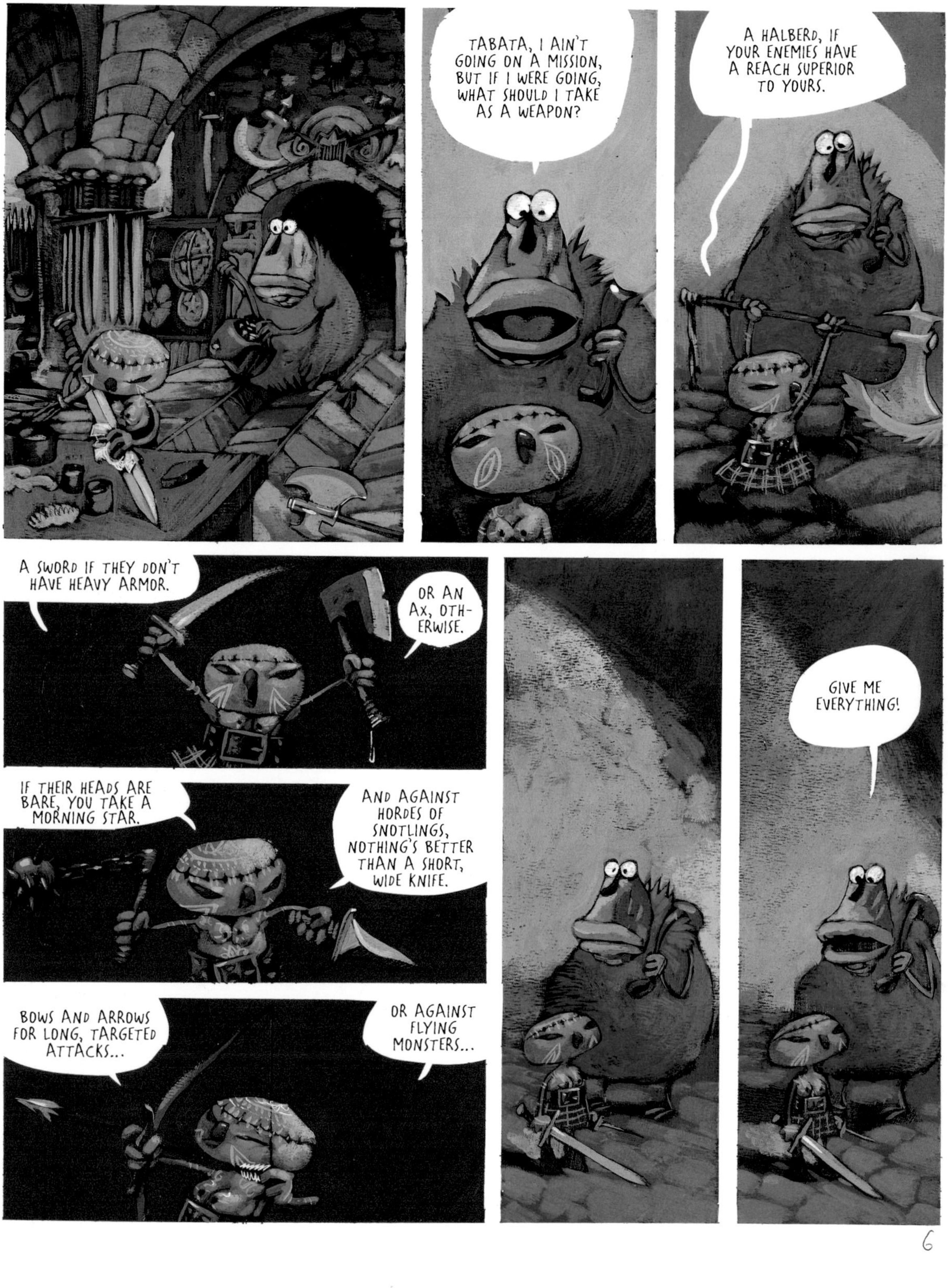
TABATA, I AIN'T GOING ON A MISSION, BUT IF I WERE GOING, WHAT SHOULD I TAKE AS A WEAPON?
A HALBERD, IF YOUR ENEMIES HAVE A REACH SUPERIOR TO YOURS.
A SWORD IF THEY DON'T HAVE HEAVY ARMOR.
OR AN AX, OTH-ERWISE.
IF THEIR HEADS ARE BARE, YOU TAKE A MORNING STAR.
AND AGAINST HORDES OF SNOTLINGS, NOTHING'S BETTER THAN A SHORT, WIDE KNIFE.
BOWS AND ARROWS FOR LONG, TARGETED ATTACKS...
OR AGAINST FLYING MONSTERS...
GIVE ME EVERYTHING!

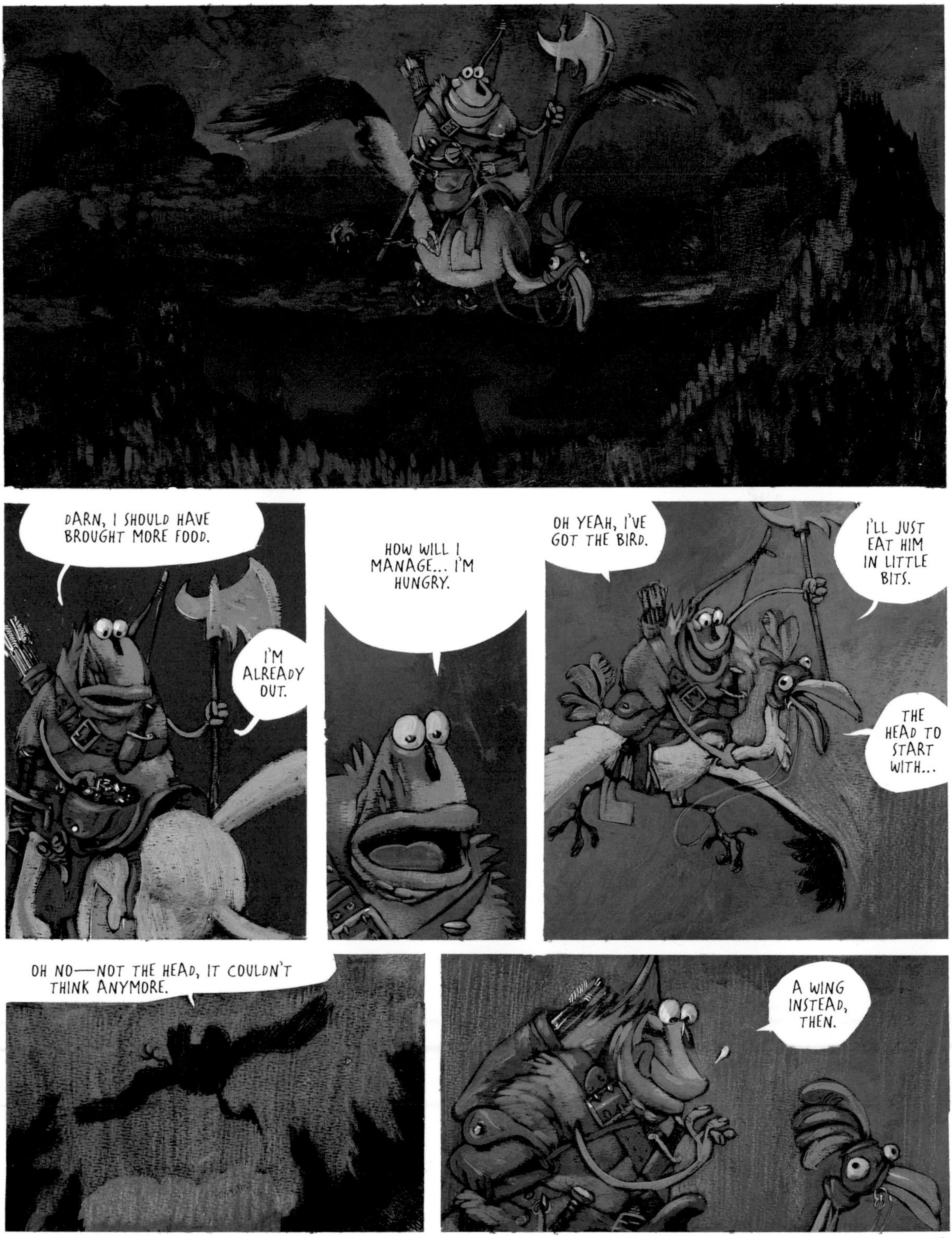
DARN, I SHOULD HAVE BROUGHT MORE FOOD.
I'M ALREADY OUT.
HOW WILL I MANAGE... I'M HUNGRY.
OH YEAH, I'VE GOT THE BIRD.
I'LL JUST EAT HIM IN LITTLE BITS.
THE HEAD TO START WITH...
OH NO—NOT THE HEAD, IT COULDN'T THINK ANYMORE.
A WING INSTEAD, THEN.

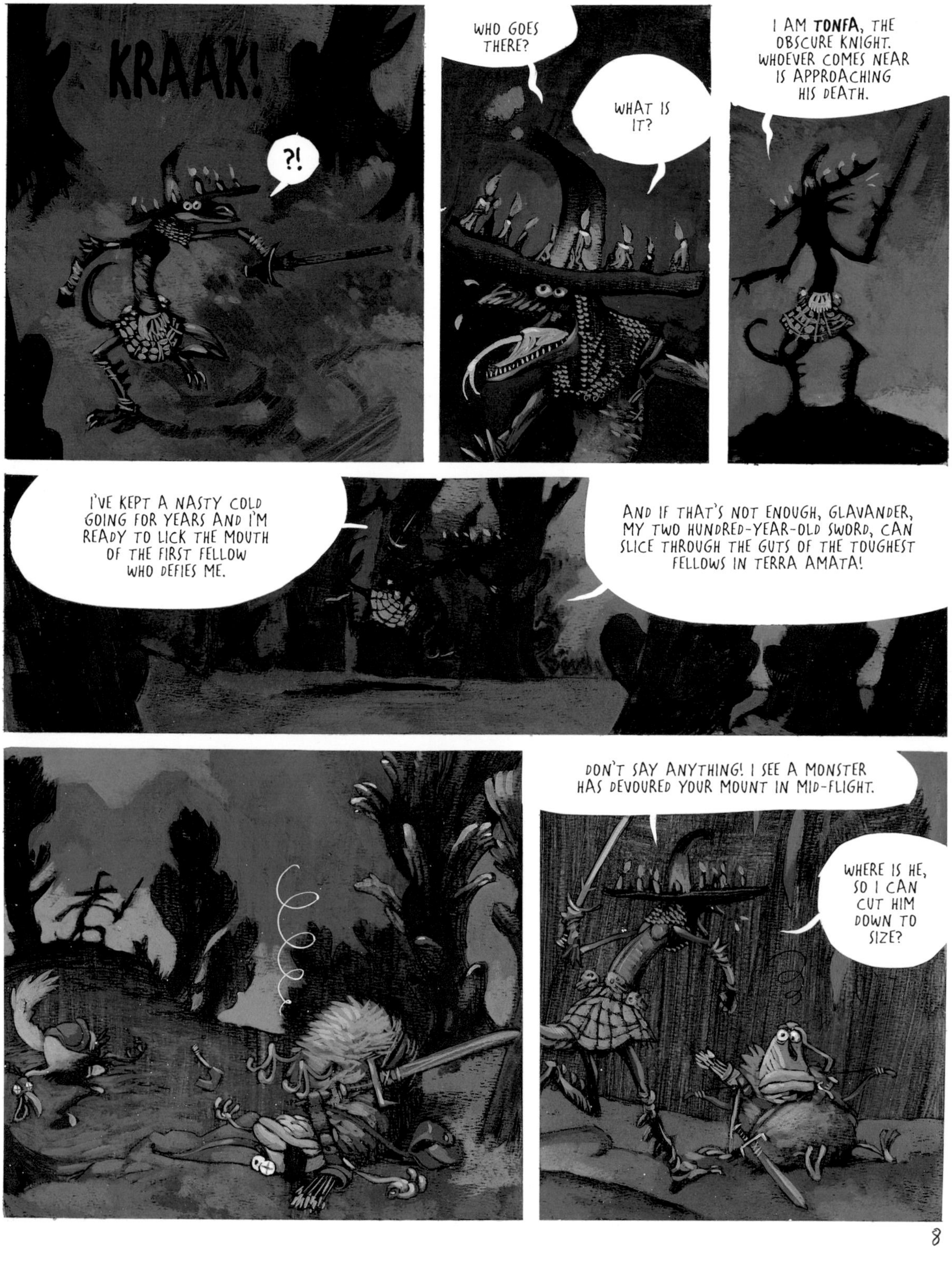
KRAAK!
?!
WHO GOES THERE?
WHAT IS IT?
I AM TONFA, THE OBSCURE KNIGHT. WHOEVER COMES NEAR IS APPROACHING HIS DEATH.
I'VE KEPT A NASTY COLD GOING FOR YEARS AND I'M READY TO LICK THE MOUTH OF THE FIRST FELLOW WHO DEFIES ME.
AND IF THAT'S NOT ENOUGH, GLAVANDER, MY TWO HUNDRED-YEAR-OLD SWORD, CAN SLICE THROUGH THE GUTS OF THE TOUGHEST FELLOWS IN TERRA AMATA!
DON'T SAY ANYTHING! I SEE A MONSTER HAS DEVOURED YOUR MOUNT IN MID-FLIGHT.
WHERE IS HE, SO I CAN CUT HIM DOWN TO SIZE?

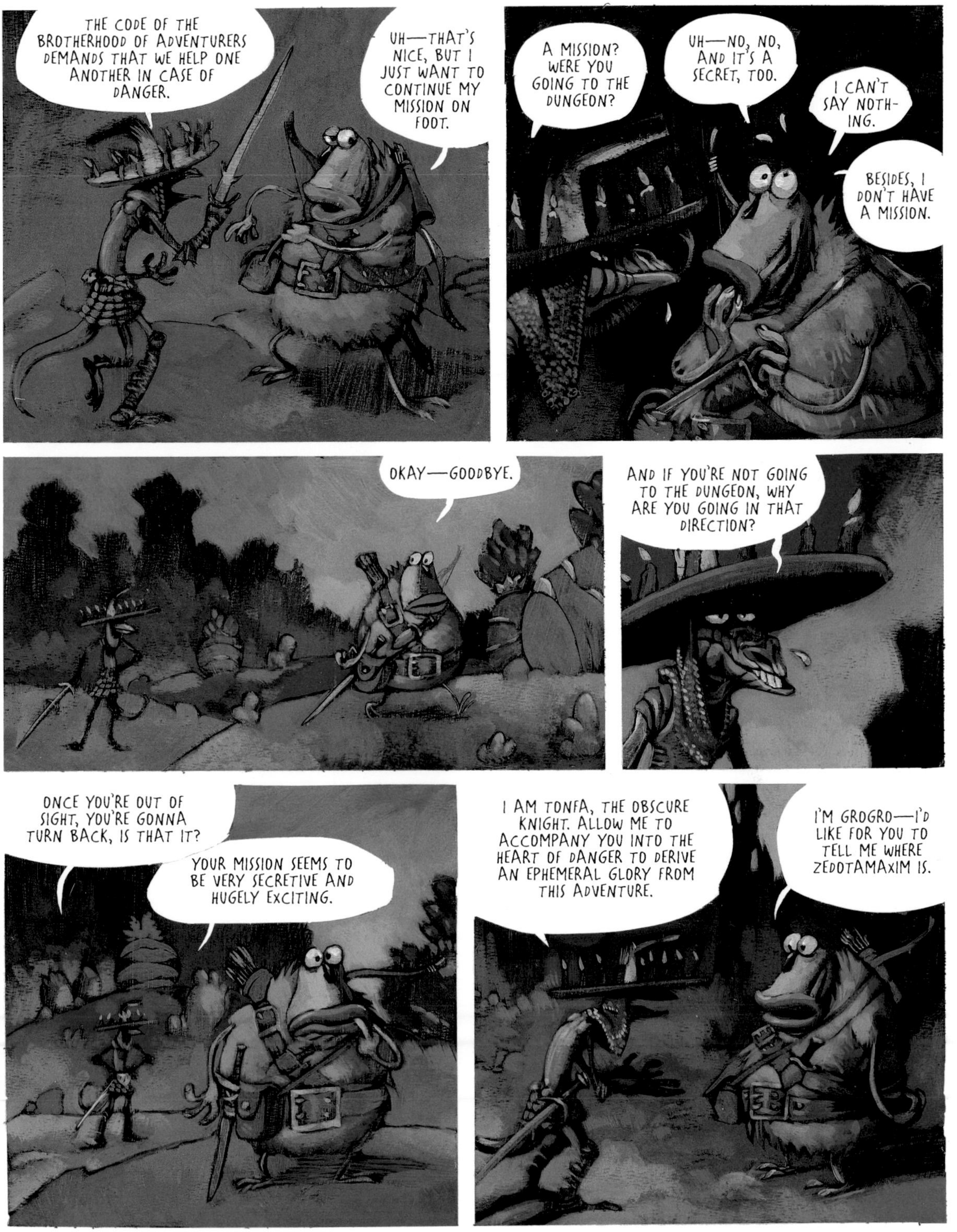
THE CODE OF THE BROTHERHOOD OF ADVENTURERS DEMANDS THAT WE HELP ONE ANOTHER IN CASE OF DANGER.
UH—THAT'S NICE, BUT I JUST WANT TO CONTINUE MY MISSION ON FOOT.
A MISSION? WERE YOU GOING TO THE DUNGEON?
UH—NO, NO, AND IT'S A SECRET, TOO.
I CAN'T SAY NOTHING.
BESIDES, I DON'T HAVE A MISSION.
OKAY—GOODBYE.
AND IF YOU'RE NOT GOING TO THE DUNGEON, WHY ARE YOU GOING IN THAT DIRECTION?
ONCE YOU'RE OUT OF SIGHT, YOU'RE GONNA TURN BACK, IS THAT IT?
YOUR MISSION SEEMS TO BE VERY SECRETIVE AND HUGELY EXCITING.
I AM TONFA, THE OBSCURE KNIGHT. ALLOW ME TO ACCOMPANY YOU INTO THE HEART OF DANGER TO DERIVE AN EPHEMERAL GLORY FROM THIS ADVENTURE.
I'M GROGRO—I'D LIKE FOR YOU TO TELL ME WHERE ZEDOTAMAXIM IS.

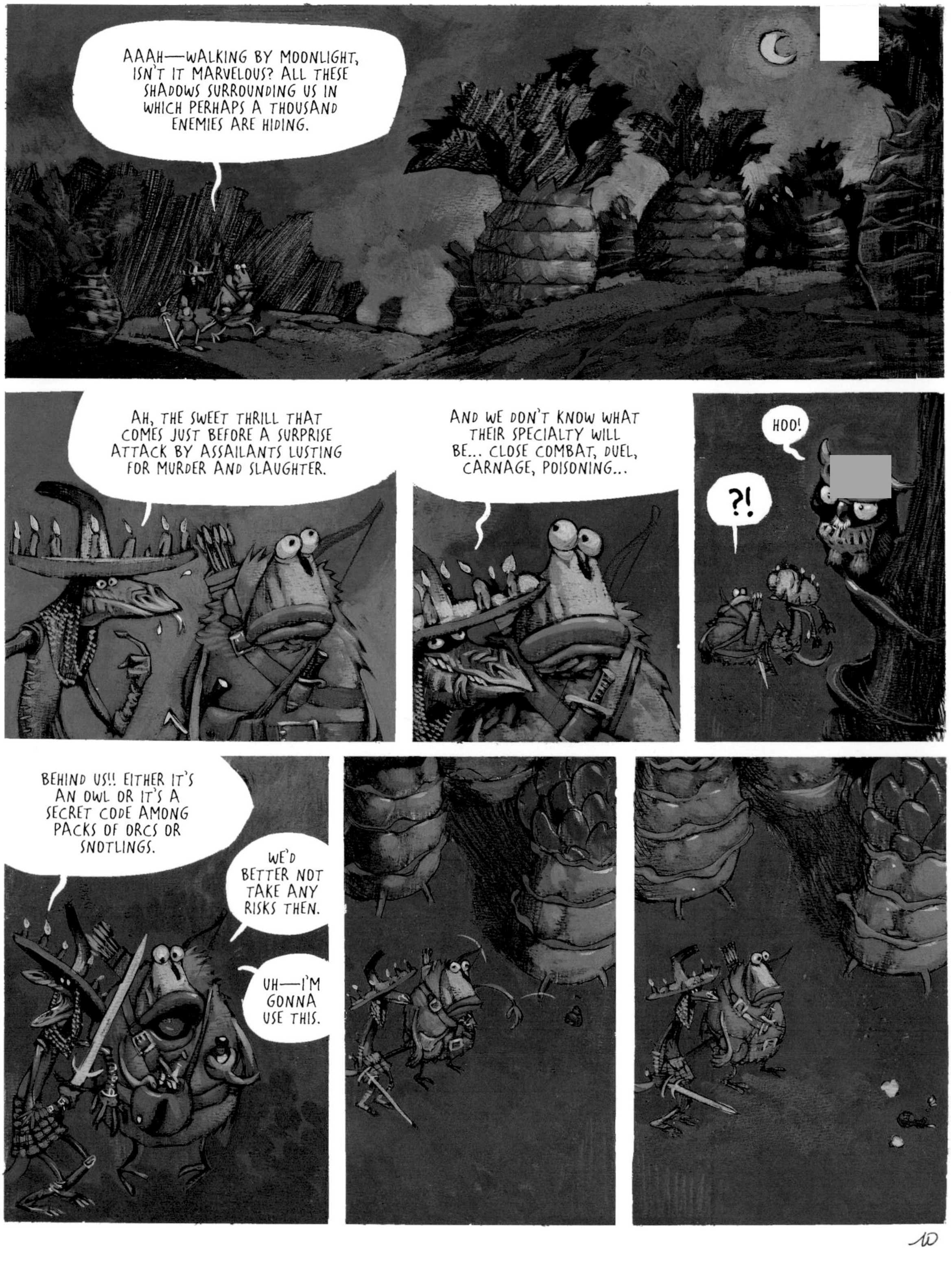
AAAH—WALKING BY MOONLIGHT, ISN'T IT MARVELOUS? ALL THESE SHADOWS SURROUNDING US IN WHICH PERHAPS A THOUSAND ENEMIES ARE HIDING.
AH, THE SWEET THRILL THAT COMES JUST BEFORE A SURPRISE ATTACK BY ASSAILANTS LUSTING FOR MURDER AND SLAUGHTER.
AND WE DON'T KNOW WHAT THEIR SPECIALTY WILL BE... CLOSE COMBAT, DUEL, CARNAGE, POISONING...
HOO!
?!
BEHIND US!! EITHER IT'S AN OWL OR IT'S A SECRET CODE AMONG PACKS OF ORCS OR SNOTLINGS.
WE'D BETTER NOT TAKE ANY RISKS THEN.
UH—I'M GONNA USE THIS.

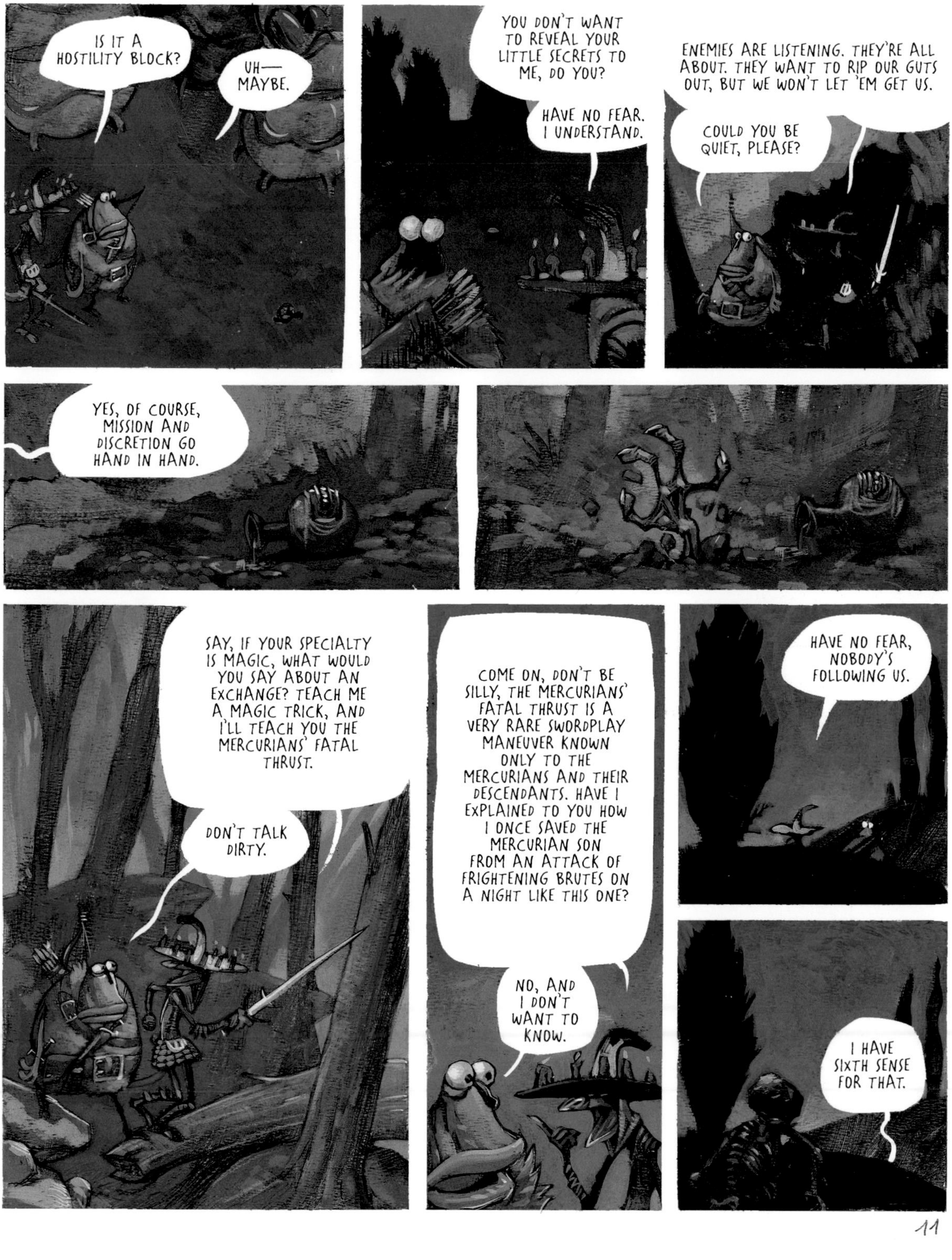
IS IT A HOSTILITY BLOCK?
UH— MAYBE.
YOU DON'T WANT TO REVEAL YOUR LITTLE SECRETS TO ME, DO YOU?
HAVE NO FEAR. I UNDERSTAND.
ENEMIES ARE LISTENING. THEY'RE ALL ABOUT. THEY WANT TO RIP OUR GUTS OUT, BUT WE WON'T LET 'EM GET US.
COULD YOU BE QUIET, PLEASE?
YES, OF COURSE, MISSION AND DISCRETION GO HAND IN HAND.
SAY, IF YOUR SPECIALTY IS MAGIC, WHAT WOULD YOU SAY ABOUT AN EXCHANGE? TEACH ME A MAGIC TRICK, AND I'LL TEACH YOU THE MERCURIANS' FATAL THRUST.
DON'T TALK DIRTY.
COME ON, DON'T BE SILLY, THE MERCURIANS' FATAL THRUST IS A VERY RARE SWORDPLAY MANEUVER KNOWN ONLY TO THE MERCURIANS AND THEIR DESCENDANTS. HAVE I EXPLAINED TO YOU HOW I ONCE SAVED THE MERCURIAN SON FROM AN ATTACK OF FRIGHTENING BRUTES ON A NIGHT LIKE THIS ONE?
NO, AND I DON'T WANT TO KNOW.
HAVE NO FEAR, NOBODY'S FOLLOWING US.
I HAVE SIXTH SENSE FOR THAT.

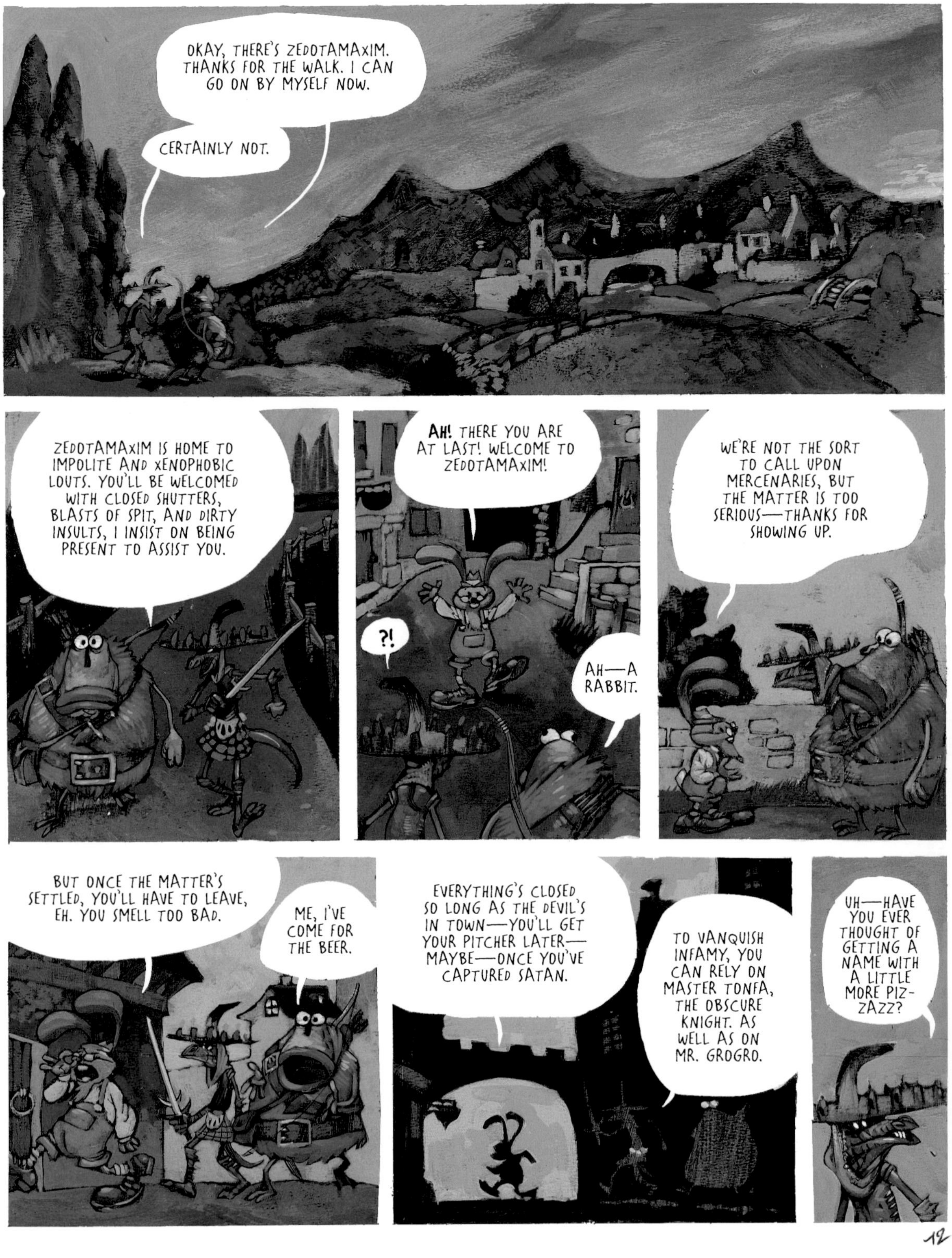
OKAY, THERE'S ZEDOTAMAXIM. THANKS FOR THE WALK. I CAN GO ON BY MYSELF NOW.
CERTAINLY NOT.
ZEDOTAMAXIM IS HOME TO IMPOLITE AND XENOPHOBIC LOUTS. YOU'LL BE WELCOMED WITH CLOSED SHUTTERS, BLASTS OF SPIT, AND DIRTY INSULTS, I INSIST ON BEING PRESENT TO ASSIST YOU.
AH! THERE YOU ARE AT LAST! WELCOME TO ZEDOTAMAXIM!
?!
AH—A RABBIT.
WE'RE NOT THE SORT TO CALL UPON MERCENARIES, BUT THE MATTER IS TOO SERIOUS—THANKS FOR SHOWING UP.
BUT ONCE THE MATTER'S SETTLED, YOU'LL HAVE TO LEAVE, EH. YOU SMELL TOO BAD.
ME, I'VE COME FOR THE BEER.
EVERYTHING'S CLOSED SO LONG AS THE DEVIL'S IN TOWN—YOU'LL GET YOUR PITCHER LATER—MAYBE—ONCE YOU'VE CAPTURED SATAN.
TO VANQUISH INFAMY, YOU CAN RELY ON MASTER TONFA, THE OBSCURE KNIGHT. AS WELL AS ON MR. GROGRO.
UH—HAVE YOU EVER THOUGHT OF GETTING A NAME WITH A LITTLE MORE PIZZAZZ?

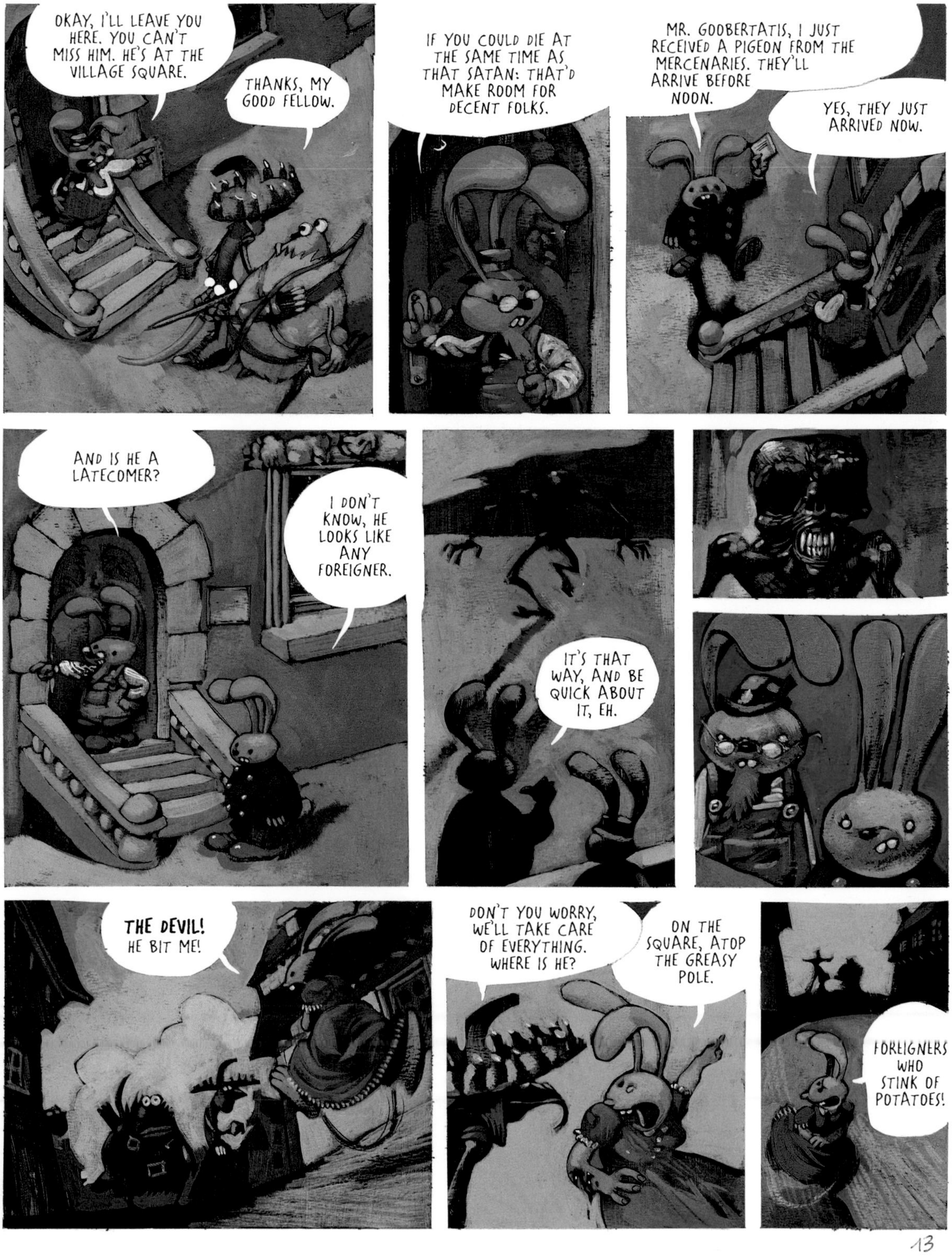
OKAY, I'LL LEAVE YOU HERE. YOU CAN'T MISS HIM. HE'S AT THE VILLAGE SQUARE.
THANKS, MY GOOD FELLOW.
IF YOU COULD DIE AT THE SAME TIME AS THAT SATAN: THAT'D MAKE ROOM FOR DECENT FOLKS.
MR. GOOBERTATIS, I JUST RECEIVED A PIGEON FROM THE MERCENARIES. THEY'LL ARRIVE BEFORE NOON.
YES, THEY JUST ARRIVED NOW.
AND IS HE A LATECOMER?
I DON'T KNOW, HE LOOKS LIKE ANY FOREIGNER.
IT'S THAT WAY, AND BE QUICK ABOUT IT, EH.
THE DEVIL! HE BIT ME!
DON'T YOU WORRY, WE'LL TAKE CARE OF EVERYTHING. WHERE IS HE?
ON THE SQUARE, ATOP THE GREASY POLE.
FOREIGNERS WHO STINK OF POTATOES!

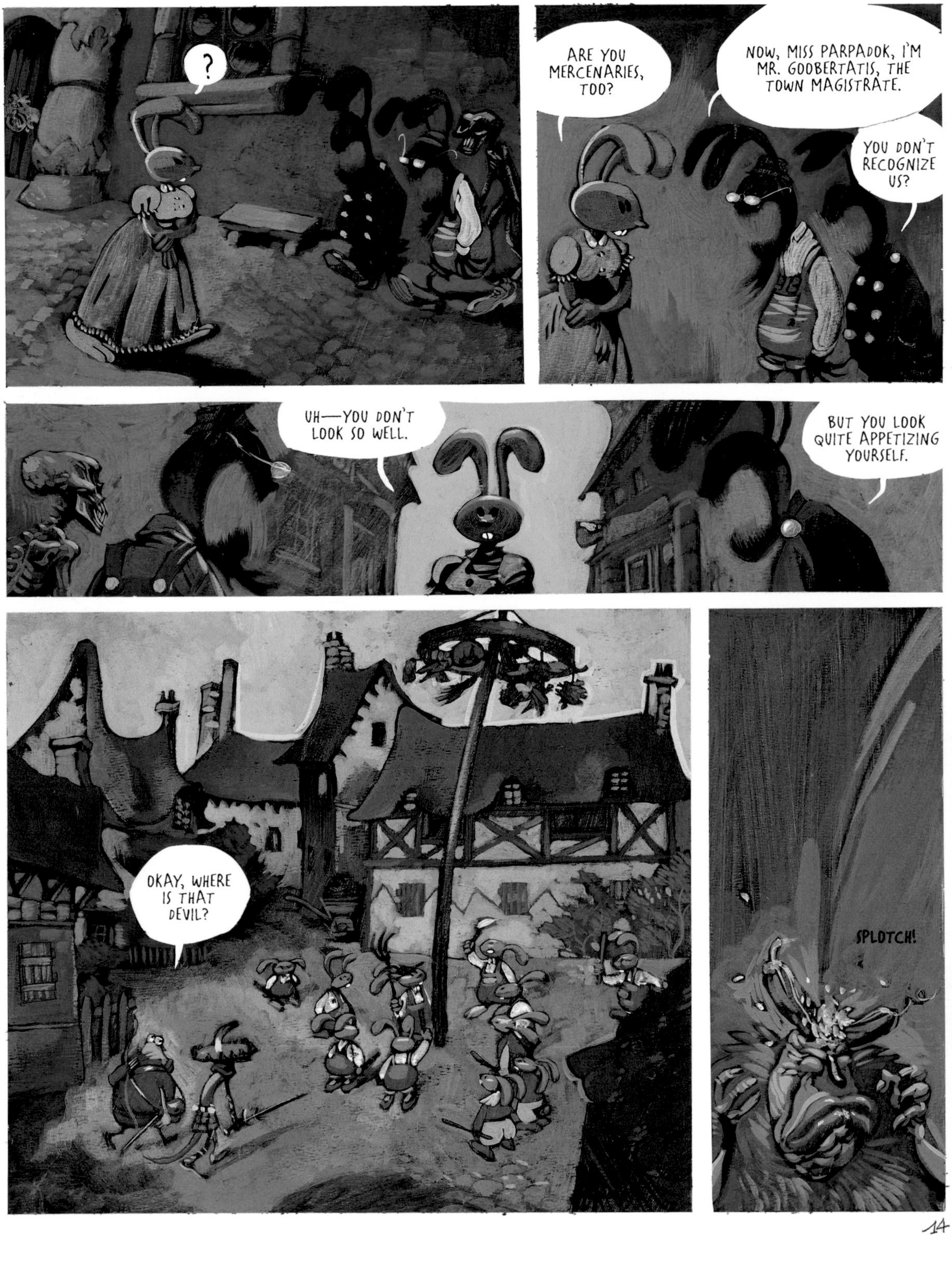
?
ARE YOU MERCENARIES, TOO?
NOW, MISS PARPADOK, I'M MR. GOOBERTATIS, THE TOWN MAGISTRATE.
YOU DON'T RECOGNIZE US?
UH—YOU DON'T LOOK SO WELL.
BUT YOU LOOK QUITE APPETIZING YOURSELF.
OKAY, WHERE IS THAT DEVIL?
SPLOTCH!

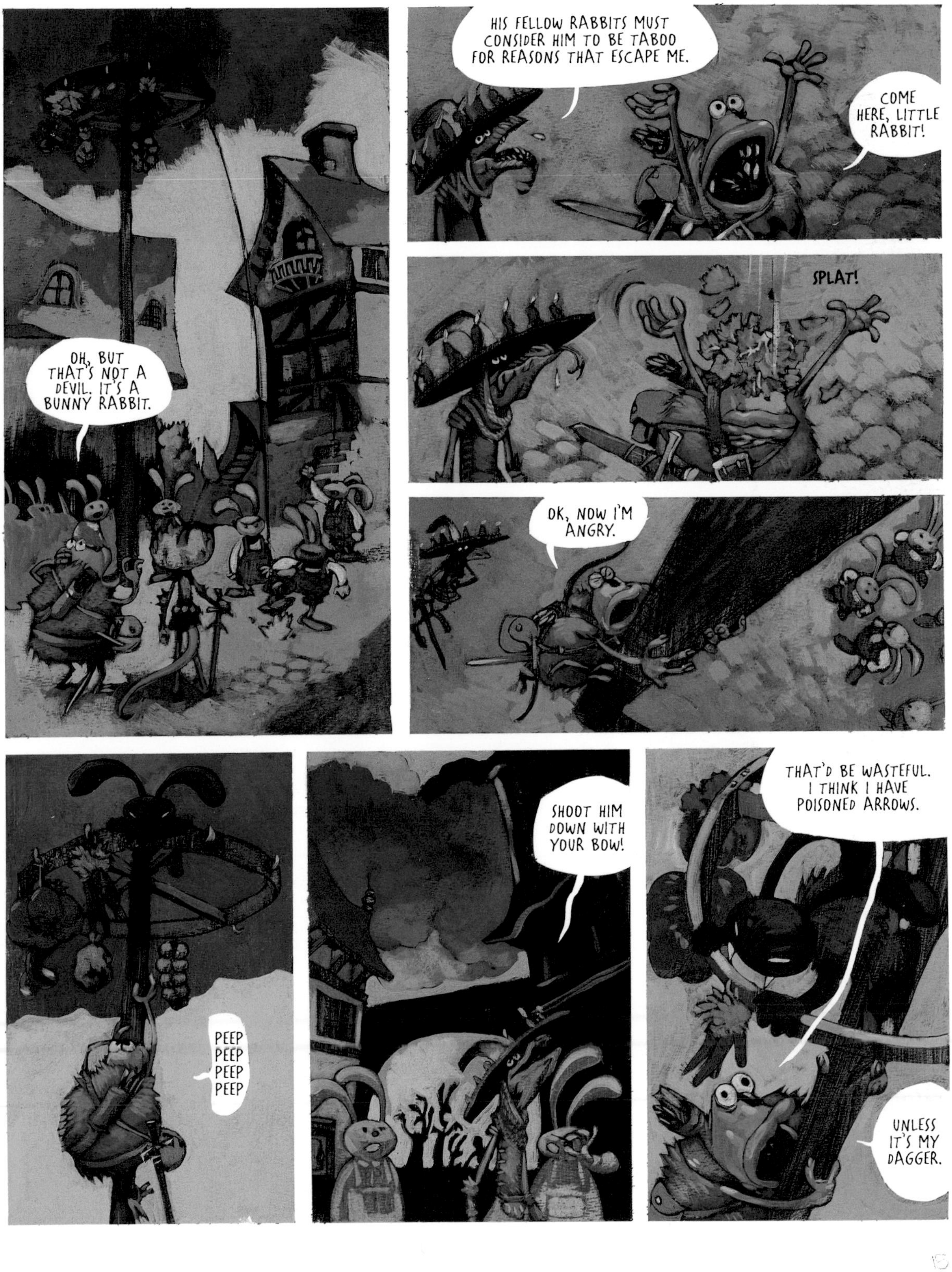
OH, BUT THAT'S NOT A DEVIL. IT'S A BUNNY RABBIT.
HIS FELLOW RABBITS MUST CONSIDER HIM TO BE TABOO FOR REASONS THAT ESCAPE ME.
COME HERE, LITTLE RABBIT!
SPLAT!
OK, NOW I'M ANGRY.
PEEP PEEP PEEP PEEP
SHOOT HIM DOWN WITH YOUR BOW!
THAT'D BE WASTEFUL. I THINK I HAVE POISONED ARROWS.
UNLESS IT'S MY DAGGER.

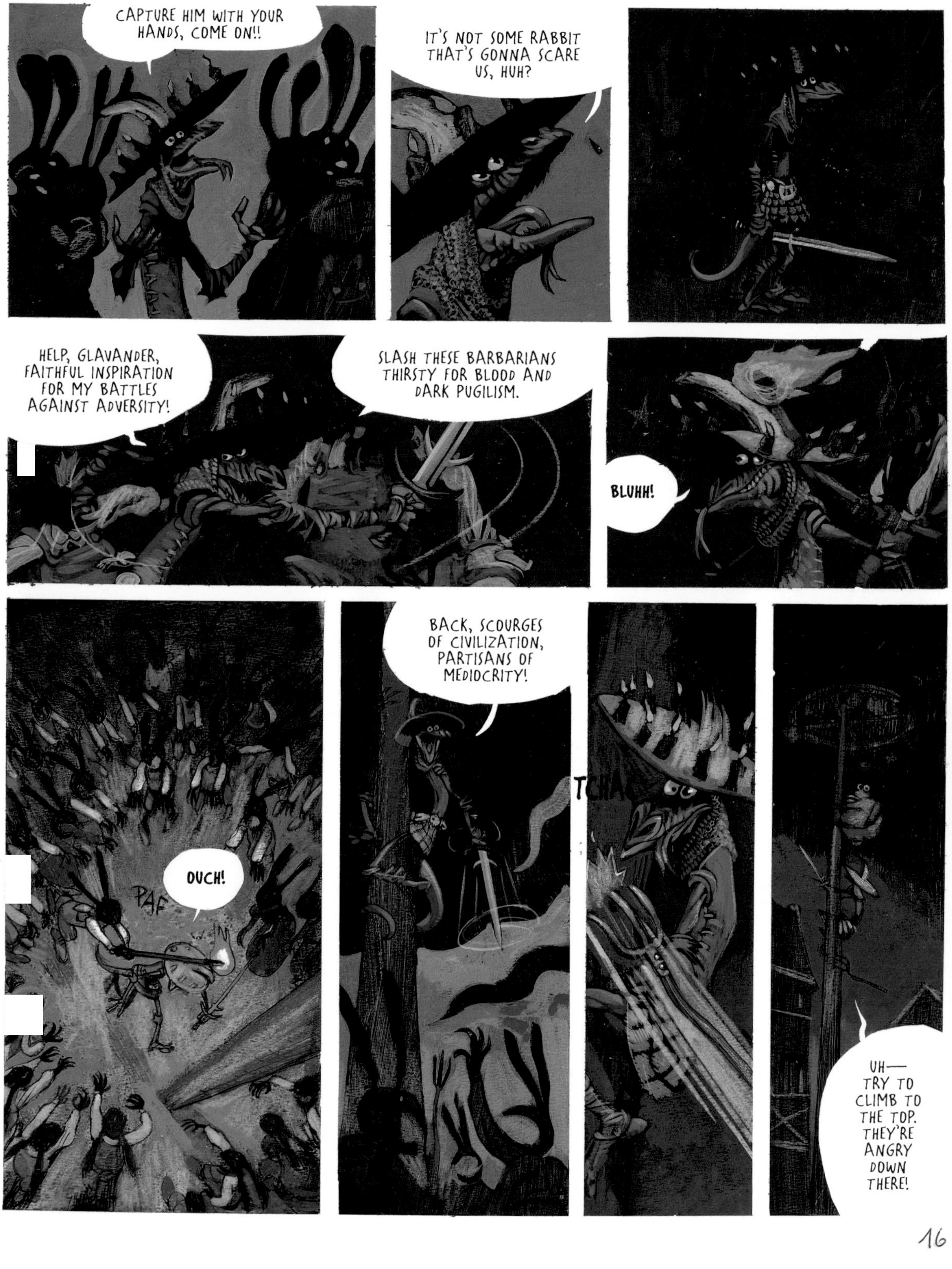
CAPTURE HIM WITH YOUR HANDS, COME ON!!
IT'S NOT SOME RABBIT THAT'S GONNA SCARE US, HUH?
HELP, GLAVANDER, FAITHFUL INSPIRATION FOR MY BATTLES AGAINST ADVERSITY!
SLASH THESE BARBARIANS THIRSTY FOR BLOOD AND DARK PUGILISM.
BLUHH!
PAF
OUCH!
BACK, SCOURGES OF CIVILIZATION, PARTISANS OF MEDIOCRITY!
UH— TRY TO CLIMB TO THE TOP. THEY'RE ANGRY DOWN THERE!

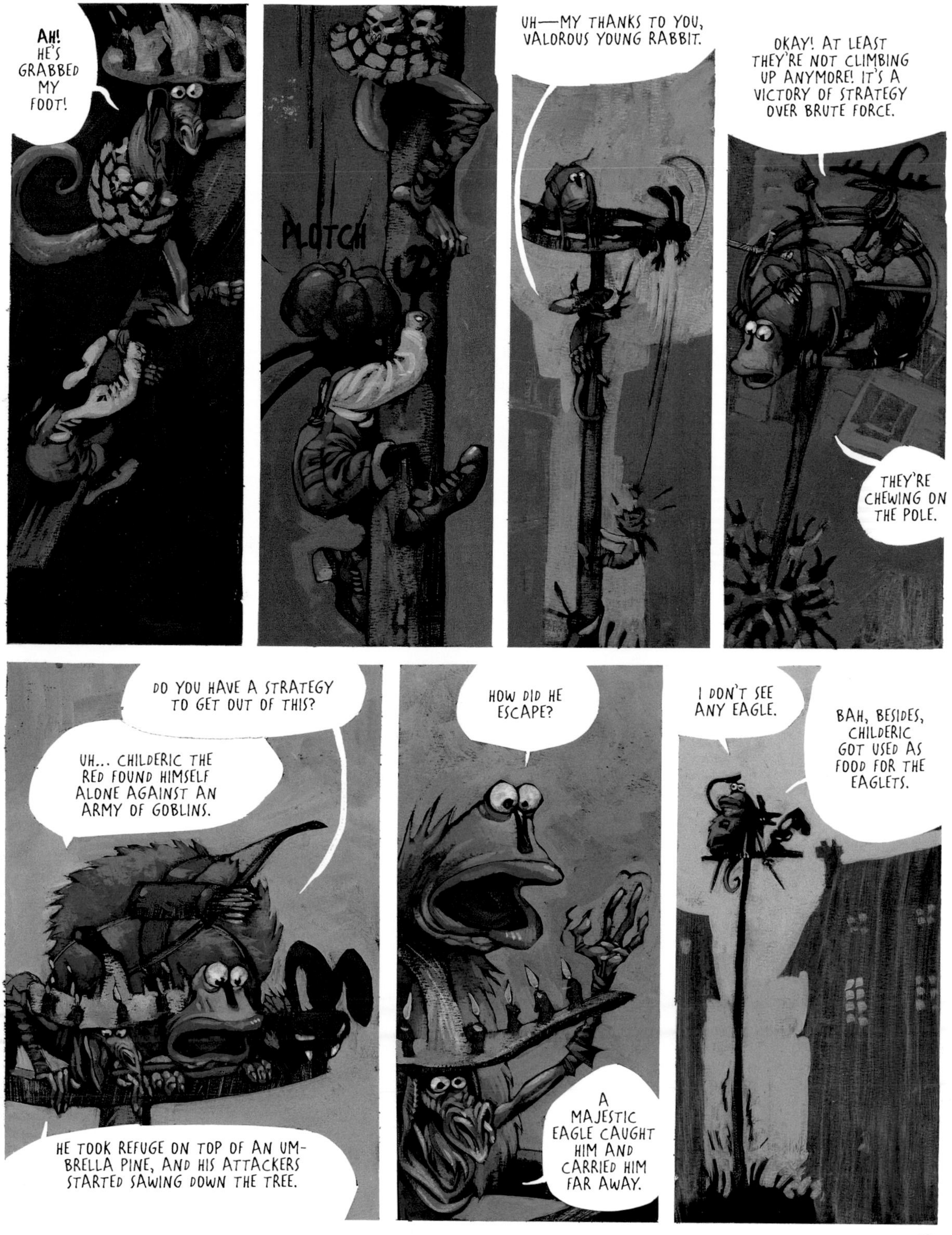
AH! HE'S GRABBED MY FOOT!
PLOTCH
UH—MY THANKS TO YOU, VALOROUS YOUNG RABBIT.
OKAY! AT LEAST THEY'RE NOT CLIMBING UP ANYMORE! IT'S A VICTORY OF STRATEGY OVER BRUTE FORCE.
THEY'RE CHEWING ON THE POLE.
DO YOU HAVE A STRATEGY TO GET OUT OF THIS?
UH... CHILDERIC THE RED FOUND HIMSELF ALONE AGAINST AN ARMY OF GOBLINS.
HE TOOK REFUGE ON TOP OF AN UM-BRELLA PINE, AND HIS ATTACKERS STARTED SAWING DOWN THE TREE.
HOW DID HE ESCAPE?
A MAJESTIC EAGLE CAUGHT HIM AND CARRIED HIM FAR AWAY.
I DON'T SEE ANY EAGLE.
BAH, BESIDES, CHILDERIC GOT USED AS FOOD FOR THE EAGLETS.

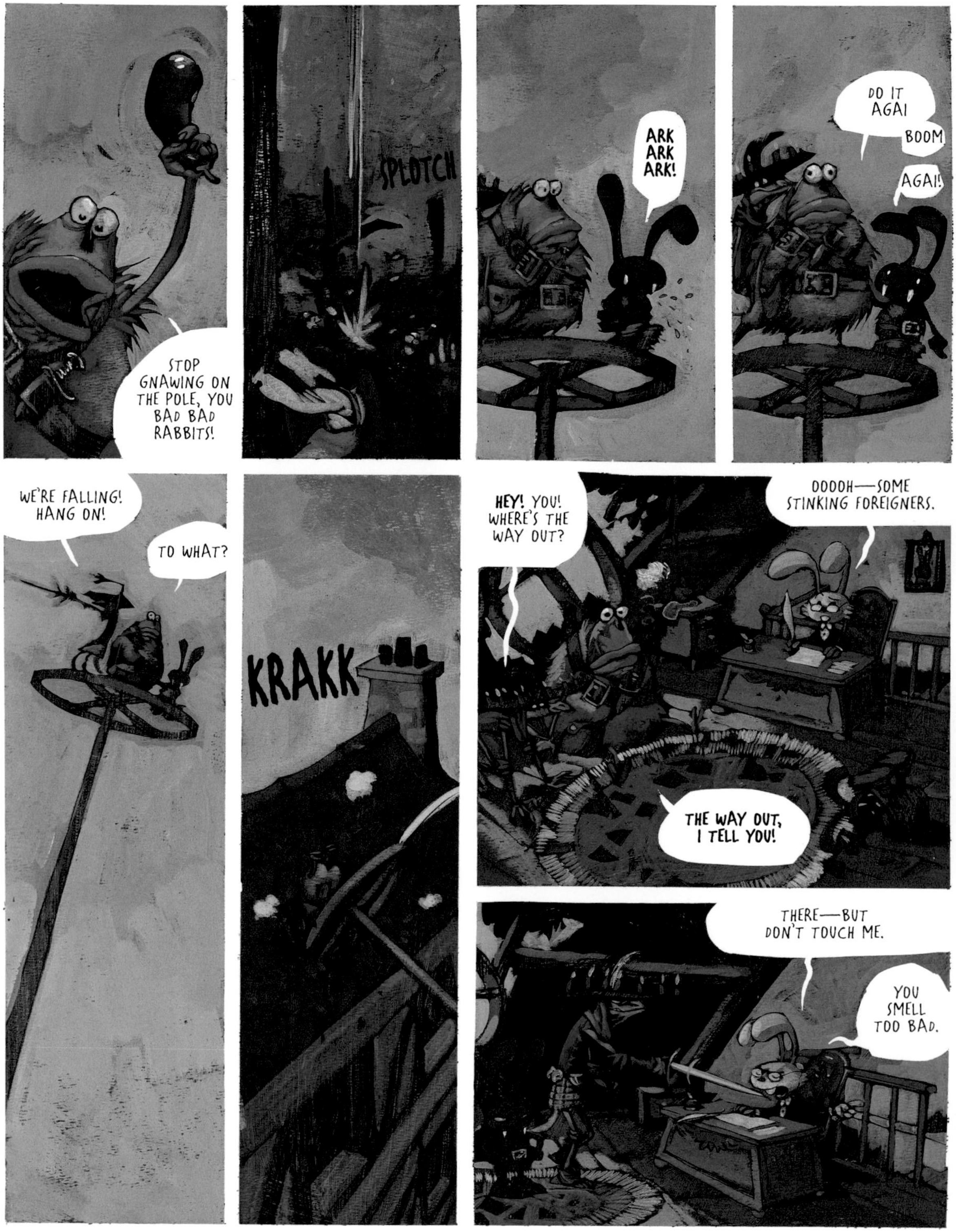
STOP GNAWING ON THE POLE, YOU BAD BAD RABBITS!
SPLOTCH
ARK ARK ARK!
DO IT AGAI
BOOM
AGAI!
WE'RE FALLING! HANG ON!
TO WHAT?
KRAKK
HEY! YOU! WHERE'S THE WAY OUT?
OOOOH—SOME STINKING FOREIGNERS.
THE WAY OUT, I TELL YOU!
THERE—BUT DON'T TOUCH ME.
YOU SMELL TOO BAD.

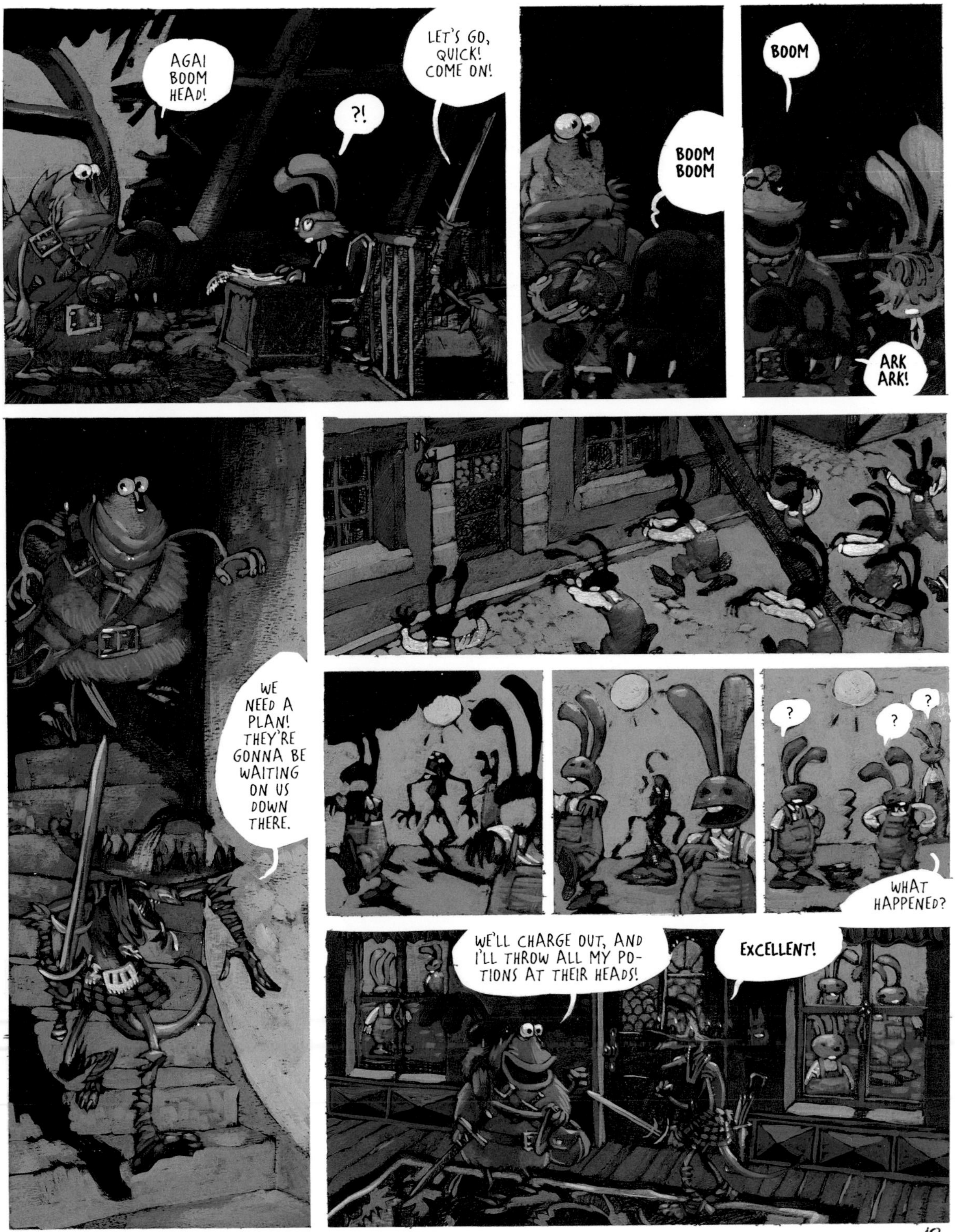
AGAI BOOM HEAD!
?!
LET'S GO, QUICK! COME ON!
BOOM BOOM
BOOM
ARK ARK!
WE NEED A PLAN! THEY'RE GONNA BE WAITING ON US DOWN THERE.
?
?
?
WHAT HAPPENED?
WE'LL CHARGE OUT, AND I'LL THROW ALL MY POTIONS AT THEIR HEADS!
EXCELLENT!

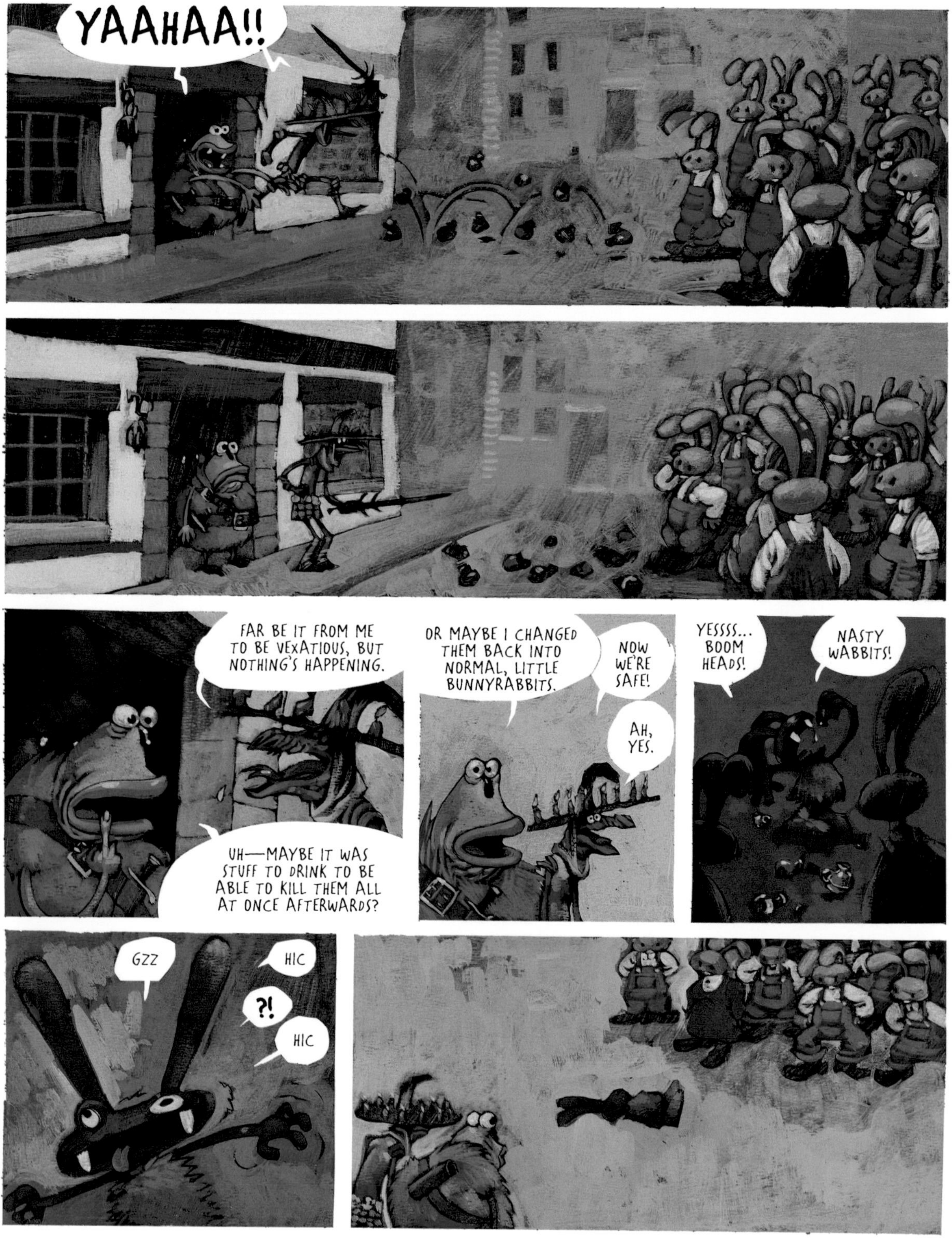

YAAHAA!!
FAR BE IT FROM ME TO BE VEXATIOUS, BUT NOTHING'S HAPPENING.
UH—MAYBE IT WAS STUFF TO DRINK TO BE ABLE TO KILL THEM ALL AT ONCE AFTERWARDS?
OR MAYBE I CHANGED THEM BACK INTO NORMAL, LITTLE BUNNYRABBITS.
NOW WE'RE SAFE!
AH, YES.
YESSSS... BOOM HEADS!
NASTY WABBITS!
GZZ
HIC
?!
HIC

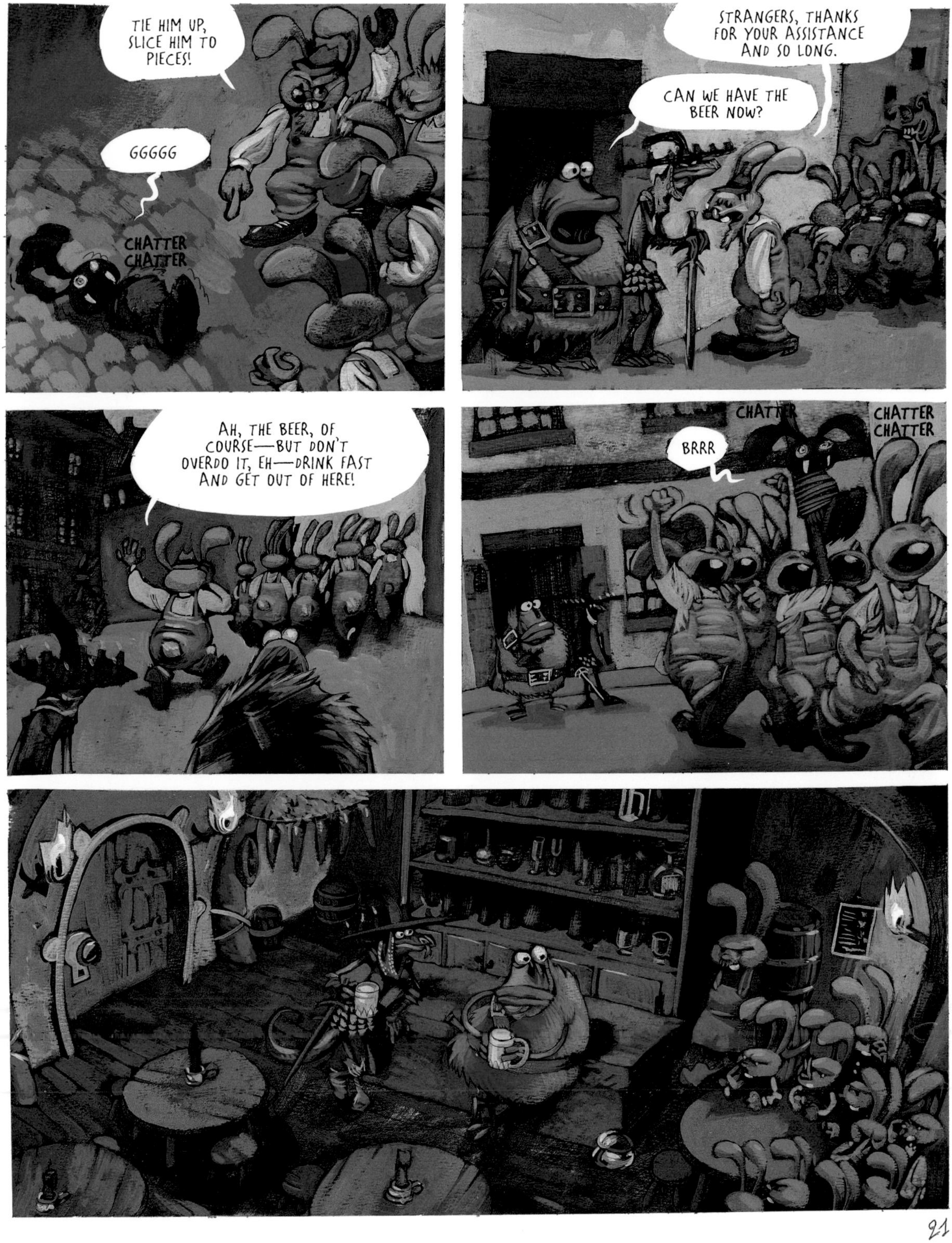
TIE HIM UP, SLICE HIM TO PIECES!
GGGGG
CHATTER CHATTER
STRANGERS, THANKS FOR YOUR ASSISTANCE AND SO LONG.
CAN WE HAVE THE BEER NOW?
AH, THE BEER, OF COURSE—BUT DON'T OVERDO IT, EH—DRINK FAST AND GET OUT OF HERE!
BRRR
CHATTER
CHATTER CHATTER

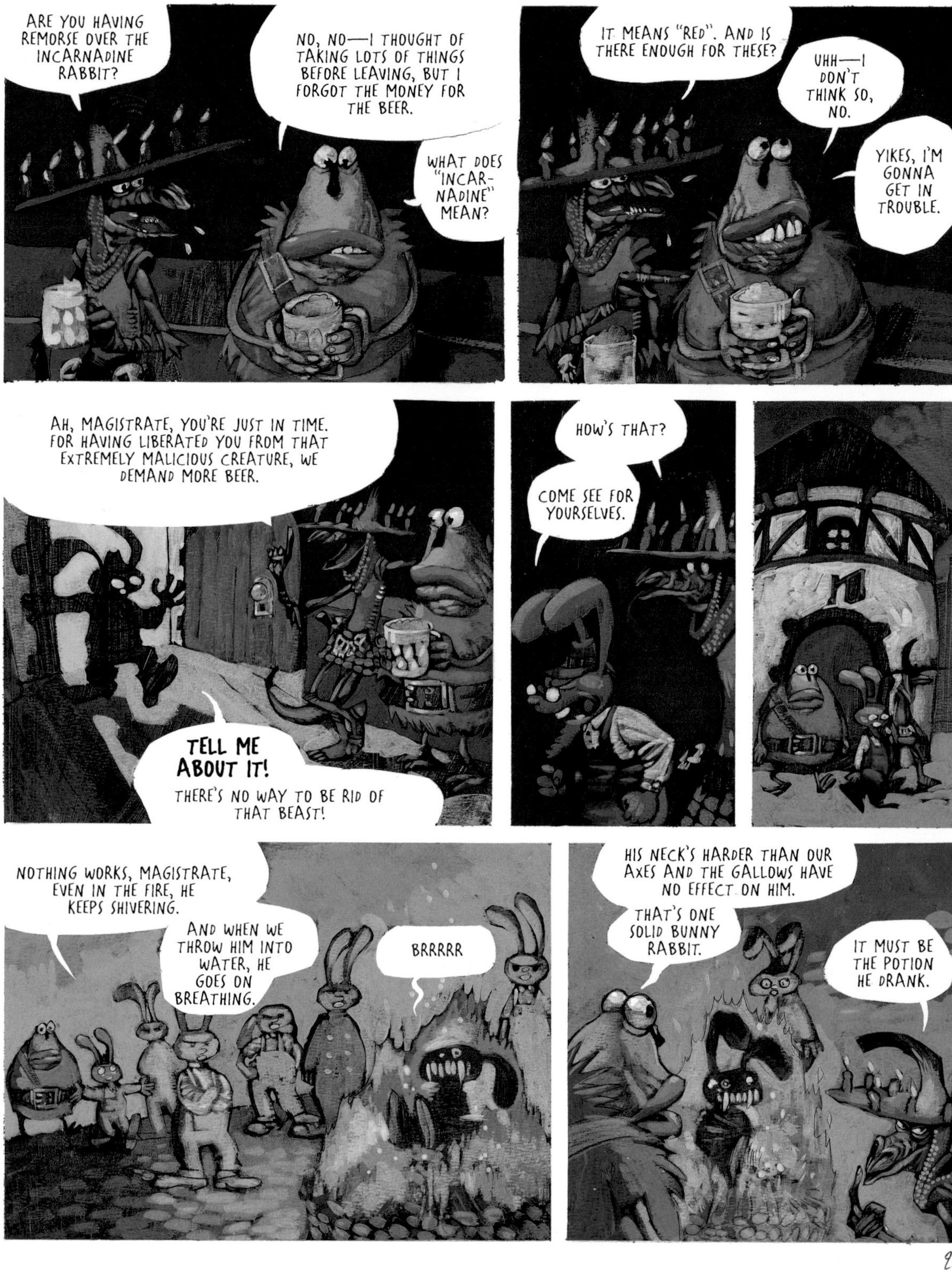
ARE YOU HAVING REMORSE OVER THE INCARNADINE RABBIT?
NO, NO—I THOUGHT OF TAKING LOTS OF THINGS BEFORE LEAVING, BUT I FORGOT THE MONEY FOR THE BEER.
WHAT DOES "INCARNADINE" MEAN?
IT MEANS "RED". AND IS THERE ENOUGH FOR THESE?
UHH—I DON'T THINK SO, NO.
YIKES, I'M GONNA GET IN TROUBLE.
AH, MAGISTRATE, YOU'RE JUST IN TIME. FOR HAVING LIBERATED YOU FROM THAT EXTREMELY MALICIOUS CREATURE, WE DEMAND MORE BEER.
TELL ME ABOUT IT!
THERE'S NO WAY TO BE RID OF THAT BEAST!
HOW'S THAT?
COME SEE FOR YOURSELVES.
NOTHING WORKS, MAGISTRATE, EVEN IN THE FIRE, HE KEEPS SHIVERING.
AND WHEN WE THROW HIM INTO WATER, HE GOES ON BREATHING.
BRRRRR
HIS NECK'S HARDER THAN OUR AXES AND THE GALLOWS HAVE NO EFFECT ON HIM.
THAT'S ONE SOLID BUNNY RABBIT.
IT MUST BE THE POTION HE DRANK.

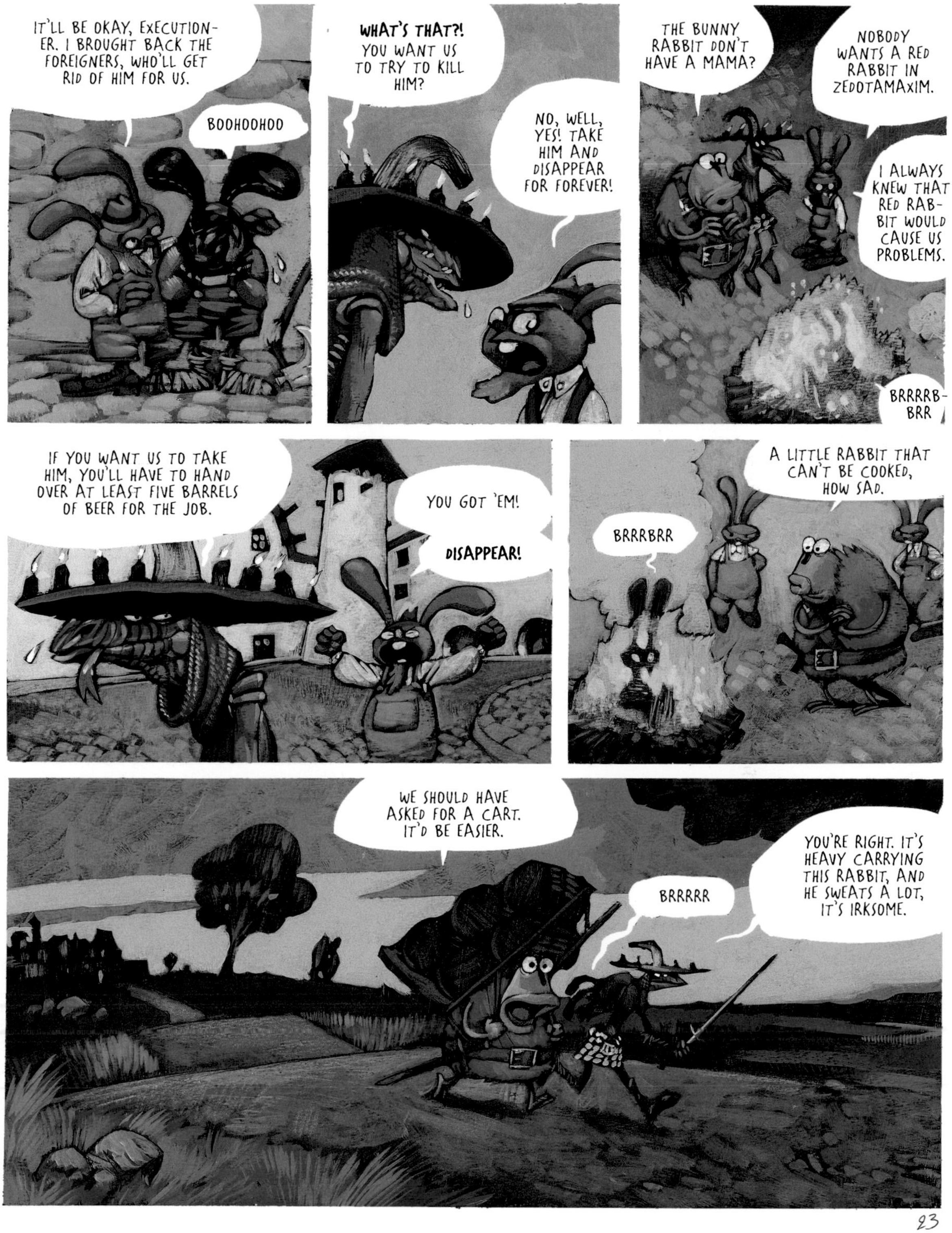

IT'LL BE OKAY, EXECUTIONER. I BROUGHT BACK THE FOREIGNERS, WHO'LL GET RID OF HIM FOR US.
BOOHOOHOO
WHAT'S THAT?! YOU WANT US TO TRY TO KILL HIM?
NO, WELL, YES! TAKE HIM AND DISAPPEAR FOR FOREVER!
THE BUNNY RABBIT DON'T HAVE A MAMA?
NOBODY WANTS A RED RABBIT IN ZEDOTAMAXIM.
I ALWAYS KNEW THAT RED RABBIT WOULD CAUSE US PROBLEMS.
BRRRRB-BRR
IF YOU WANT US TO TAKE HIM, YOU'LL HAVE TO HAND OVER AT LEAST FIVE BARRELS OF BEER FOR THE JOB.
YOU GOT 'EM!
DISAPPEAR!
A LITTLE RABBIT THAT CAN'T BE COOKED, HOW SAD.
BRRRBRR
WE SHOULD HAVE ASKED FOR A CART. IT'D BE EASIER.
BRRRRR
YOU'RE RIGHT. IT'S HEAVY CARRYING THIS RABBIT, AND HE SWEATS A LOT, IT'S IRKSOME.

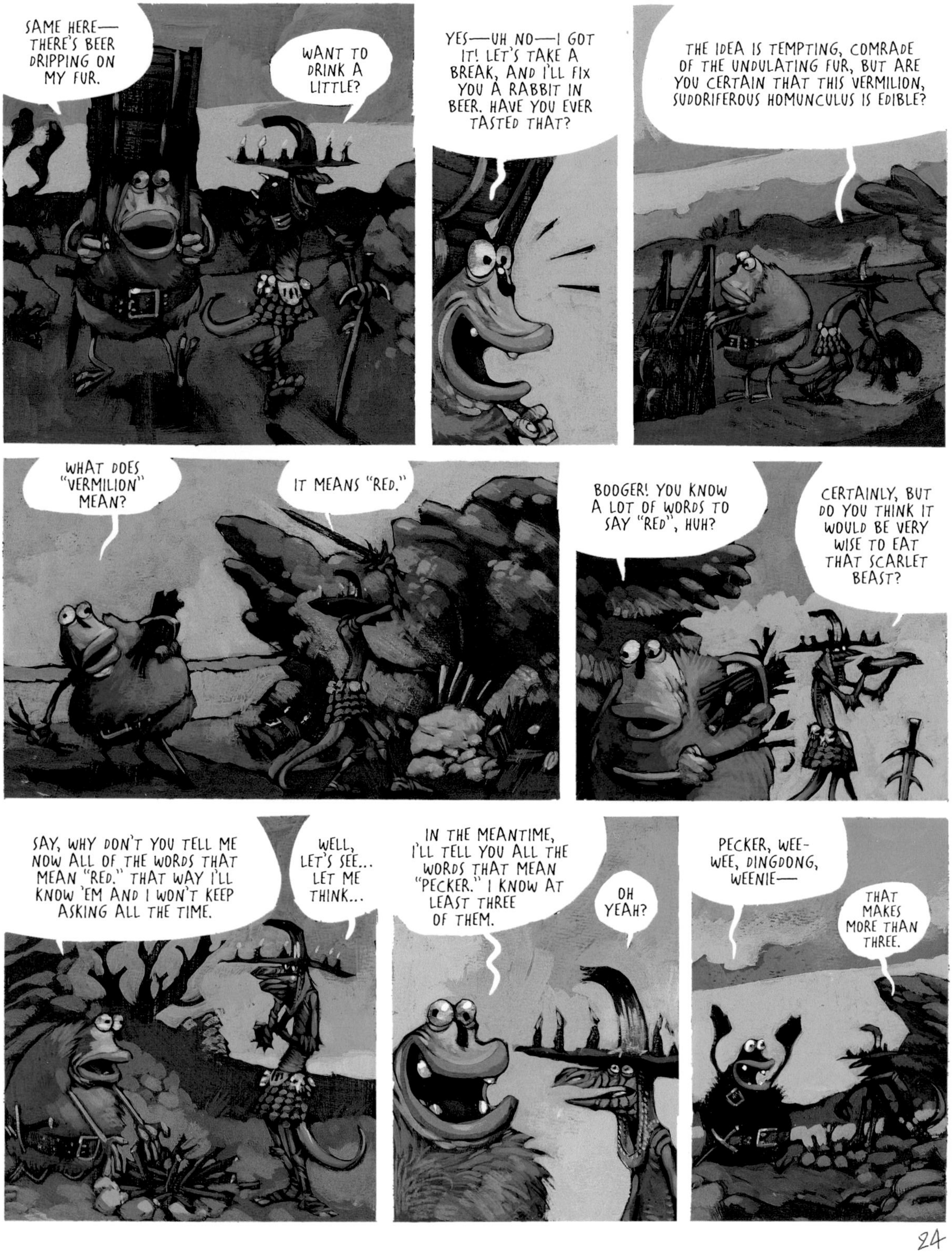
SAME HERE— THERE'S BEER DRIPPING ON MY FUR.
WANT TO DRINK A LITTLE?
YES—UH NO—I GOT IT! LET'S TAKE A BREAK, AND I'LL FIX YOU A RABBIT IN BEER. HAVE YOU EVER TASTED THAT?
THE IDEA IS TEMPTING, COMRADE OF THE UNDULATING FUR, BUT ARE YOU CERTAIN THAT THIS VERMILION, SUDORIFEROUS HOMUNCULUS IS EDIBLE?
WHAT DOES "VERMILION" MEAN?
IT MEANS "RED."
BOOGER! YOU KNOW A LOT OF WORDS TO SAY "RED", HUH?
CERTAINLY, BUT DO YOU THINK IT WOULD BE VERY WISE TO EAT THAT SCARLET BEAST?
SAY, WHY DON'T YOU TELL ME NOW ALL OF THE WORDS THAT MEAN "RED." THAT WAY I'LL KNOW 'EM AND I WON'T KEEP ASKING ALL THE TIME.
WELL, LET'S SEE... LET ME THINK...
IN THE MEANTIME, I'LL TELL YOU ALL THE WORDS THAT MEAN "PECKER." I KNOW AT LEAST THREE OF THEM.
OH YEAH?
PECKER, WEE-WEE, DINGDONG, WEENIE—
THAT MAKES MORE THAN THREE.

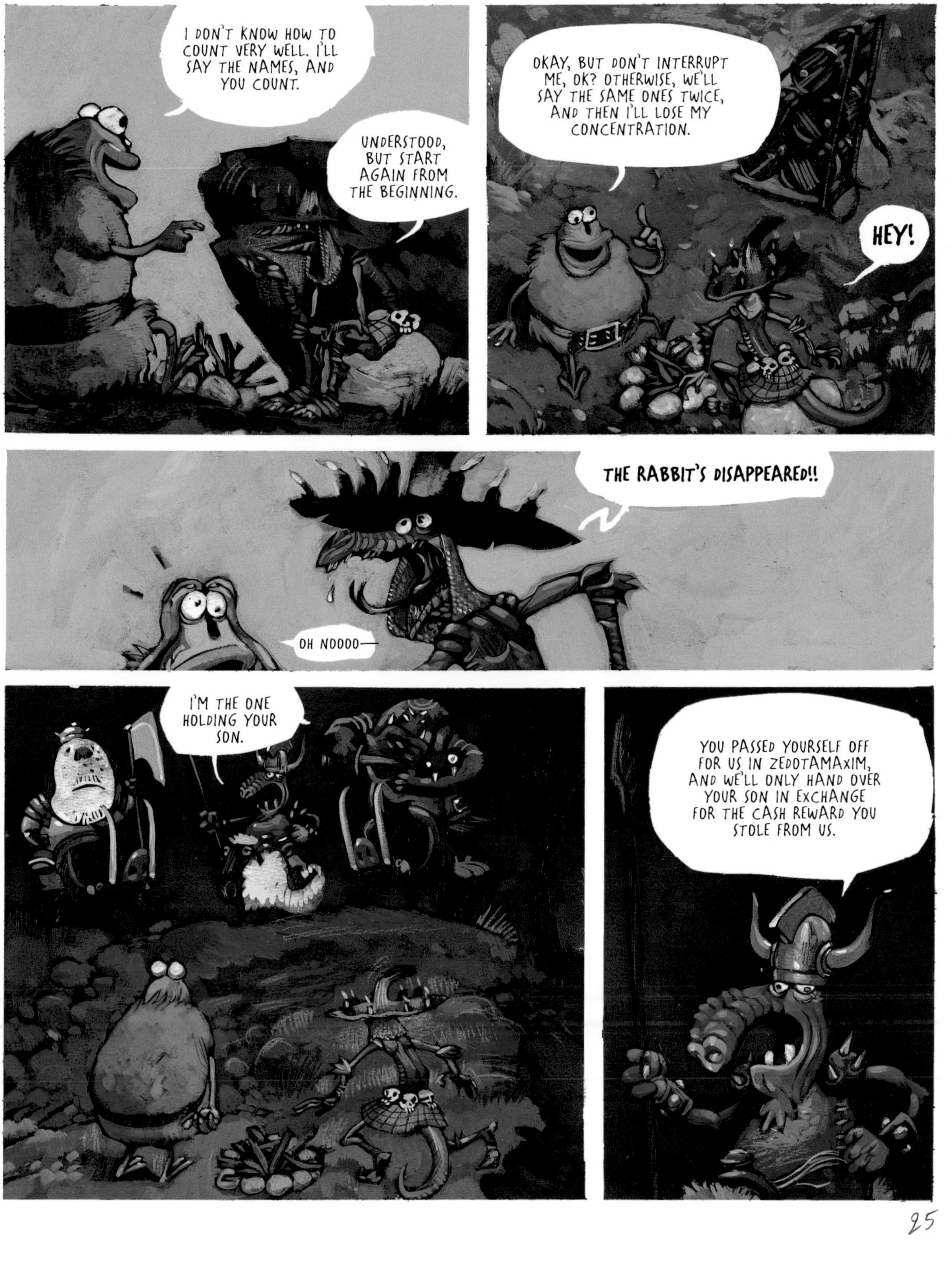
I DON'T KNOW HOW TO COUNT VERY WELL. I'LL SAY THE NAMES, AND YOU COUNT.
UNDERSTOOD, BUT START AGAIN FROM THE BEGINNING.
OKAY, BUT DON'T INTERRUPT ME, OK? OTHERWISE, WE'LL SAY THE SAME ONES TWICE, AND THEN I'LL LOSE MY CONCENTRATION.
HEY!
THE RABBIT'S DISAPPEARED!!
OH NOOOO—
I'M THE ONE HOLDING YOUR SON.
YOU PASSED YOURSELF OFF FOR US IN ZEDOTAMAXIM, AND WE'LL ONLY HAND OVER YOUR SON IN EXCHANGE FOR THE CASH REWARD YOU STOLE FROM US.

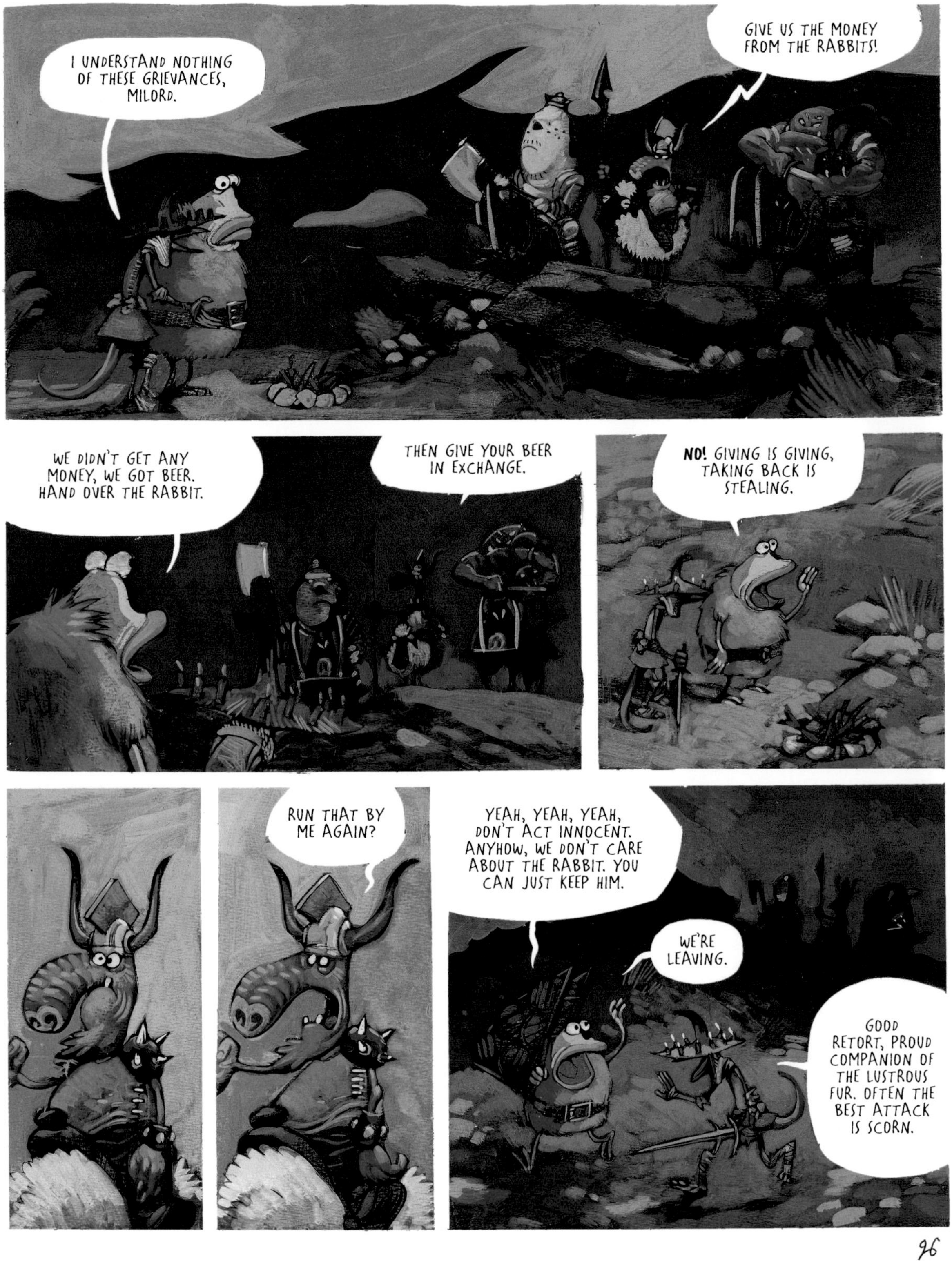
I UNDERSTAND NOTHING OF THESE GRIEVANCES, MILORD.
GIVE US THE MONEY FROM THE RABBITS!
WE DIDN'T GET ANY MONEY, WE GOT BEER. HAND OVER THE RABBIT.
THEN GIVE YOUR BEER IN EXCHANGE.
NO! GIVING IS GIVING, TAKING BACK IS STEALING.
RUN THAT BY ME AGAIN?
YEAH, YEAH, YEAH, DON'T ACT INNOCENT. ANYHOW, WE DON'T CARE ABOUT THE RABBIT. YOU CAN JUST KEEP HIM.
WE'RE LEAVING.
GOOD RETORT, PROUD COMPANION OF THE LUSTROUS FUR. OFTEN THE BEST ATTACK IS SCORN.

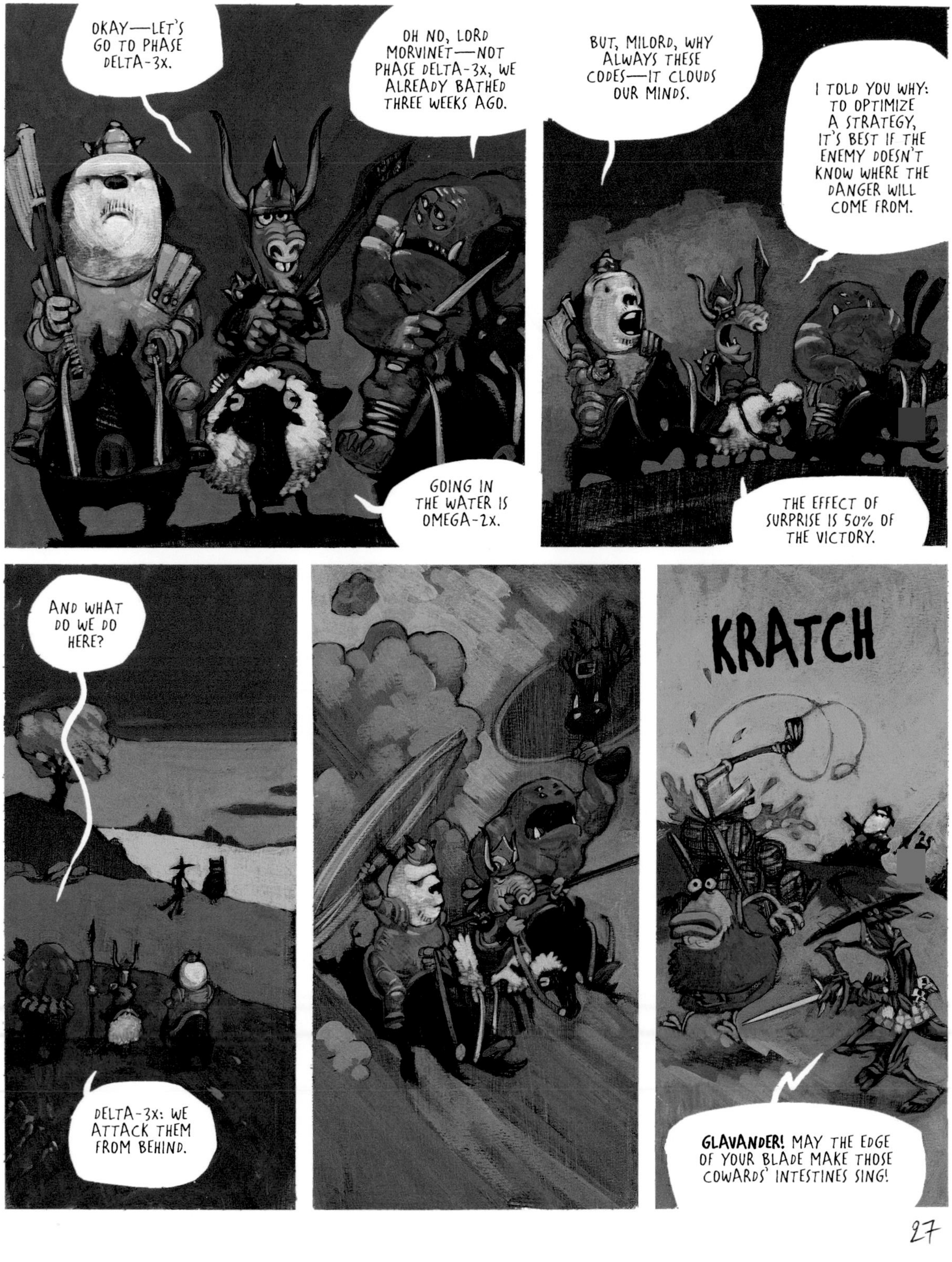
OKAY—LET'S GO TO PHASE DELTA-3X.
OH NO, LORD MORVINET—NOT PHASE DELTA-3X, WE ALREADY BATHED THREE WEEKS AGO.
GOING IN THE WATER IS OMEGA-2X.
BUT, MILORD, WHY ALWAYS THESE CODES—IT CLOUDS OUR MINDS.
I TOLD YOU WHY: TO OPTIMIZE A STRATEGY, IT'S BEST IF THE ENEMY DOESN'T KNOW WHERE THE DANGER WILL COME FROM.
THE EFFECT OF SURPRISE IS 50% OF THE VICTORY.
AND WHAT DO WE DO HERE?
DELTA-3X: WE ATTACK THEM FROM BEHIND.
KRATCH
GLAVANDER! MAY THE EDGE OF YOUR BLADE MAKE THOSE COWARDS' INTESTINES SING!

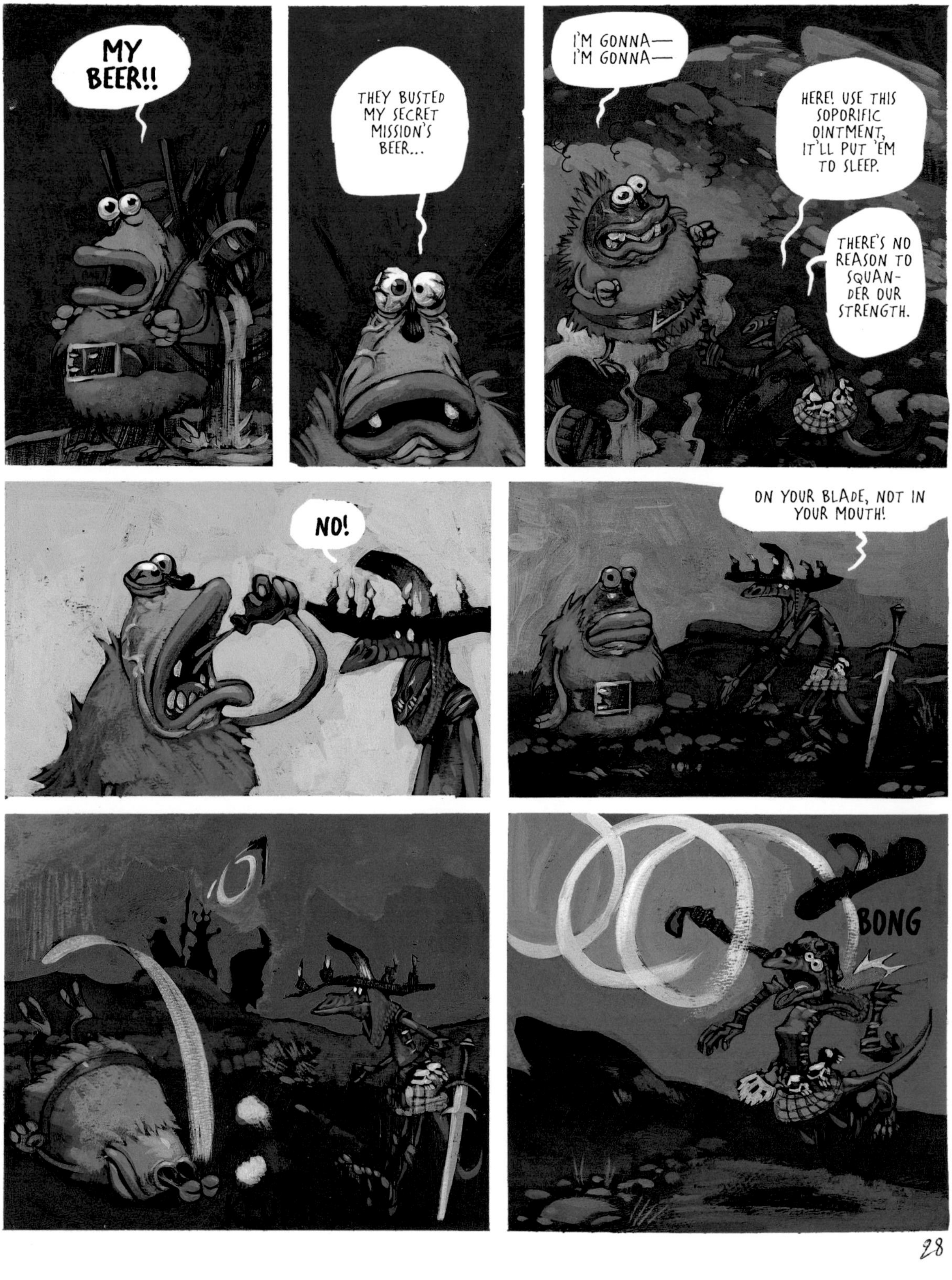
MY BEER!!
THEY BUSTED MY SECRET MISSION'S BEER...
I'M GONNA— I'M GONNA—
HERE! USE THIS SOPORIFIC OINTMENT, IT'LL PUT 'EM TO SLEEP.
THERE'S NO REASON TO SQUANDER OUR STRENGTH.
NO!
ON YOUR BLADE, NOT IN YOUR MOUTH!
BONG

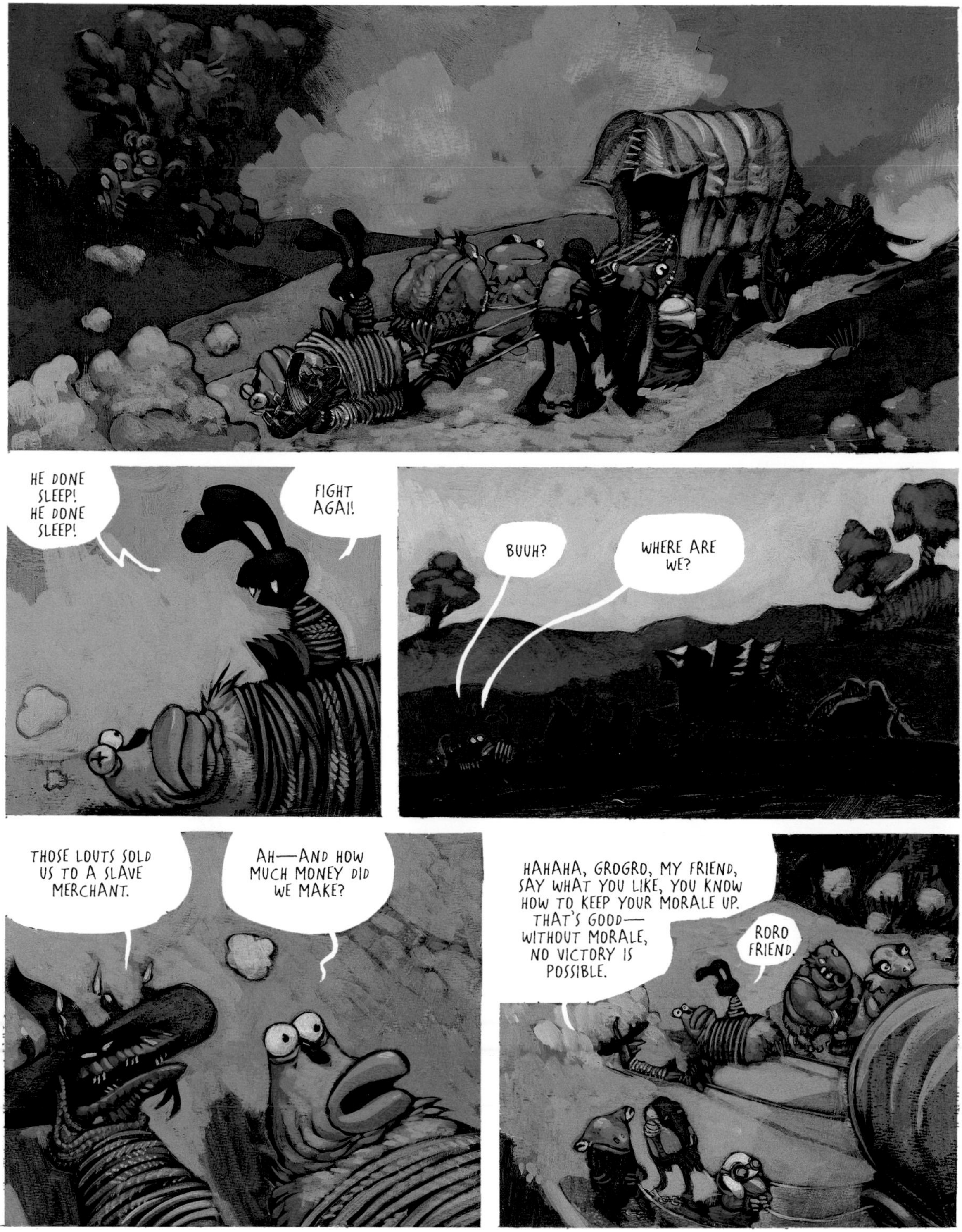
HE DONE SLEEP! HE DONE SLEEP!
FIGHT AGAI!
BUUH?
WHERE ARE WE?
THOSE LOUTS SOLD US TO A SLAVE MERCHANT.
AH—AND HOW MUCH MONEY DID WE MAKE?
HAHAHA, GROGRO, MY FRIEND, SAY WHAT YOU LIKE, YOU KNOW HOW TO KEEP YOUR MORALE UP. THAT'S GOOD—WITHOUT MORALE, NO VICTORY IS POSSIBLE.
RORO FRIEND.

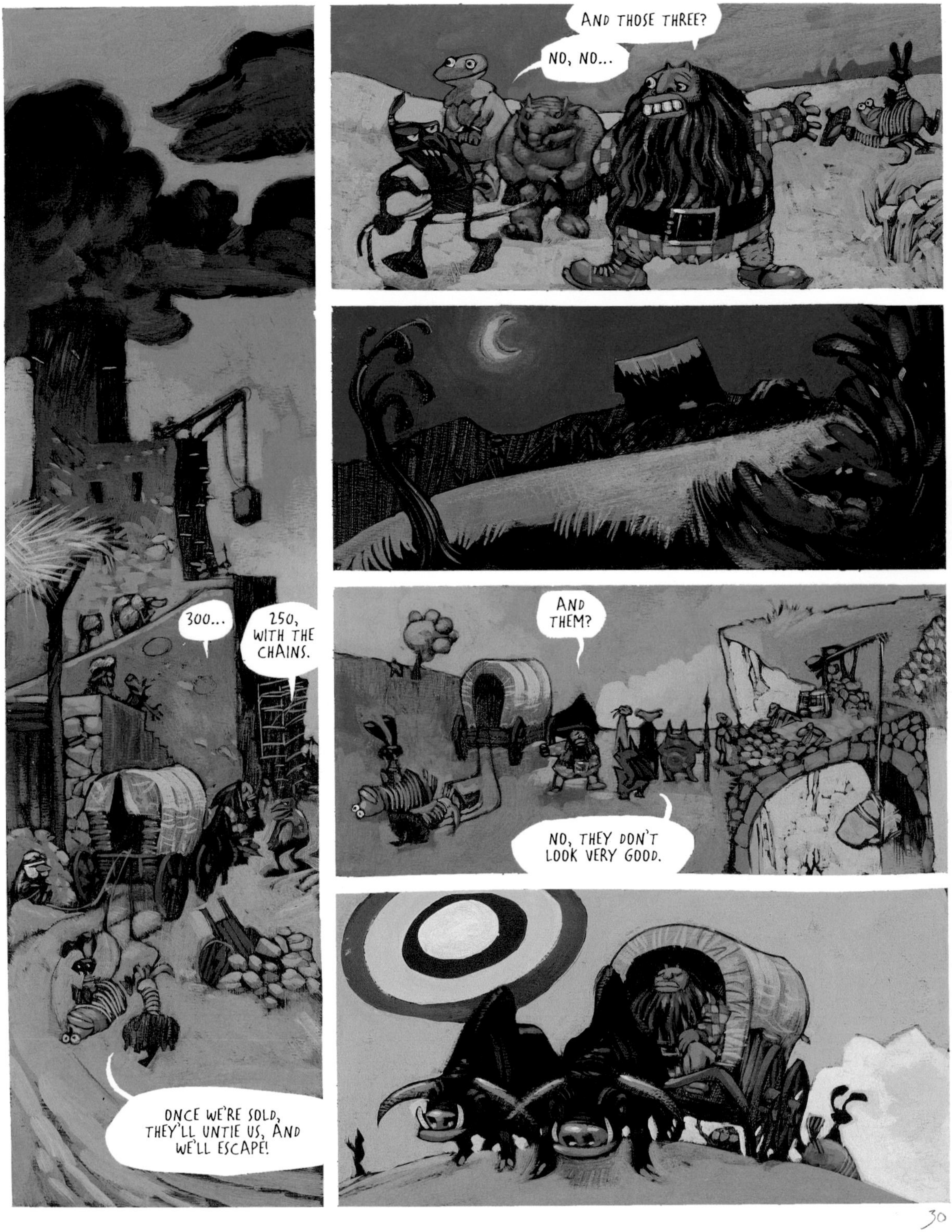
300...
250, WITH THE CHAINS.
ONCE WE'RE SOLD, THEY'LL UNTIE US, AND WE'LL ESCAPE!
AND THOSE THREE?
NO, NO...
AND THEM?
NO, THEY DON'T LOOK VERY GOOD.

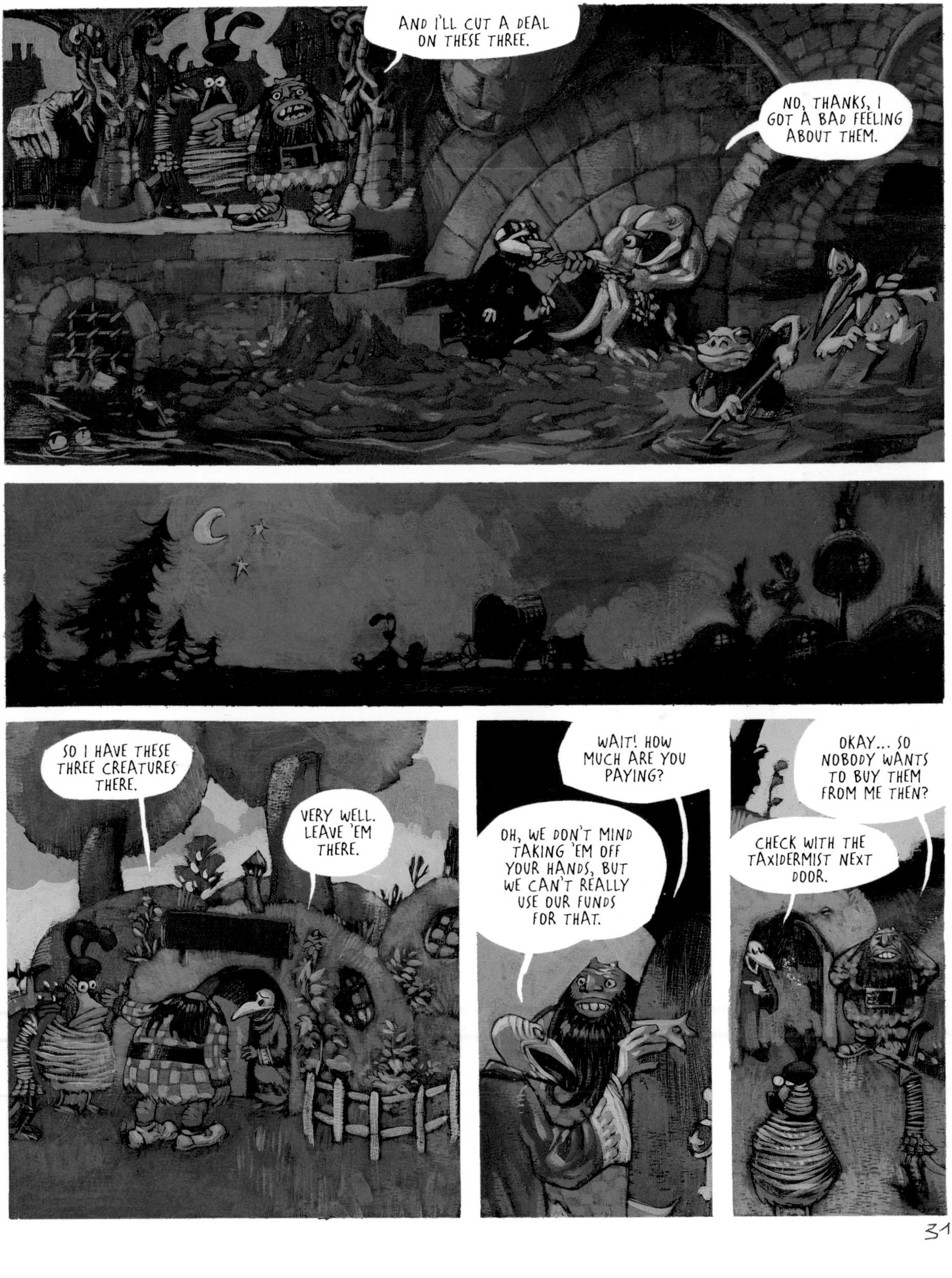
AND I'LL CUT A DEAL ON THESE THREE.
NO, THANKS, I GOT A BAD FEELING ABOUT THEM.
SO I HAVE THESE THREE CREATURES THERE.
VERY WELL. LEAVE 'EM THERE.
WAIT! HOW MUCH ARE YOU PAYING?
OH, WE DON'T MIND TAKING 'EM OFF YOUR HANDS, BUT WE CAN'T REALLY USE OUR FUNDS FOR THAT.
OKAY... SO NOBODY WANTS TO BUY THEM FROM ME THEN?
CHECK WITH THE TAXIDERMIST NEXT DOOR.

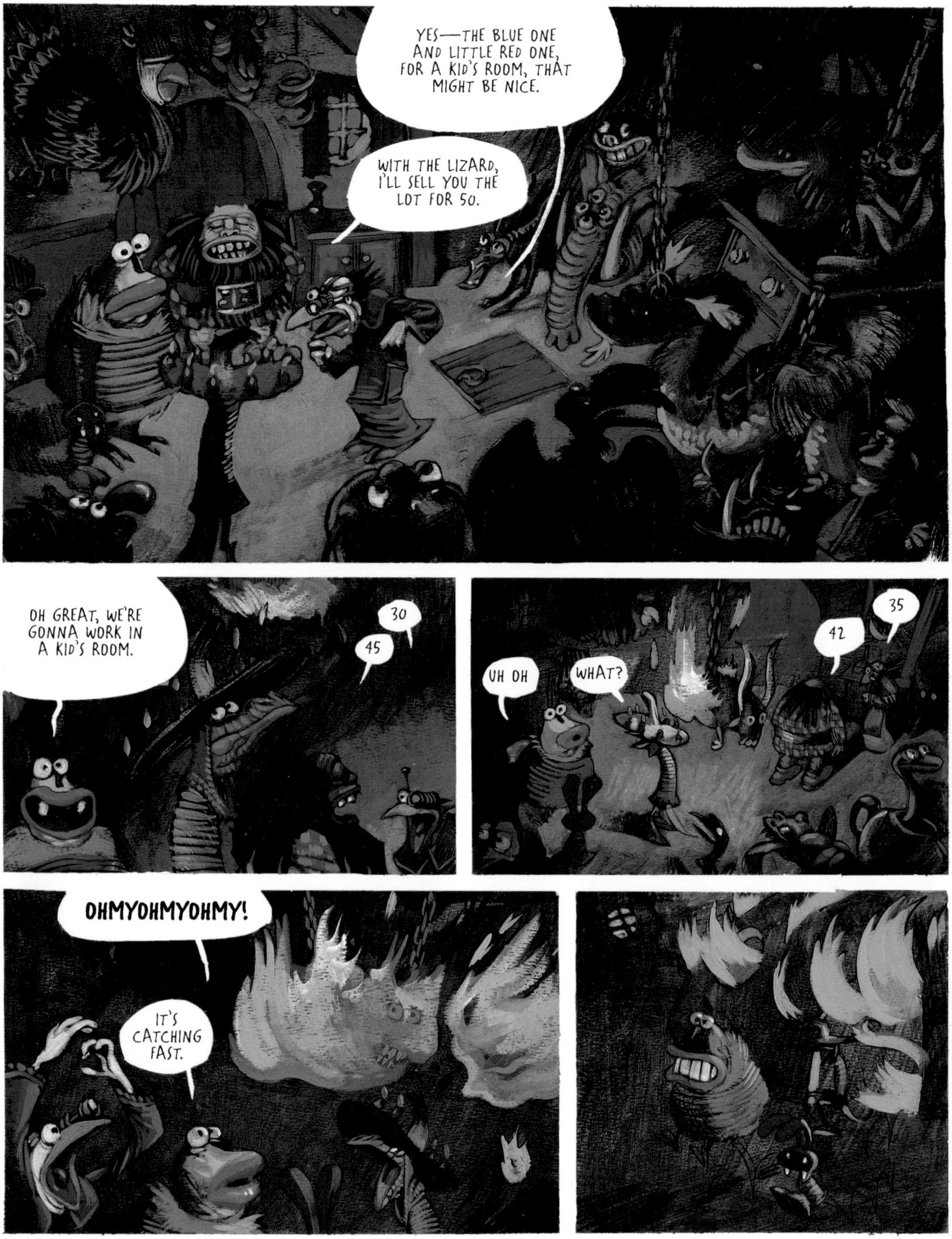
YES—THE BLUE ONE AND LITTLE RED ONE, FOR A KID'S ROOM, THAT MIGHT BE NICE.
WITH THE LIZARD, I'LL SELL YOU THE LOT FOR 50.
OH GREAT, WE'RE GONNA WORK IN A KID'S ROOM.
30
45
UH OH
WHAT?
42
35
OHMYOHMYOHMY!
IT'S CATCHING FAST.

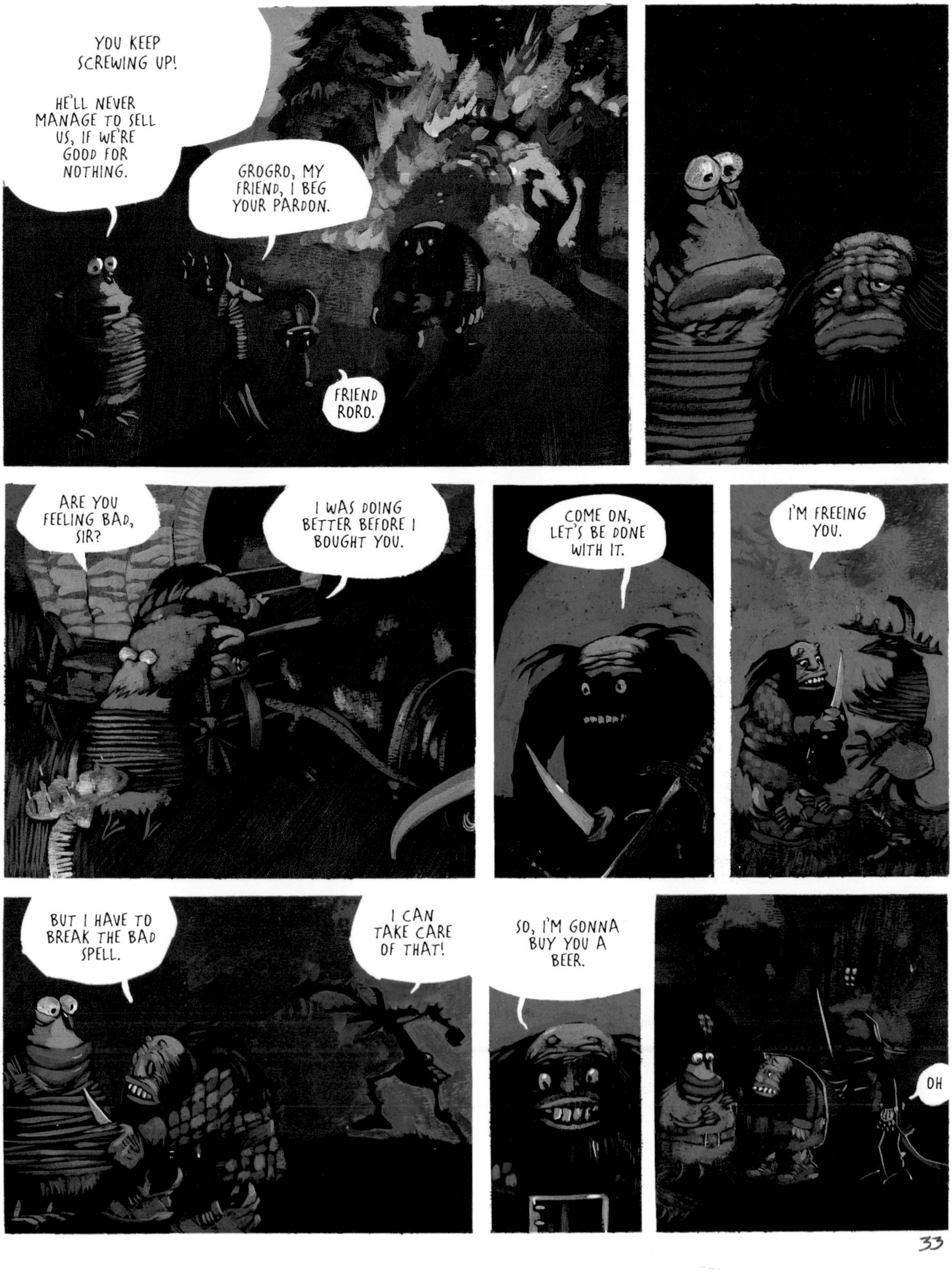
YOU KEEP SCREWING UP!
HE'LL NEVER MANAGE TO SELL US, IF WE'RE GOOD FOR NOTHING.
GROGRO, MY FRIEND, I BEG YOUR PARDON.
FRIEND RORO.
ARE YOU FEELING BAD, SIR?
I WAS DOING BETTER BEFORE I BOUGHT YOU.
COME ON, LET'S BE DONE WITH IT.
I'M FREEING YOU.
BUT I HAVE TO BREAK THE BAD SPELL.
I CAN TAKE CARE OF THAT!
SO, I'M GONNA BUY YOU A BEER.
OH

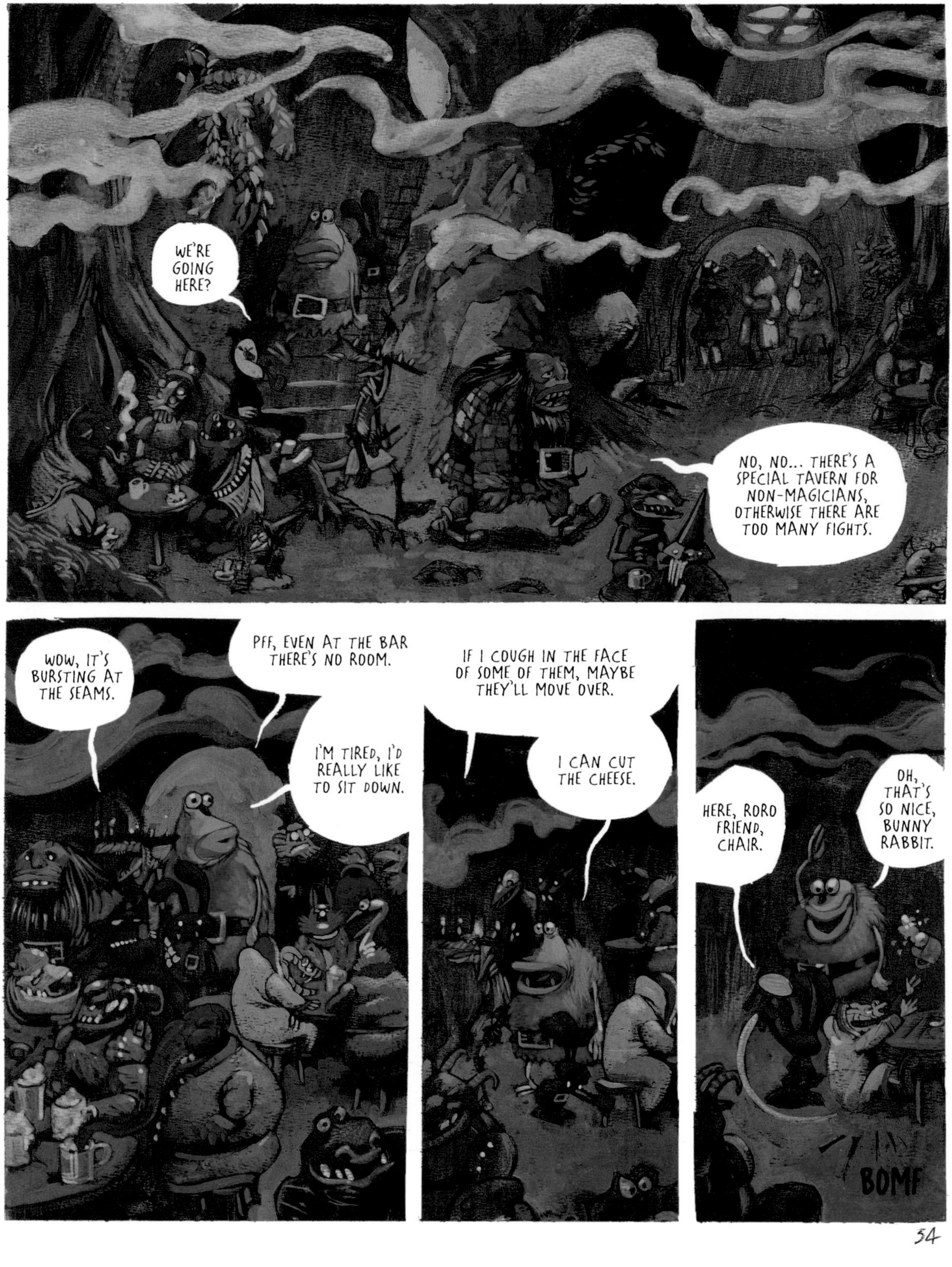
WE'RE GOING HERE?
NO, NO... THERE'S A SPECIAL TAVERN FOR NON-MAGICIANS, OTHERWISE THERE ARE TOO MANY FIGHTS.
WOW, IT'S BURSTING AT THE SEAMS.
PFF, EVEN AT THE BAR THERE'S NO ROOM.
I'M TIRED, I'D REALLY LIKE TO SIT DOWN.
IF I COUGH IN THE FACE OF SOME OF THEM, MAYBE THEY'LL MOVE OVER.
I CAN CUT THE CHEESE.
HERE, RORO FRIEND, CHAIR.
OH, THAT'S SO NICE, BUNNY RABBIT.
BOMF

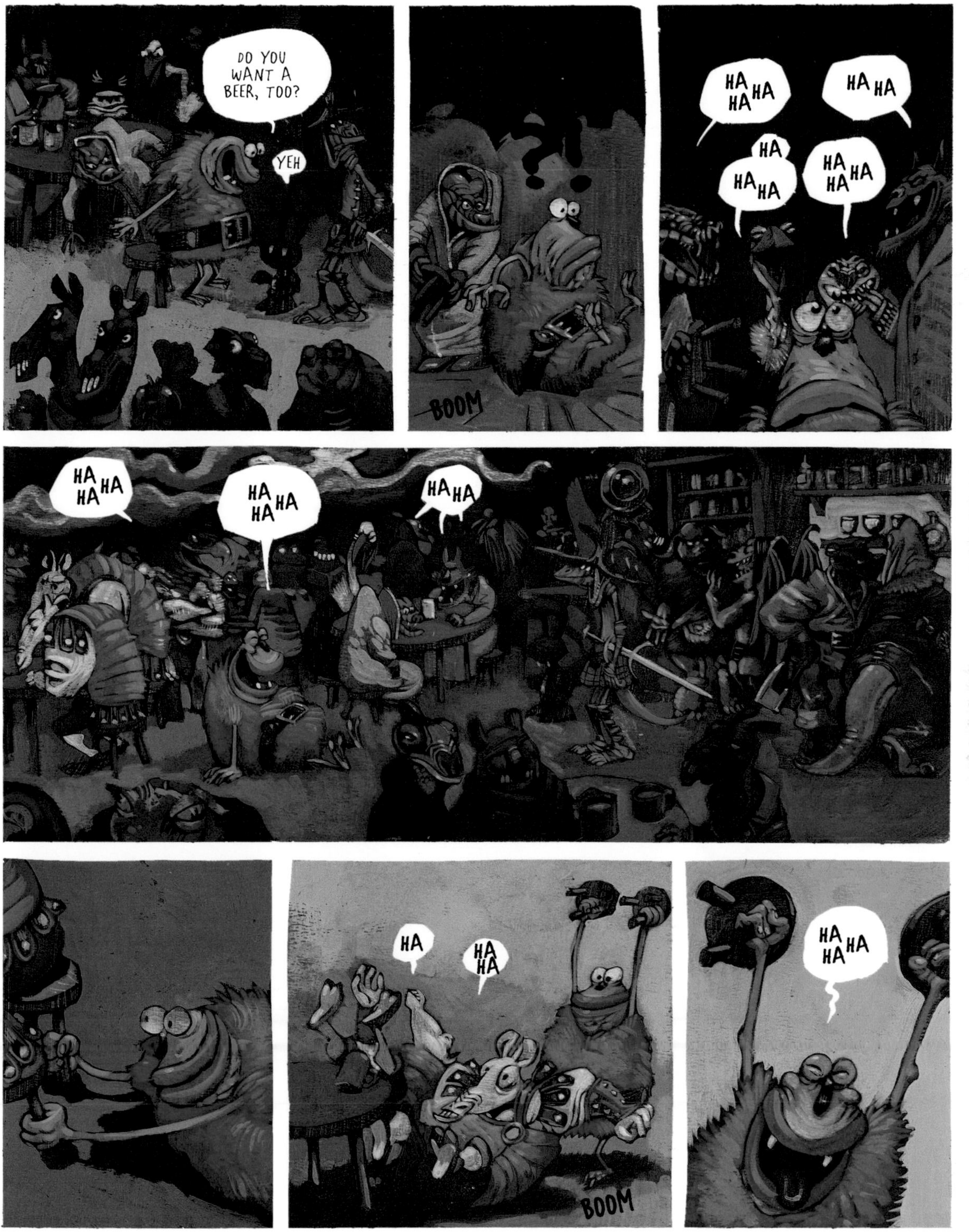
DO YOU WANT A BEER, TOO?
YEH
BOOM
HA HA HA
HA HA
HA
HA HA
HA HA HA
HA HA HA
HA HA HA
HA HA
HA
HA HA
BOOM
HA HA HA

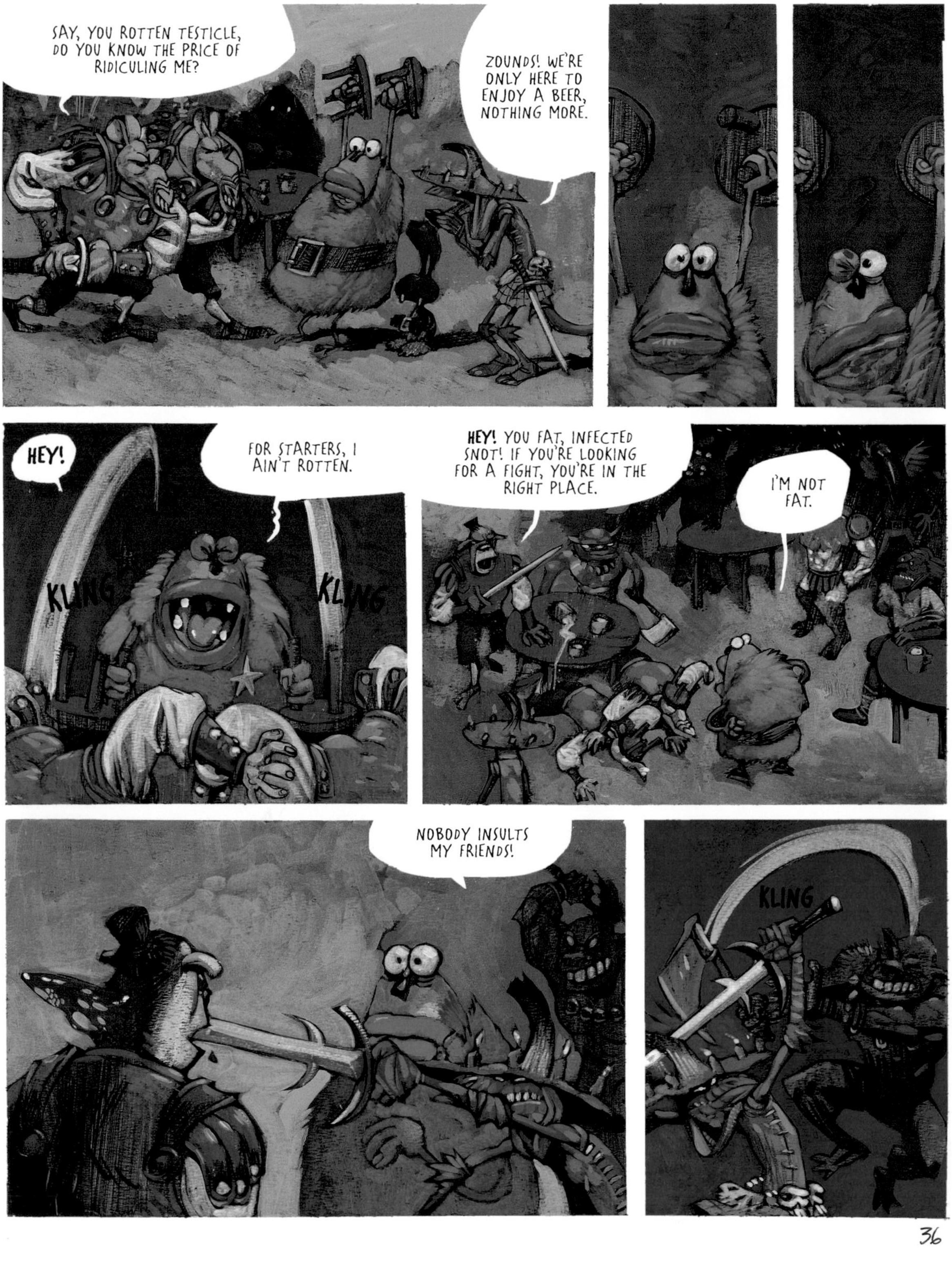
SAY, YOU ROTTEN TESTICLE, DO YOU KNOW THE PRICE OF RIDICULING ME?
ZOUNDS! WE'RE ONLY HERE TO ENJOY A BEER, NOTHING MORE.
HEY!
FOR STARTERS, I AIN'T ROTTEN.
KLING
KLING
HEY! YOU FAT, INFECTED SNOT! IF YOU'RE LOOKING FOR A FIGHT, YOU'RE IN THE RIGHT PLACE.
I'M NOT FAT.
NOBODY INSULTS MY FRIENDS!
KLING

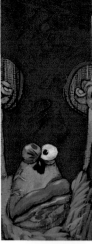

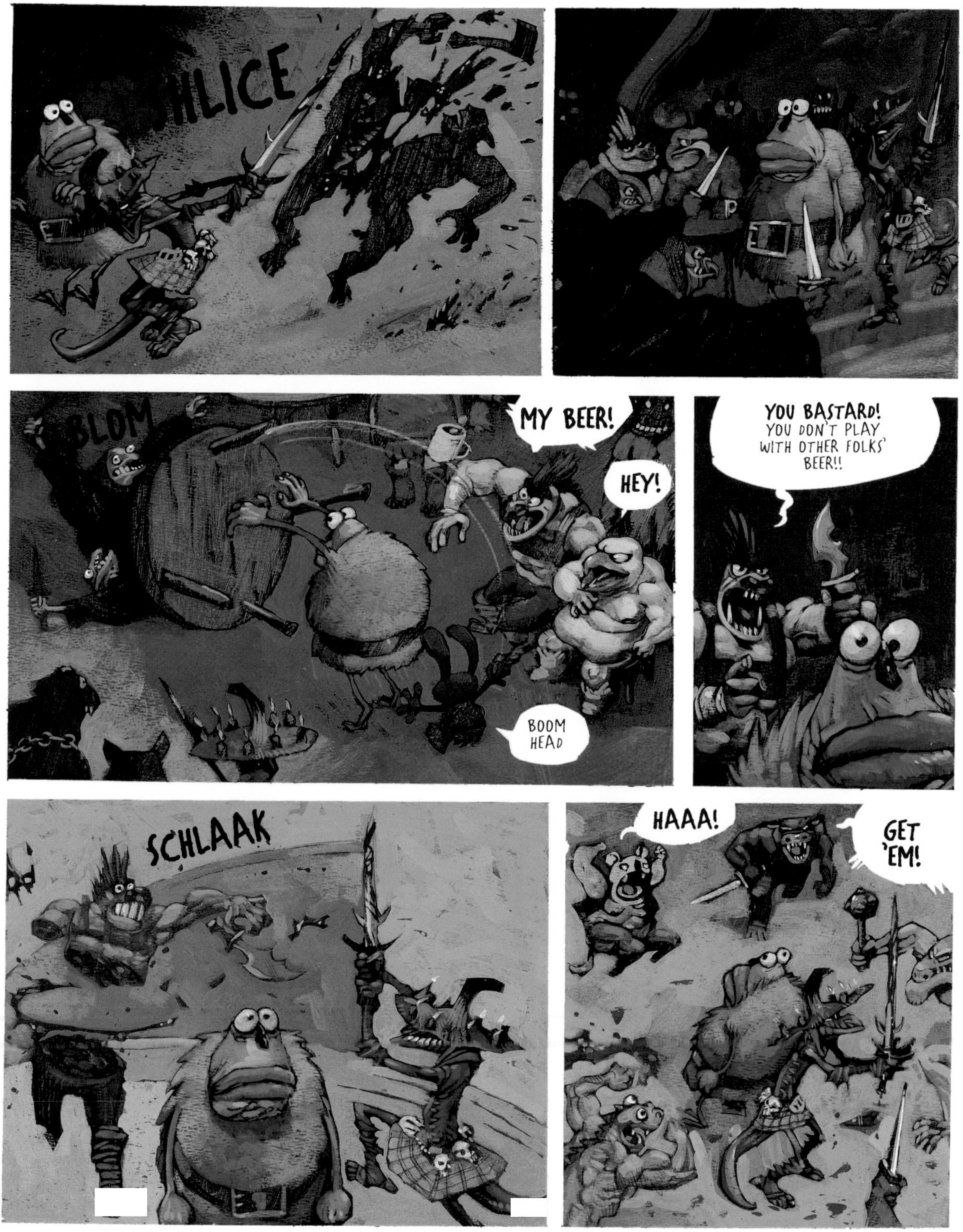
SHLICE
BLOM
MY BEER!
HEY!
BOOM HEAD
YOU BASTARD! YOU DON'T PLAY WITH OTHER FOLKS' BEER!!
SCHLAAK
HAAA!
GET 'EM!

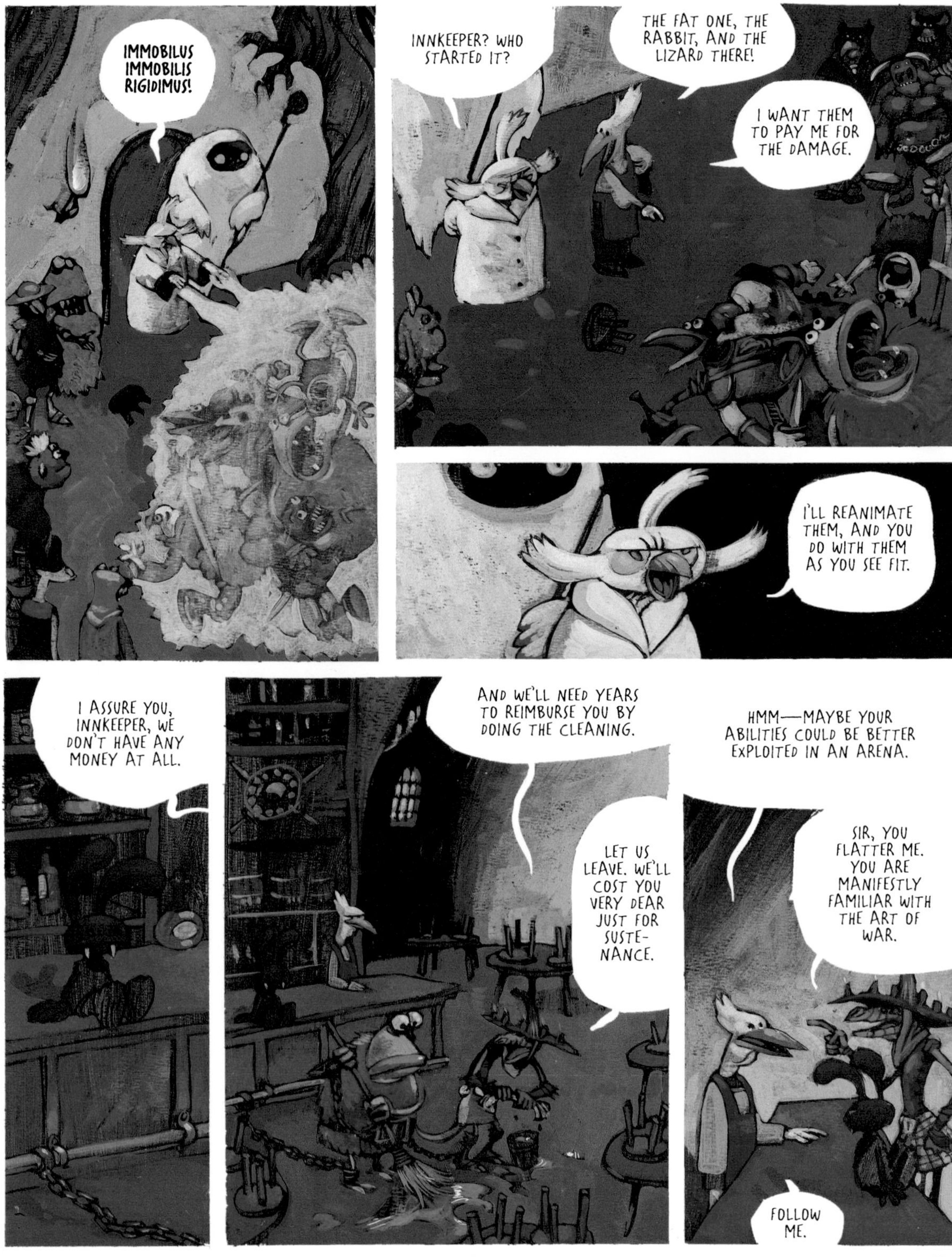
IMMOBILUS IMMOBILIS RIGIDIMUS!
INNKEEPER? WHO STARTED IT?
THE FAT ONE, THE RABBIT, AND THE LIZARD THERE!
I WANT THEM TO PAY ME FOR THE DAMAGE.
I'LL REANIMATE THEM, AND YOU DO WITH THEM AS YOU SEE FIT.
I ASSURE YOU, INNKEEPER, WE DON'T HAVE ANY MONEY AT ALL.
AND WE'LL NEED YEARS TO REIMBURSE YOU BY DOING THE CLEANING.
LET US LEAVE. WE'LL COST YOU VERY DEAR JUST FOR SUSTE-NANCE.
HMM—MAYBE YOUR ABILITIES COULD BE BETTER EXPLOITED IN AN ARENA.
SIR, YOU FLATTER ME. YOU ARE MANIFESTLY FAMILIAR WITH THE ART OF WAR.
FOLLOW ME.

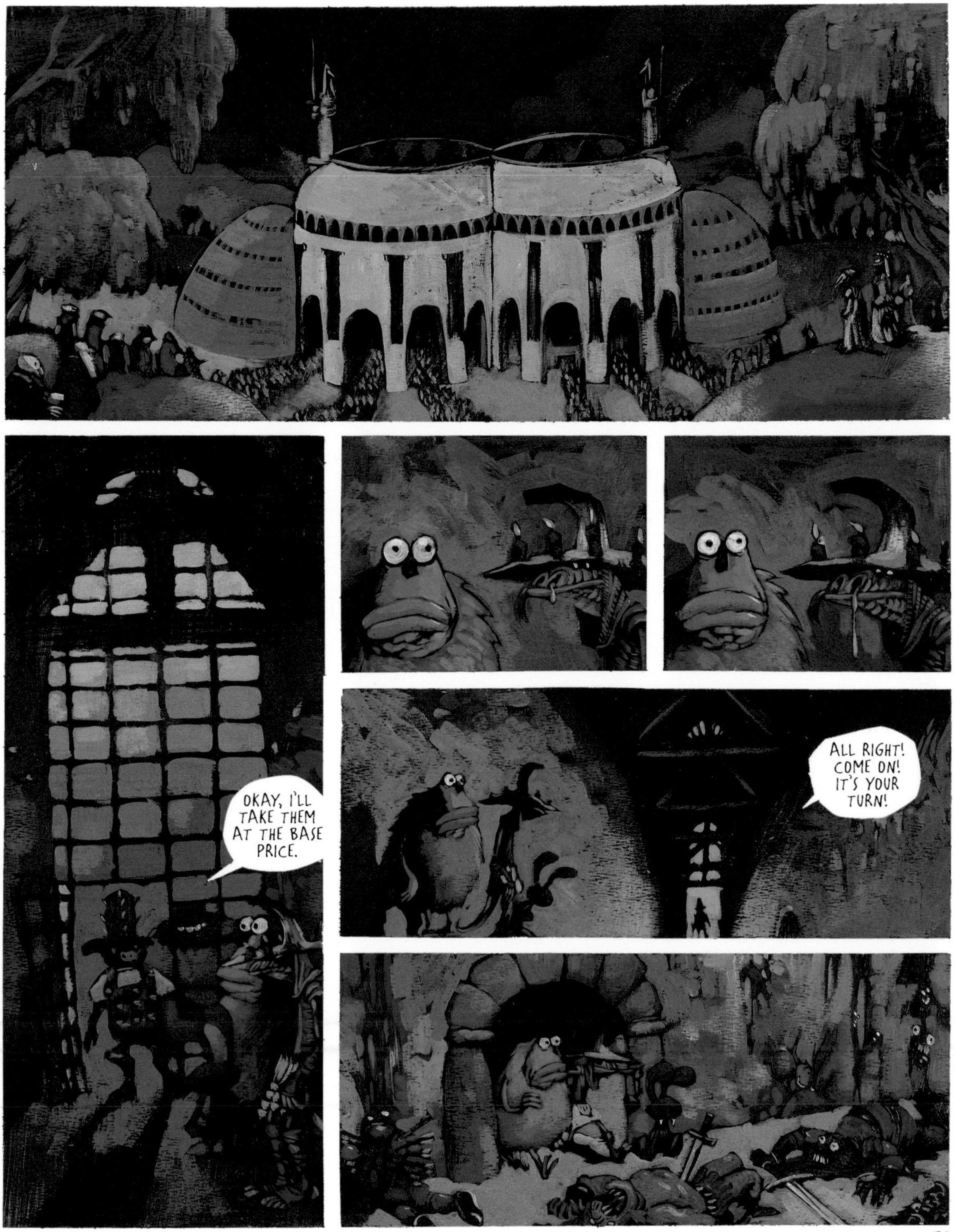
OKAY, I'LL TAKE THEM AT THE BASE PRICE.
ALL RIGHT! COME ON! IT'S YOUR TURN!

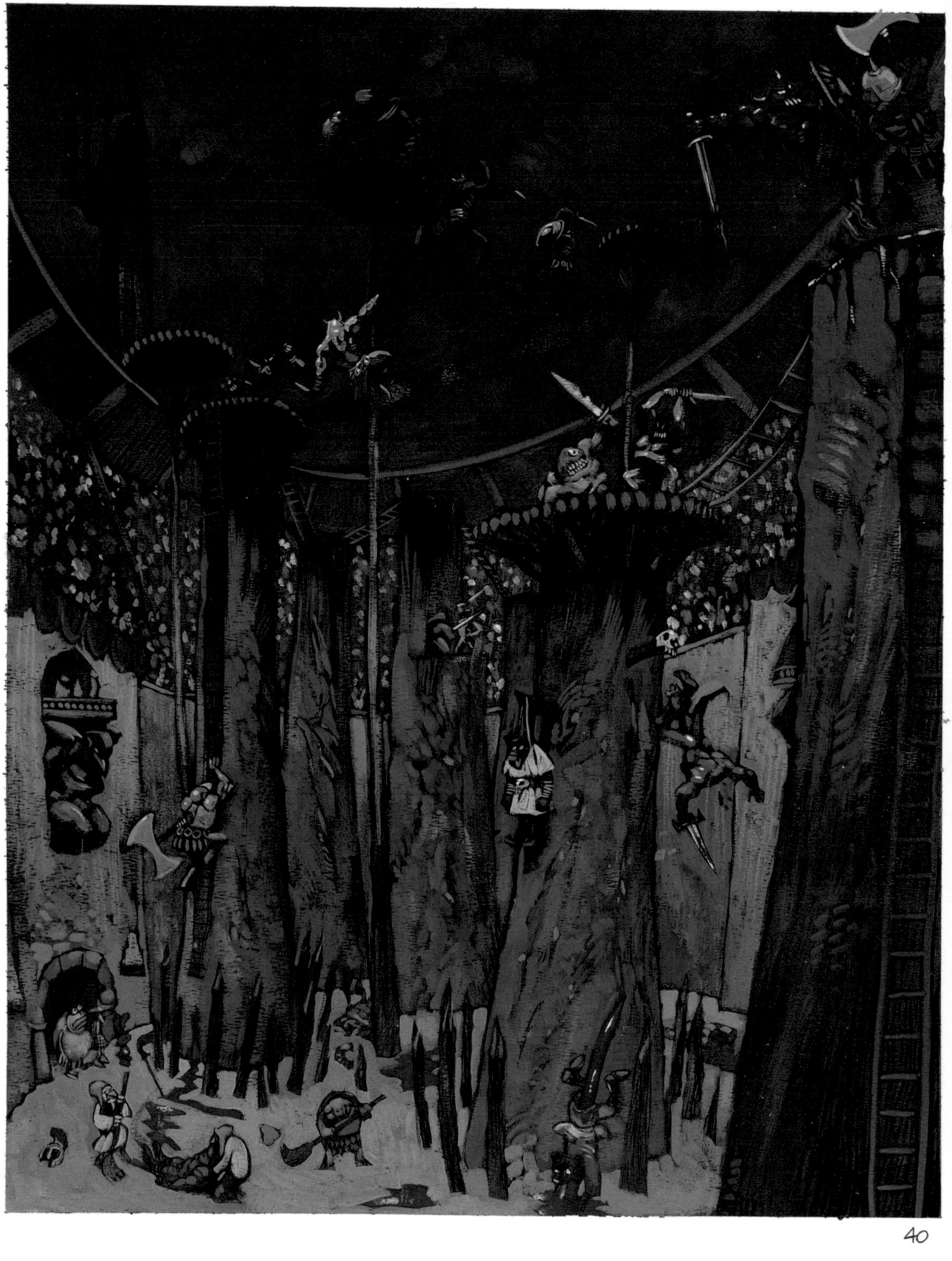

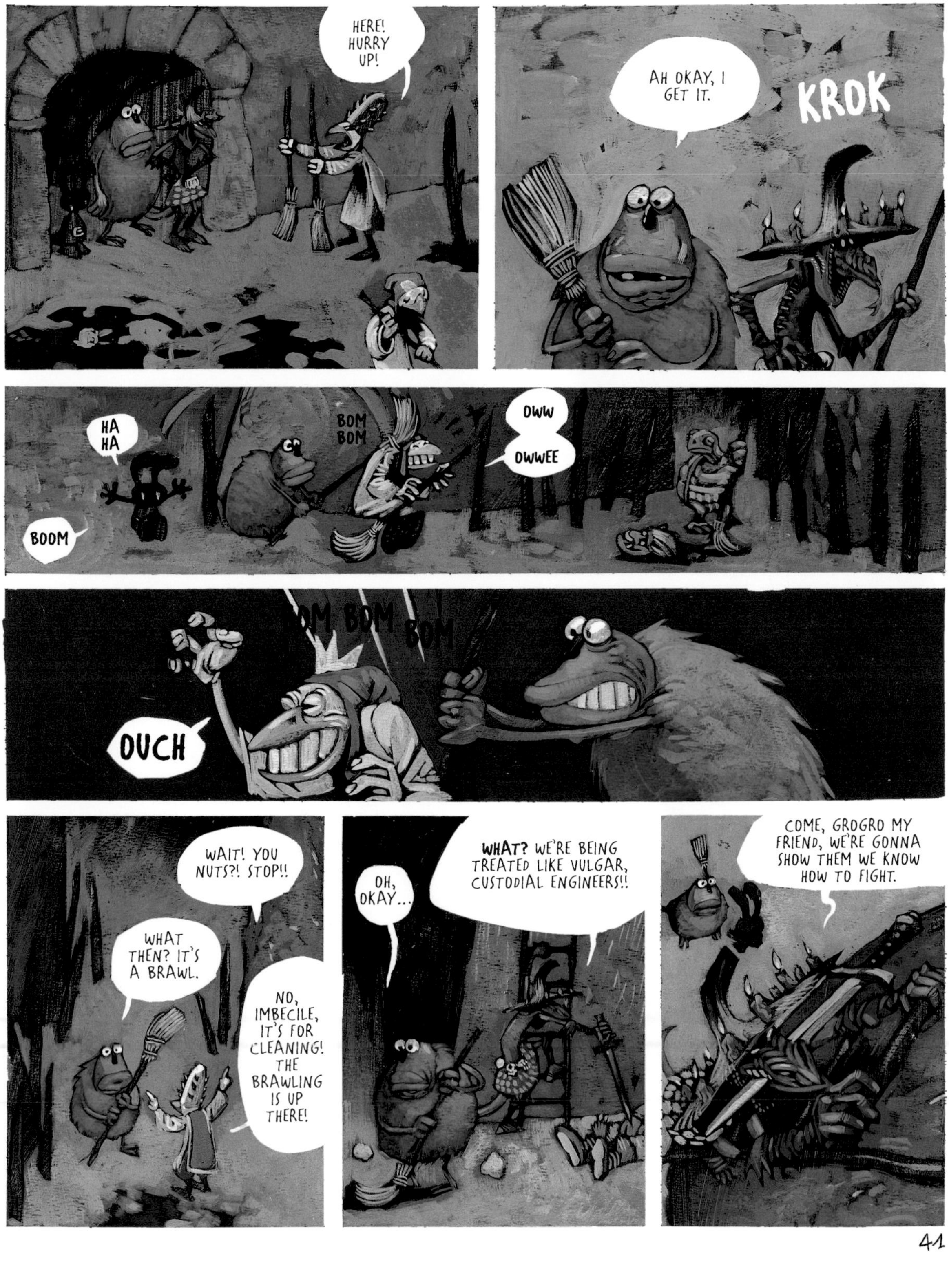
HERE! HURRY UP!
AH OKAY, I GET IT.
KROK
HA HA
BOOM
BOM BOM
OWW
OWWEE
BOM BOM BOM
OUCH
WAIT! YOU NUTS?! STOP!!
WHAT THEN? IT'S A BRAWL.
NO, IMBECILE, IT'S FOR CLEANING! THE BRAWLING IS UP THERE!
OH, OKAY...
WHAT? WE'RE BEING TREATED LIKE VULGAR, CUSTODIAL ENGINEERS!!
COME, GROGRO MY FRIEND, WE'RE GONNA SHOW THEM WE KNOW HOW TO FIGHT.

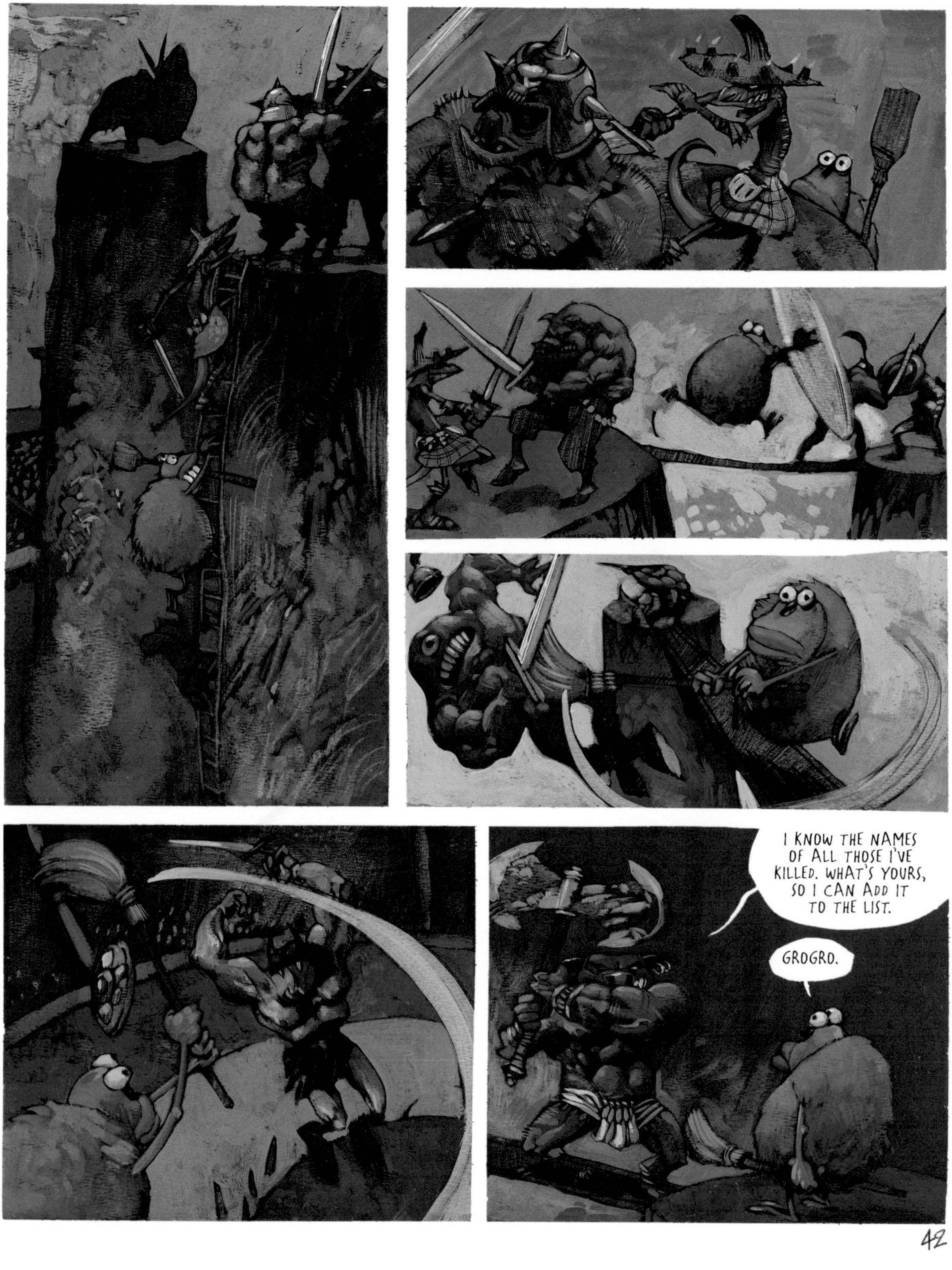
I KNOW THE NAMES OF ALL THOSE I'VE KILLED. WHAT'S YOURS, SO I CAN ADD IT TO THE LIST.
GROGRO.

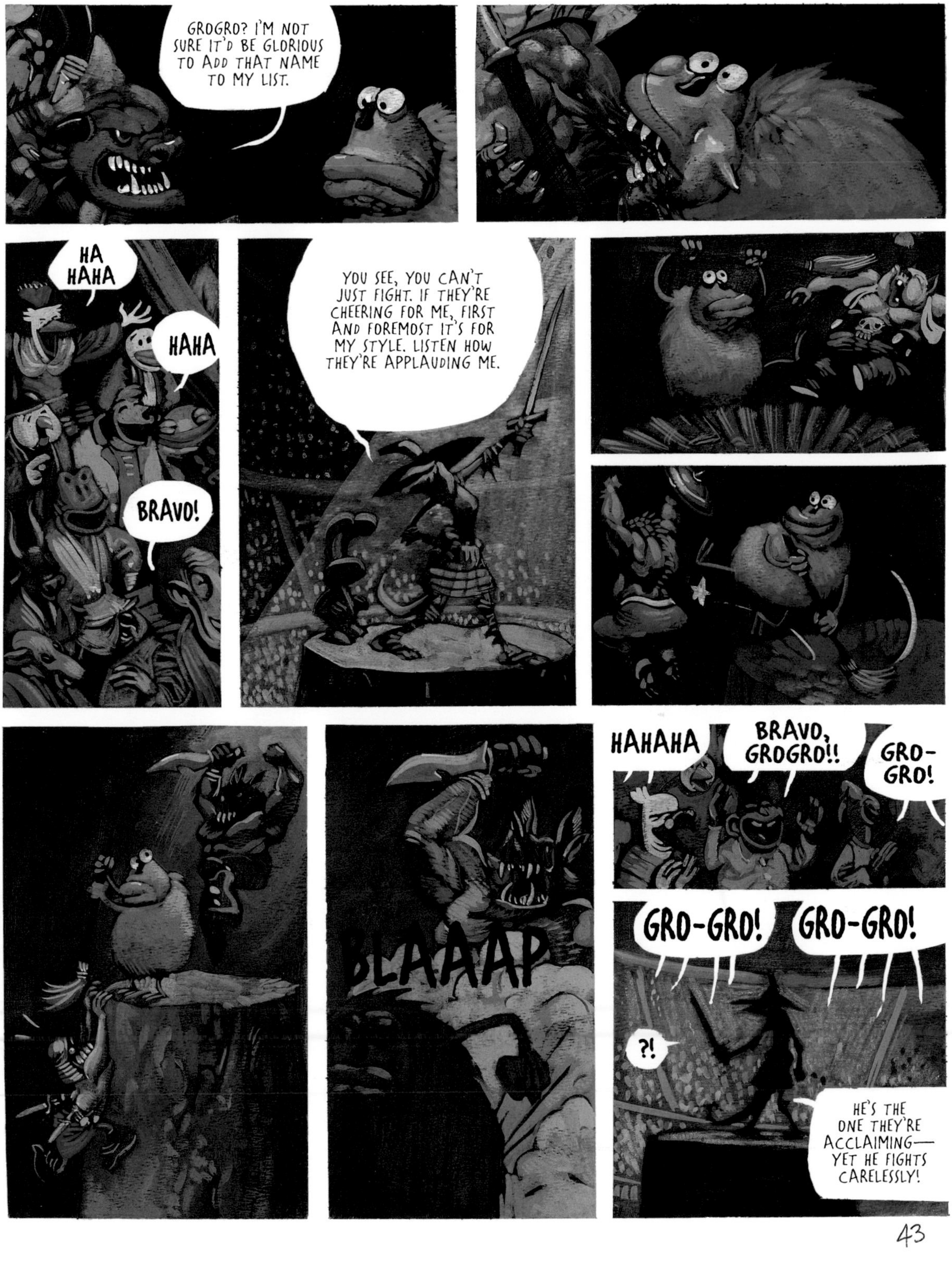

GROGRO? I'M NOT SURE IT'D BE GLORIOUS TO ADD THAT NAME TO MY LIST.
HA HAHA
HAHA
BRAVO!
YOU SEE, YOU CAN'T JUST FIGHT. IF THEY'RE CHEERING FOR ME, FIRST AND FOREMOST IT'S FOR MY STYLE. LISTEN HOW THEY'RE APPLAUDING ME.
BLAAAP
HAHAHA
BRAVO, GROGRO!!
GRO-GRO!
GRO-GRO!
GRO-GRO!
?!
HE'S THE ONE THEY'RE ACCLAIMING— YET HE FIGHTS CARELESSLY!

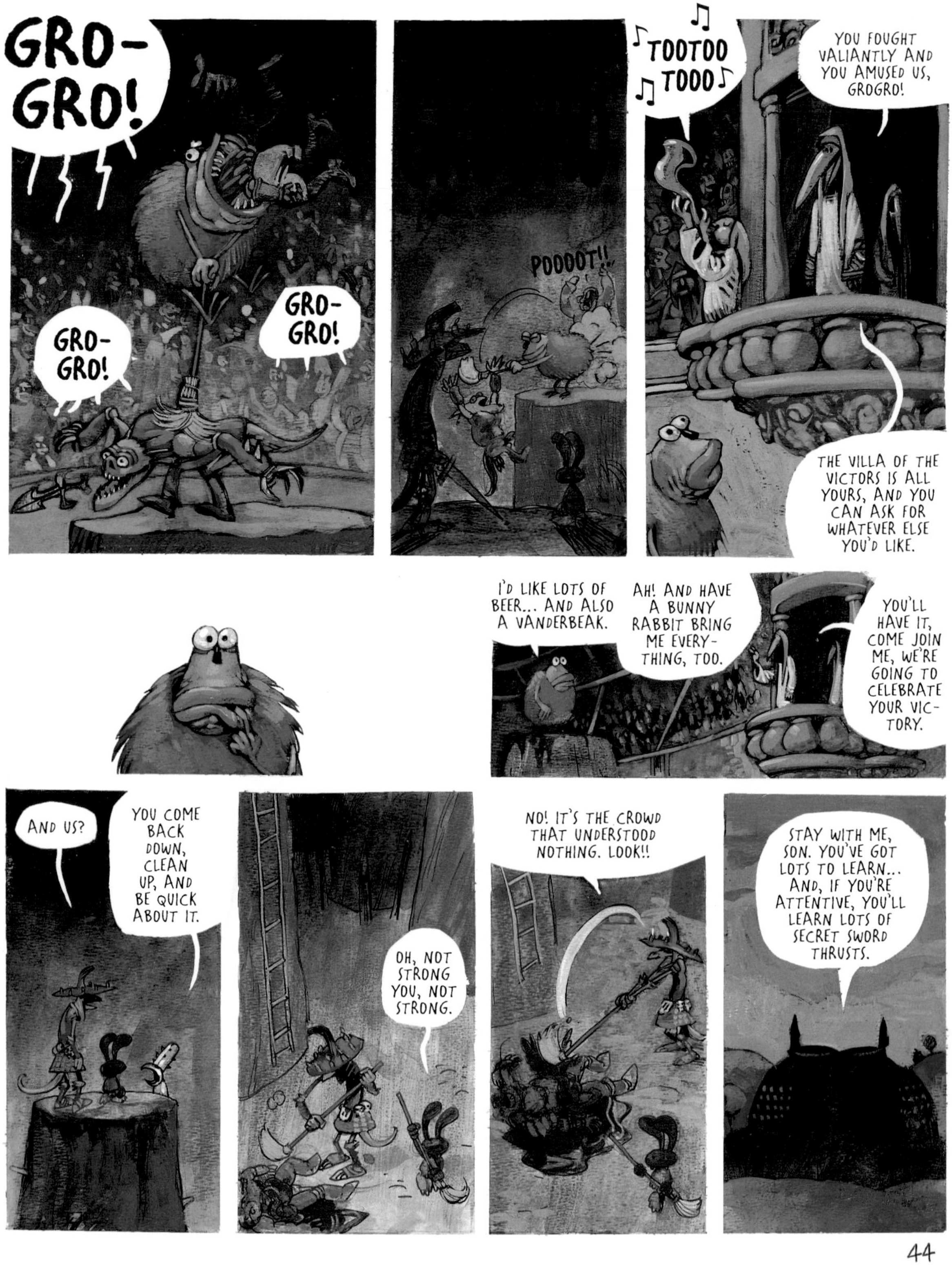
GRO-GRO!
GRO-GRO!
GRO-GRO!
POOOOT!!
TOOTOO TOOO
YOU FOUGHT VALIANTLY AND YOU AMUSED US, GROGRO!
THE VILLA OF THE VICTORS IS ALL YOURS, AND YOU CAN ASK FOR WHATEVER ELSE YOU'D LIKE.
I'D LIKE LOTS OF BEER... AND ALSO A VANDERBEAK.
AH! AND HAVE A BUNNY RABBIT BRING ME EVERYTHING, TOO.
YOU'LL HAVE IT, COME JOIN ME, WE'RE GOING TO CELEBRATE YOUR VICTORY.
AND US?
YOU COME BACK DOWN, CLEAN UP, AND BE QUICK ABOUT IT.
OH, NOT STRONG YOU, NOT STRONG.
NO! IT'S THE CROWD THAT UNDERSTOOD NOTHING. LOOK!!
STAY WITH ME, SON. YOU'VE GOT LOTS TO LEARN... AND, IF YOU'RE ATTENTIVE, YOU'LL LEARN LOTS OF SECRET SWORD THRUSTS.

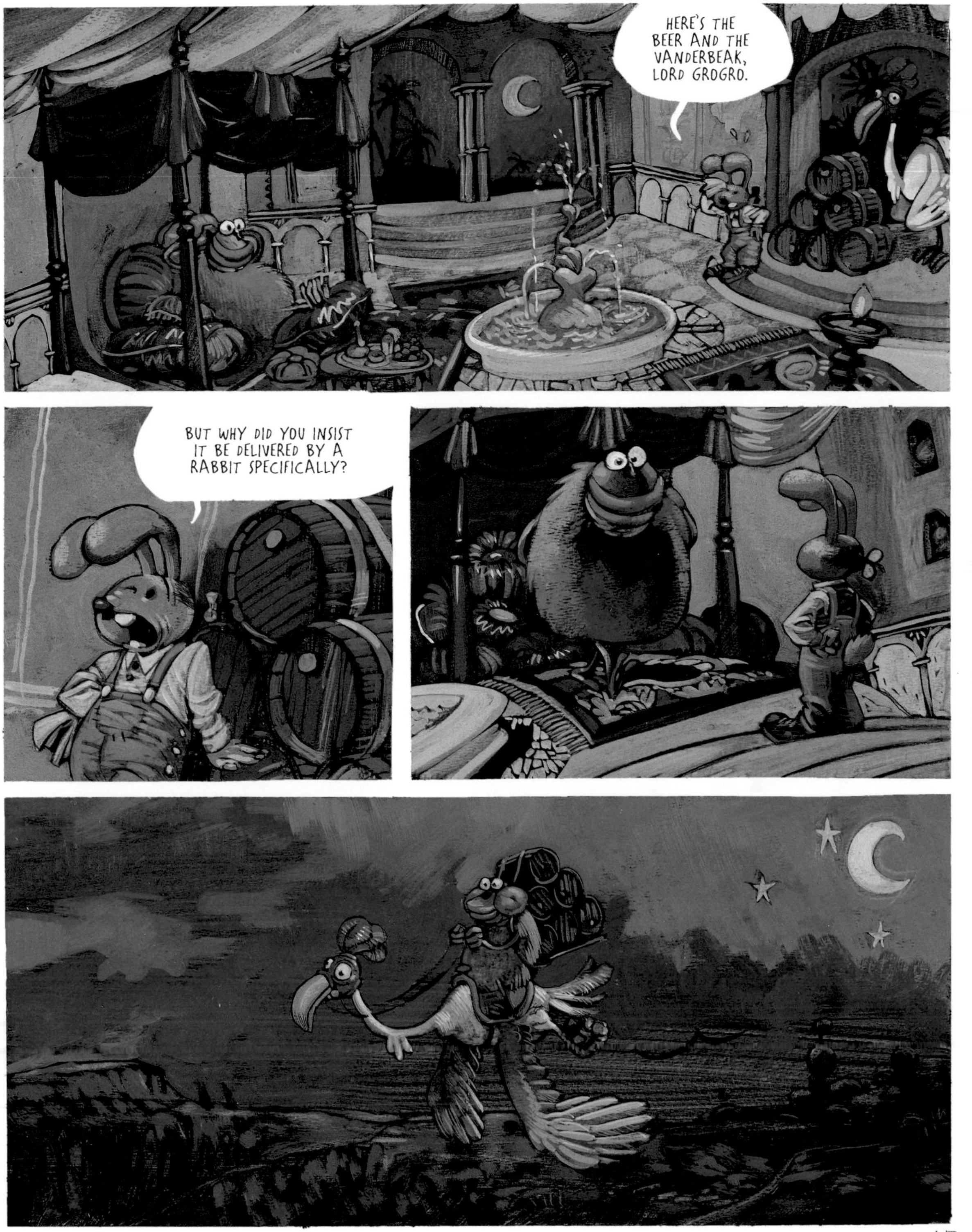
HERE'S THE BEER AND THE VANDERBEAK, LORD GROGRO.
BUT WHY DID YOU INSIST IT BE DELIVERED BY A RABBIT SPECIFICALLY?

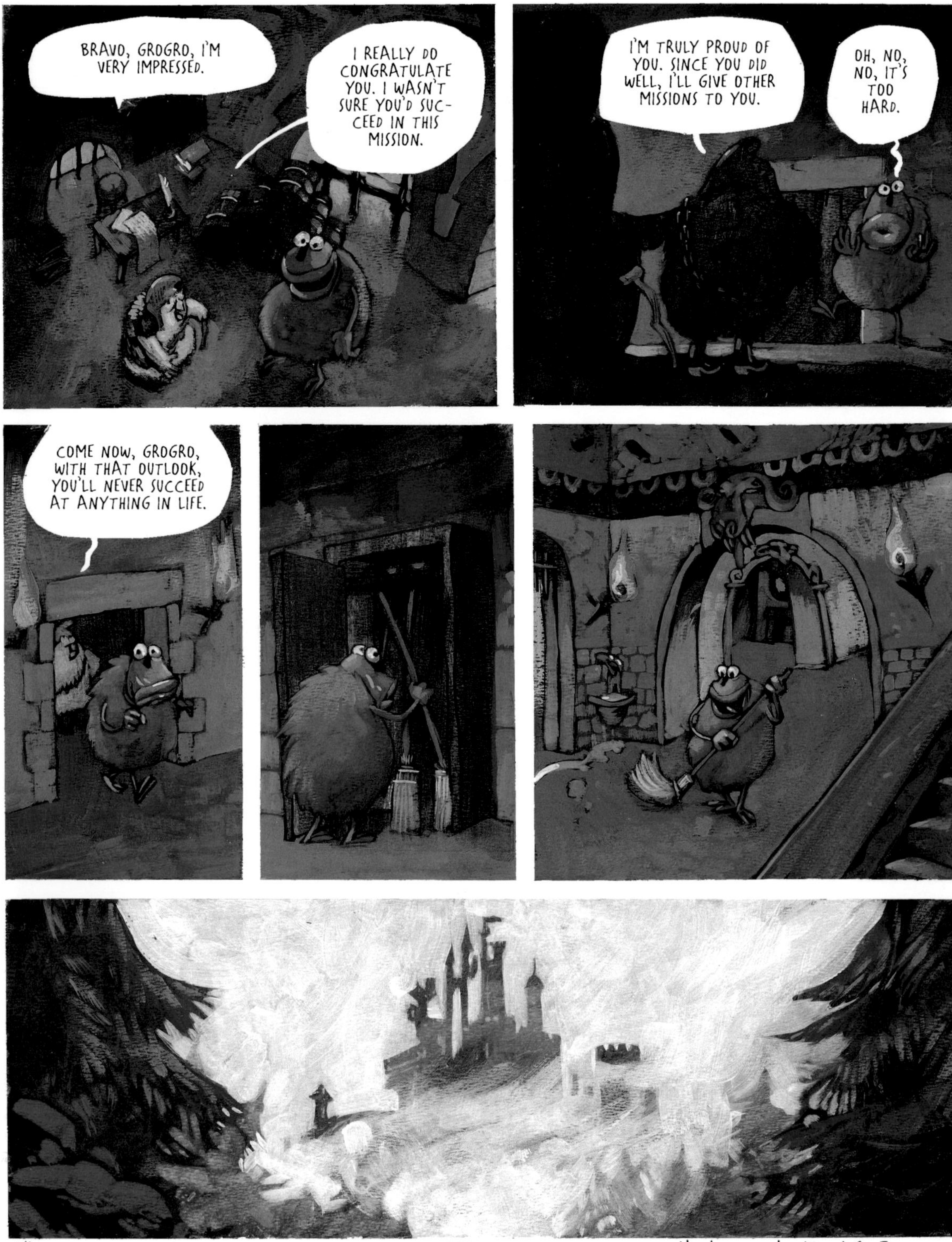
BRAVO, GROGRO, I'M VERY IMPRESSED.
I REALLY DO CONGRATULATE YOU. I WASN'T SURE YOU'D SUCCEED IN THIS MISSION.
I'M TRULY PROUD OF YOU. SINCE YOU DID WELL, I'LL GIVE OTHER MISSIONS TO YOU.
OH, NO, NO, IT'S TOO HARD.
COME NOW, GROGRO, WITH THAT OUTLOOK, YOU'LL NEVER SUCCEED AT ANYTHING IN LIFE.

Joann Sfar

FIN

Nantes le 15-01-2003